Allusions in *Omeros*

UNIVERSITY PRESS OF FLORIDA

Florida A&M University, Tallahassee
Florida Atlantic University, Boca Raton
Florida Gulf Coast University, Ft. Myers
Florida International University, Miami
Florida State University, Tallahassee
New College of Florida, Sarasota
University of Central Florida, Orlando
University of Florida, Gainesville
University of North Florida, Jacksonville
University of South Florida, Tampa
University of West Florida, Pensacola

Allusions in

Omeros

Notes and a Guide to Derek Walcott's Masterpiece

❖ Maria McGarrity

University Press of Florida
Gainesville · Tallahassee · Tampa · Boca Raton
Pensacola · Orlando · Miami · Jacksonville · Ft. Myers · Sarasota

This book may be available in an electronic edition.

20 19 18 17 16 15   6 5 4 3 2 1

Library of Congress Cataloging-in-Publication Data
McGarrity, Maria, 1970– author.
Allusions in *Omeros* : notes and a guide to Derek Walcott's masterpiece /
Maria McGarrity.
pages cm
Includes bibliographical references and index.
ISBN 978-0-8130-6100-9
1. Walcott, Derek. Omeros. 2. Caribbean literature (English)—History and criticism.
3. West Indies—In literature. 4. Epic poetry, English—History and criticism. I. Title.
PR9272.9.W3O4438 2015
811'.54—dc23
2014045495

The University Press of Florida is the scholarly publishing agency for the State
University System of Florida, comprising Florida A&M University, Florida Atlantic
University, Florida Gulf Coast University, Florida International University, Florida
State University, New College of Florida, University of Central Florida, University of
Florida, University of North Florida, University of South Florida, and University of
West Florida.

University Press of Florida
15 Northwest 15th Street
Gainesville, FL 32611-2079
http://www.upf.com

Contents

Preface

This book provides information rather than a traditional literary analysis or interpretation. It is a collection of historical, literary, and cultural notes for Derek Walcott's highly allusive and challenging poetic tour de force, *Omeros*. In its pedagogical design and methodology, it is modeled on a classic reference source for readers and scholars of James Joyce: Don Gifford's and Robert Seidman's *Ulysses Annotated*. Criticism on Walcott's *Omeros* has focused on the broad strokes and cultural paradigms, but there is no such go-to resource for the range of readers, from the beginner to the scholar, of *Omeros* like there is for *Ulysses*.

In the fall of 2006, I taught a graduate seminar on postcolonial literature during which I assigned *Omeros*. Although I had taught *Ulysses* successfully in several seminars, both to undergraduate and graduate students, *Omeros* seemed to challenge to the point of disaffection even the most diligent of readers. The issue, however, is not with the text but rather with the lack of an apparatus for readers to enter the network of references. *Ulysses* is a similarly complicated and even longer work. Yet the issues that face the readers of Joyce have been dealt with by nearly a century of critical and scholarly work on various editions and guides to the text. Walcott's status within global literatures rivals Joyce's position at this point, yet Walcott's work has not received the sustained diligent attention to allusive detail that it also demands.

The chapters that follow provide a guide to, and offer glimpses into, an allusive network that readers may use to chart their own voyages amid Walcott's famed journey. While I have tried to be as thorough as possible, the entries vary in length and specificity. For example, the entry for Queen Victoria is brief; her historical position is commonly known, and readers will not struggle to find information about her role in the British Empire. Yet, the entry for Chrysostom is more detailed because his role in the reception of the Philoctetes story is largely unclear to contemporary readers and can be confusing because of the two distinct figures, the Greek Sophist and the Christian Saint, who share the name. I invite readers to use the entries provided in the following chapters to spark new routes through Walcott's text. The entries are organized by page and line numbers from the standard Farrar, Straus and Giroux and Faber and Faber editions. This work generally provides information from the public domain and offers insights into Walcott's networks of meaning, which multiple scholars have noted, sometimes repeatedly or even simultaneously. Thus the volume eschews parenthetical citations to avoid creating a virtually endless series of attributions. Yet, the volume is also limited in its scope since no single list of allusions and notes can incorporate every possible meaning. I trust that those who use this resource will add to it through their own insightful readings, through creating further scholarship on Walcott, and perhaps most importantly through widening the appreciation for the remarkable achievement that is *Omeros*.

Acknowledgments

I have relied on the extraordinary community of Walcott, Caribbean, and postcolonial scholars in shaping this volume. Sandra Pouchet Paquet encouraged the project from the beginning and has been a model of scholarly generosity. A special thanks goes to Joyce Zonana for her enduring friendship and for reading the manuscript at several points. Joanna Johnson provided not only detailed information for the British allusions but also remains a continuing source of good cheer. I thank Rosemary Mayer for her knowledge of painting and ancient epics. I thank Josh Brewer for his knowledge of poetry and the Caribbean. I owe a debt of gratitude to Greg Winston for his recommendation of the University Press of Florida as a publisher. My graduate assistants, Kate Danyo and Charles Thorne, were remarkable for their dedication and perseverance. This book would not have been completed without the support I received for research and travel to St. Lucia and Trinidad through Faculty Development Grants and the Long Island University community, specifically Gale Stevens Haynes, Jeff Kane, and David Cohen. The Folk Research Center in Castries, St. Lucia, provided access to manuscripts and translation services. I thank John Robert Lee for his nuanced insight on St. Lucian literature and Gregor Williams for his superb knowledge of St. Lucian history. McDonald Dixon also offered a critical source for a colonial image of the Caribbean. I thank Dunstan St. Omer for his willingness to speak about his work so candidly. I am grateful for the friendship and encouragement of Alison Donnell and Evelyn O'Callaghan. Finally, I must thank all of those readers, poets, and critics whose works on *Omeros* are compiled in the bibliography and have formed the basis of this book. This endeavor would not be possible without the guidance of such a generous community. To thank everyone individually for their insights would take another chapter at minimum, and so these few words are offered instead. Let the brevity of this acknowledgment not be mistaken for its depth.

A Note

N.B. The following entries correspond to the page and line numbers [page.line] of the Farrar, Straus and Giroux (North America) and Faber and Faber (E.U., U.K., and Commonwealth) editions of Derek Walcott's *Omeros*.

❖ Introduction

Derek Walcott's *Omeros* has captivated and confounded readers with its delightful complexity since its publication in 1990. *Omeros* occupies a fundamental place within modern Caribbean, global English, and post-colonial literatures. Yet, Walcott's work remains challenging for many who wish to read it. In an interview with D.J.R. Bruchner, Walcott claims not to have written "a conundrum for scholars"; however, his systemic but fluid matrix of allusion is both subtle in its references and highly complex in its intricacy, both for the general reader and frequently for the specialist (*New York Times*, October 9, 1990). This book charts Walcott's allusive network in a systematic manner. It also clarifies his exploration of the various intertextual routes within this most challenging narrative poem. Walcott's significant poetic achievement has situated him as the preeminent Caribbean writer studied worldwide. *Omeros* is a radical reconceptualization of the juxtaposition between the modern experience of individual and collective identity formation and the most ancient experiences of exile and homecoming. *Omeros* is central to both the Nobel Prize winner's oeuvre and world literature. In this work, which incorporates the multivocal, culturally syncretistic, and profoundly engaging histories in the archipelago, the poet presents the wondrousness of the Caribbean to the world.

LIFE AND WORKS

Born in 1930, Derek Walcott came of age amid a vibrant cultural and linguistic matrix in Castries, St. Lucia, the capital of the island. In striking ways, the Walcotts, who were Methodist and English-speaking, stood apart from the society in which they found themselves, which was largely Roman Catholic and French Creole/Kwéyòl-speaking. Walcott, as well as his twin, Roderick, and sister, Pamela, was also marked by the dramatic loss of his father, Warwick, at too young an age (Derek and Roderick were just infants at his passing). Their mother, Alix, taught at the local Methodist school and took in sewing to support the family. In this way, she stitched together not only the materials of her neighbors but also the economic means of her family. She also gave the young Derek the money to publish his first poems (*25 Poems*) in 1948. The mentorship of Harry Simmons and Walcott's friendships with Garth St. Omer, the writer, and Dunstan St. Omer, the painter, deeply influenced his artistic development. Simmons' belief in celebrating indigenous art forms and making local culture the subject of great art profoundly influenced Derek. Although Walcott used the pen rather than the brush as his primary artistic tool, visual culture, both in painting and dramatic performance, remains central to his world and his work.

Unlike many of Walcott's contemporaries, who moved to Britain for university, Walcott remained in the Caribbean and undertook his studies at the University [College] of the West Indies, in Mona, Jamaica. As a part of his artistic development, Walcott struggled to overcome Manichean positions and the facile (but often imposed) choice between identifying with African or European cultures. Those tensions were particularly strong during the global wave of decolonization movements after World War II. While in university, he composed a poem about the Mau Mau Rebellion in Kenya, "A Far Cry from Africa." He writes of the dilemma of being between cultures:

> I who am poisoned with the blood of both,
> Where shall I turn, divided to the vein?
> I who have cursed
> The drunken officer of British rule, how choose
> Between this Africa and the English tongue I love?
> Betray them both, or give back what they give?
> How can I face such slaughter and be cool?
> How can I turn from Africa and live?
>   (lines 26–33)

In fact, Walcott does not turn away. As his later works evidence, he accepts his African heritage just as he accepts his European heritage.

After taking his degree and teaching at posts in Jamaica, St. Lucia, and Grenada in the late 1950s and 1960s, Walcott moved to Trinidad and in 1959 undertook the formation of the Little Carib Basement Theatre, which ultimately became the Trinidad Theater Workshop (Walcott directed the theater until 1976). Drama, both in writing and performance production, has been crucial to Walcott's artistic formation. Many of his plays focus on important aspects of Caribbean history. This productive period yielded the play *Dream on Monkey Mountain* (1967) as well as the poetry of *The Castaway* (1965) and *The Gulf* (1969). Walcott continued to write poetry and to take on increasingly sophisticated narrative structures. His publication in 1973 of *Another Life*, his story of an artist coming of age written as a novel in verse, signified an important advance in poetic form. The work is a striking marker of Walcott's maturing vision, particularly as it relates to the struggles of personal identity and colonial history. It is also his first successful experiment with a book-length narrative poem, a form that he will perfect in *Omeros*. In his 1974 essay "The Muse of History," Walcott explains his remarkably intimate view of Caribbean history: "I say to the ancestor who sold me, and to the ancestor who bought me, I have no father. . . . Exiled from your own Edens you have placed me in the wonder of another, and that was my inheritance and your gift" (64). While he does not ignore the brutality of past suffering, he refuses to be circumscribed by its legacies. In his personal politics he finds the New World to be an Adamic geography just as the Caribbean serves as a new Garden of Eden. The Caribbean represents a paradisiacal imagined archipelago in which the traumas of history are not elided but integrated into the islands, thereby enriching their generative, creative soils.

Throughout the 1980s, after earning a MacArthur "Genius Grant," and with many ensuing readings, travels, and appointments worldwide, Walcott moved between his home island and his various posts, including a professorship at Boston University. He published several poetry volumes, *The Fortunate Traveller* (1981), *Midsummer* (1984), and *The Arkansas Testament* (1987), all of which reveal the poet's increasingly nuanced struggles with departure and return, both individual and collective. In 1984 his *Haitian Earth* premiered to mark the 150th anniversary of the world's first successful slave revolution (the Haitian Revolution in 1804), and in 1989 *The Ghost Dance*, a play dealing with the U.S. expansion to the West and its tragic effects on American Indians, premiered.* *The Ghost Dance* and its central figures are alluded to in *Omeros* in a heartbreaking acknowledgment of cultural displacement and personal loss. A critical year for the poet was 1990, with the death of his beloved mother, Alix Walcott, and the publication of *Omeros*. World-wide readership and acclaim followed with the Nobel Prize in 1992. Yet, despite or perhaps because of his life and travels abroad, St. Lucia and the Caribbean remain central to his artistic vision.

Walcott is deeply conscious of the neocolonial economic structures of dependence that remain in the Caribbean. The plantation economies of the Great House(s) have been replaced with tourist economies of the resort(s). Walcott's critique of the conditions that perpetuate the continued subservience of Caribbean peoples to foreign tourists is evident in *Omeros* with Helen's refusal to work as a waitress and to allow herself to be touched for the pleasure of those she is asked to serve. Yet, Walcott's economic critique also relates to his love of his island. The Jalousie Resort between the two Pitons, or peaks that so dominate the landscape of St. Lucia, was the focus of much of his concern. The resort was not only yet another example of foreign investment that served outside interests (and that created substantial local jobs only in low-paying service positions: cooks, waitresses, maids, porters) but also located in the symbolic core of the island, between the peaks that residents affectionately refer to as the island's breasts. Moreover, Walcott has expressed concern about the environmental impact of such business ventures (Walcott 2005, 127–39). St. Lucia in reality was unable to do what Walcott's Helen does in *Omeros*, that is, refuse to be touched; despite much public outcry and opposition, the resort was opened in 1992.

Walcott's works celebrate the quotidian concerns of common people on his island and places them within the eternal conversation of the global literary tradition. *The Bounty* (1997) is an important volume of

---

* The decision to use the term *American Indian* to refer to indigenous peoples in the United States reflects the preference of many people who previously would have been referred to as *Native American* as well as the recommendation of the *Chicago Manual of Style*.

poetry in that vein; it joins the global tradition with an intimate sense of loss relating to the passing of Walcott's mother, Alix. The end of the twentieth century saw both the death of Walcott's brother, Roderick, and the publication of *Tiepolo's Hound* (2000). This is his most significant volume since *Omeros*. It takes Camille Pissarro, the son of Sephardic Jewish immigrants to St. Thomas, and imagines Walcott's and Pissarro's artistic journeys as linked. His subsequent volumes of poetry, *The Prodigal* (2004) and *White Egrets* (2011), show a writer coming to terms with both a return to home and the culmination of a life in art. Walcott's technique remains challenging in these late works. As Adrian Augier notes in a review of *The Prodigal*, "only a fool moves casually over a page of Walcott" (2006, 148).

Walcott's play, *O Starry Starry Night*, premiered in 2013. This work continues the celebration of visual art in Walcott's works and uses two impressionists, Paul Gauguin and Vincent van Gogh, as its central characters. Gauguin briefly lived and painted in Martinique, the island directly north of St. Lucia that is visible from St. Lucia on a clear day. In the final moments of the play, Van Gogh confesses, "[d]espite my ambitions I have always been afraid that I might produce a masterpiece" (99). What does one do after creating a masterpiece? While the character is surely referencing his own *Starry Night*, Walcott (and his readers) may very well consider such an aftermath in terms of *Omeros*. Walcott has completed a stage version of *Omeros* that premiered in 2014. Walcott's *Omeros*, in print and now on stage, has reached an audience across the globe. His subsequent efforts, though highly regarded, must navigate its enduring wake.

CONTEXTUALIZING CARIBBEAN WRITING

Walcott's work as a Caribbean writer operates within a long tradition of artistic production in the archipelago. Walcott reaches back to early paradigms both within and beyond the precincts of Caribbean culture(s). Writing in the Caribbean ranges from pre-Columbian markings left by indigenous peoples to early accounts and letters from enslaved African subjects, settlers, and colonial administrators. Early Caribbean women such Mary Prince, whose *History* as an enslaved woman who suffered cruelty in the West Indies riveted audiences, and Mary Seacole, a complex cultural figure who moved from Jamaica to Central America and then Britain and published her *Wonderful Adventures of Mrs. Seacole in Many Lands*, in which she acknowledges that some have termed her "a female Ulysses" (1990, 1), show that Caribbean identities and cultural positions are nuanced, intricate, and belie any easy assessment.

In the twentieth century, the period when Caribbean writing entered its postwar boom with both the Windrush generation (the first wave of Caribbean immigrants to Britain, a group named for the ship on which the journey was undertaken) and subsequent global diasporic migrations (to Canada, the United States, and beyond), well-known writers such as V. S. Naipaul, George Lamming, Sam Selvon, Aimé Césaire, and Kamau [Edward] Brathwaite represent the Caribbean well beyond its maritime and cultural borders. Walcott resides in this noticeably masculine ensemble of writers who portray not merely the elites of the settler classes but critically everyday folk. Despite the impressive number of Caribbean writers who subsequently have gained attention and readership—these now include Robert Antoni, David Dabydeen, Edwidge Danticat, Jamaica Kincaid, Caryl Phillips, and Jean Rhys, among many others—Walcott's career in the Caribbean is framed predominantly by comparisons to two contemporaries: his fellow Caribbean Nobel laureate for literature, the Trinidadian novelist V. S. Naipaul, and Kamau Brathwaite, the Barbadian poet. Both of these writers have chosen in their own ways to journey in directions unlike that of Walcott. For Naipaul, his envisioning and celebration of British identity has taken over his oeuvre to such a degree that he has famously rejected the Caribbean as a location that can produce art. Brathwaite, perhaps Walcott's greatest rival and *compère*, was noticeably more African in his focus. Walcott, in contrast to Brathwaite's Africanist emphasis, is more interested in multiple, rhizomatic forms of Caribbean identity and connection than in sourcing a single root. Walcott has been critiqued for his acceptance of European identity as a part of Caribbean identity. Yet, his broader framework certainly has become reflected in the cultural mélange of the contemporary Caribbean. Walcott's inclusive vision endures, whereas the cultural separatism in vogue earlier has somewhat fallen away, at least at the level of identity politics.

The question of postcolonial literature(s) remains a challenging one. Early postcolonial theories, emerging out of Commonwealth literary studies, examined cultural dynamics amid the periods of colonization, imperial occupation, and decolonization. They asserted global tropes that unified the literatures of such diverse geographies and histories as Africa, Asia, Australia, Latin America, and, of course, the Caribbean. A groundbreaking work of this movement, *The Empire Writes Back: Theory and Practice in Post-colonial Literatures*, by Bill Ashcroft, Gareth Griffiths, and Helen Tiffin, appeared in 1989. After this initial assembling and organizing movement, more recent postcolonial theories have searched for not only global strokes but also more precision in the unique specificities of postcolonial experiences across the globe. They seek not to reject global paradigms but to pay attention to the subtle differences of national/linguistic/cultural variations. The nuances of multiple voices that write neither in European tongues nor terms have become new centers of discourse and learning in important ways that reach outside of conventional publishing and academic confines. By the turn of the twenty-first century, the University of the West Indies, in Cave Hill, Barbados, was hosting a Caribbean Culture conference (June 2001) where Edward Baugh examined the nexus between literary theory and Caribbean cultural theory. The theoretical frameworks for Caribbean and postcolonial studies have emerged to become powerful paradigms within global culture(s).

LANGUAGE

In Anglophone postcolonial studies, Walcott's artistry transcends the limits of nation and geography, perhaps ironically due to the very dominance of the British Empire and its ultimate collapse, which has allowed English to become a global tongue or lingua franca. Walcott's choice to write in English in many ways mirrors the choice of his literary idol, James Joyce, who also chose to write in English rather than the Irish of the Gaelic movement's cultural and political nationalism. Walcott's decision, however, should not be read as absolute. His English is highly informed by the French–based Creole/Kwéyòl (or what he terms a "patois" or "patwa") dominant in St. Lucia, both in its rhythms and its vocabulary. While he chooses, like Joyce, an international readership and artistic community, he celebrates the everyday speech of the Caribbean as well.

The notion of a "West Indian" literature (before the 1950s a term derived from and associated with British colonies) has evolved toward the more modern and contemporary notion of pan-Caribbean literature, which includes in the regions beyond the English-speaking those writers working in French, Dutch, Spanish, and more critically the Creoles or nation languages of everyday speech in these islands. Both terms describe full and complex languages; yet, the term "nation language" is overtly celebratory of the wondrousness of what some term "non-standard" languages. In a vivid moment early in *Omeros*, Walcott appears to destabilize the notion of a central linguistic heritage when Ma Kilman encounters Seven Seas. He writes, "his words were not clear / They were Greek to her. Or old African babble" (18.2–3). Walcott's unwillingness to distinguish or establish hierarchies between African and Greek languages simultaneously demonstrates his decentering of Caribbean cultural origins and his inclusive notions of linguistic possibility.

The movement in terminology from West Indian to Caribbean literature(s), written in many nation languages, emerges in the period of decolonization of following World War II and takes hold firmly in the 1970s. In this movement, there is a general interest in forming networks within the archipelago rather than merely responding to the power dynamics of old colonial masters abroad; the turn toward a reconfiguration of literary and cultural identity at home rests upon previously overlooked links found between islands and peoples, cultural roots in Africa, India, and China, and ultimately in the celebration of indigeneity, which privileges the precolonial cultural markers that contribute to the *creolité* of the contemporary Caribbean. The open forms of cultural hybridity and positive syncretism that so characterize Caribbean cultures have become in recent years a model for examining transnational and diasporic cultures and histories across the larger postcolonial world, even as this model negotiates the harsh neocolonial economic realities that confront formerly colonized peoples.

CRITICAL RECEPTION AND THE EPIC QUESTION

Omeros met with immediate acclamation for its formidable language and elegant narrative. According to the reviewer Mary Lefkowitz for the *New York Times*, *Omeros* is a work of "extraordinary power" (October 7, 1990). *Omeros* has been called a tour de force and a triumph of form, artistry, and narrative. According to Bernard Knox in the *New York Review of Books*, the work is "a constant source of surprise and delight from stanza to stanza, a music so subtle, so varied, so exquisitely right that it never once, in more than eight thousand lines, strikes a false note" (March 7, 1991). This celebratory tone is not uncommon in the initial assessments of the work. The reviewer John Lucas calls it "one of the great poems of our time" (*New Statesman & Society* 36). Another critic calls *Omeros* "a monumental achievement": "One can propose a catalogue of features that earn it this distinction: its virtuosic versification combining a kind of hexameter with a Dantesque terza rima; its complex narrative; its subtle and polyvalent reflexiveness; the sheer variety of its registers of diction and plot, the wealth and resonance of its imagery" (Melas 2005, 147).

Beyond the initial (largely laudatory) reviews, the critical debate surrounding *Omeros* has focused habitually on the question of epic. The range of response has varied from a complete celebration of the traditional qualities and forms of the work from classicists who stress conventional epic markers to critics who accept that designation to a degree but argue that Walcott remakes the epic in a unique Caribbean frame through his celebration of folk traditions, everyday language, and radical cultural inclusivity, or what Jahan Ramazani terms Walcott's "intercultural inheritance" (1997, 409). The issue with calling *Omeros* an epic is the presumed appropriation of the epic form by European imperialists. As Joseph Farrell notes, it is "the notion that the European epic speaks with the voice of the accumulated authority of generations of White imperialist culture that leads many readers to deny *Omeros* any meaningful association with the epic genre, while in the open polyphony of novelistic genres they find a quality better suited to the creolization of language, the racial and literary miscegenation that characterizes the poem" (1997, 251). Walcott, however, sees the epic genre not merely in terms of European forms. At the moment of his greatest professional triumph, during his Nobel lecture, "The Antilles: Fragments of Epic Memory," Walcott foregrounded not the Homeric epics but the Hindu epic, *Ramayana*, and its performance, *Ramleela*, in the small town of Felicity, Trinidad, as "elation, [and] delight" performed habitually on the Caroni plain by the descendants of South Asian indentured peoples (December 7, 1992). Notably, in *Omeros* he also invokes the ancient Mesopotamian *Epic of Gilgamesh*.

Most startling perhaps amid these vibrant critical debates is the position of Walcott himself, who has accepted and refused the epic designation as a way to negotiate the controversy over form. He explains in his essay "Reflections on *Omeros*" that "the book is really not about a model of another poem; it is really about associations, or references, because that is what we are in the Americas: we are a culture of references, not certainties" (1997, 239). Walcott suggests that *Omeros* revels in an exponential assemblage of meaning in this culture of references. Such an expansive creative vision both resists linear history and represents the travails and triumphs of individual characters as it celebrates ordinary lives.

Walcott's ambivalence about labeling his work an "epic" has been reflected to varying degrees by several noted scholars. However, convincingly, Joseph Farrell reminds Walcott's readers of "the genre's capacity to reinvent itself through inversion, opposition to epic predecessors, and ironic self-reflexion" (1997, 262). The poem operates on multiple levels simultaneously. Paul Breslin has acknowledged the challenge of an easy epic designation. He notes, "too many parts . . . seem sincerely invested in the Homeric analogy critiqued elsewhere" (272). Walcott's work celebrates and undermines any straightforward categorization of epic form. He plays with such conventions as he reimagines them.

In fact, *Omeros* is a text that, on one level, occupies the highest and most exclusive of cultural and literary genres, the epic, while, on another level, it represents the most everyday expression of modern culture. Farrell acknowledges that there is "considerable anxiety among critics and on the part of the poet himself about the generic affinities of *Omeros*" (1997, 250–51). Yet, the remarkable quotidian concerns that fill Walcott's stanzas would stun any reader expecting a text of classical mimicry.

Walcott invokes the ancient Greek epics not in an effort to exclude other cultural models but to incorporate that literary heritage (among many others) into his creation of a radically new one. Walcott has returned to Greek poetry throughout his career, from his early "Origins" to the later "Homecoming: Anse La Raye" and *The Odyssey: A Stage Version*, which he published after *Omeros*. Although ancient Greek arts are now central to the European cultural and intellectual tradition, as Edward Said avers in *Culture and Imperialism*, ancient Greek culture was more oriented toward Northern Africa and the ancient Near East than toward Europe. To read the Homeric epics as simply European is to overlook their complicated historical contexts. Walcott suggests that the debts to Greece and Rome that seem so evident to his readers are in fact "overpaid accounts" (1997, 239). What he gestures toward and arguably achieves in *Omeros* is at once an erasure of that debt and a celebration of inheritance. His balance sheets, written in verse form, are made out not simply to Europe or to Africa but to a global poetic consciousness.

ISLAND IMAGINARY

Decades before *Omeros* was published, Walcott seemed to be struggling toward a reconfiguration of the island as a location of his imaginary. He opens an essay "Isla Incognita" with a striking mandate to his readers and himself: "Erase everything, even the name of this island, if it is to be rediscovered. It is the only way to begin. We will try to pretend that we have seen none of it before. It will be impossible, of course, for how can we tell whether our feeling on seeing that rock and its bay, is nostalgia or revelation? Well, combine both and the illumination made by their igniting would be discovery" (2005, 51). The "discovery," a charged term for a poet of the postcolonial world, is one of regeneration and cleansing. In *Omeros*, a roving journey of ultimate homecoming, the boundaries of St. Lucia between land and sea, earth and sky, highlight the importance of periphery. The sea is an ever present, dynamic force, a daily fact of life in island cultures, particularly Caribbean cultures. Its presence continually suggests a certain expectation of place that values margins. The landscapes and seascapes create an island imaginary, though they remain in flux; these outside edges become crucial for Walcott (McGarrity 2008,

80–120). In his geographic imaginings, the zones of the beach become as critical as the hearts of the island landscapes or even the center of Castries. Walcott's radical inclusivity reflects his geography, which, for this poet, is an intimate expression of writing (*graphia*) the world (*geo*). Walcott notes in an early poem, "by a country's cast / topography delineates its verse" ("Homage to Edward Thomas" 1–2). Geography bonds the writer to home while allowing his journey across the sea. David Farrier poetically notes of Walcott's profoundly liquid imaginary: "The sea is an archive in constant flux. Its histories coexist simultaneously rather than sequentially, making the presence of all Atlantic journeys legible in the action of the surf. However, what the surf writes is transitory. Just as one configuration of the shoreline is completed, the backwash, that leaves only detritus in which the poet can read meaning or construct a culture, alters it" (2003, 25). Walcott's island location becomes global and local at once. St. Lucia, lovingly drawn by the poet, operates as an island metaphor, a repeating signifier of cultural syncretism. Its beaches and waters become repeating yet fluid zones. The poet rejects absolutes and certainties. Yet, the sea serves as a repository for history and a location of possibility for the poetic imagination. For Walcott, the sea takes, preserves, and yields matter to the poet, who transforms it into art.

GLOBAL AND LOCAL, HIGH AND LOW, AT ONCE

The questioning of margins, however, leads us into a discussion of the various elements within *Omeros*. Alongside Helen, Achille, Hector, Philoctete, all easy marks for any student who has read some of the ancient Greek texts, Walcott places another structure of meaning drawn from everyday life. Dare we call this structure at the heart of *Omeros* a highly local or popular culture? References to the Coal Market, which has been out of commission since the end of World War II, and to the enduring Cathedral of the Immaculate Conception in Castries are local cultural allusions. These highly local references often uniquely characterize the figures around which they appear.

The central protagonist, Achille, is remarkable in this view. Although the allusions that are attached to his character are both highly local and related to the ancient Greek epics, there are relatively few cultural allu-sions associated with him in the text. Of course, *In God We Troust*, the name of his boat and a phrase that reappears frequently in the text, is derived from the phrase "In God We Trust" on American money. We have the reference to "Soul Brothers" (111.27) as having lost their soul and selling out, much as Achille thinks that Helen has sold herself to the tourists. The Soul Brothers are a popular South African band that formed in 1974 with three members and now comprises thirteen musi-cians. This is also the name of a Ray Charles and Milt Jackson album from 1958. The song lyrics, "Marley reggae—/ 'Buffalo Soldier.' Thud. 'Heart of America'" (161.6–7) occupy Achille when he thinks about the connections between what Walcott terms "Red Indians bouncing to a West Indian rhythm" (161.19). Finally, there is the Lifebuoy soap, an allegorical name that seems self-evident, that Achille uses to wash after he has reunited with Helen (274.11). In spite of the relative dearth of popular cultural allusions for Achille, his character remains throughout the text a deeply rooted and profoundly authentic presence, and it is he who will make a symbolic voyage to Africa and back in order to untangle and fully assume the diverse threads of his identity.

In contrast, the large numbers of popular cultural references associ-ated with the Major and Maud Plunkett suggest their very dislocation and alienation from the island-scape. For example, we have the Land Rover of the Major and Maud. Walcott repeatedly invokes the vehicle that they use to traverse the island in high colonial fashion. Guinness, the beer, seems to represent Plunkett himself. Guinness is not just good for you, to make an advertising tag line useful for a moment, but rep-resents your social status. Walcott's use of Guinness is much like his description of martini olives and snooker balls: it serves to suggest the Major's cultural positioning amid the lower middle class of colonial set-tler strivers, excluded from the higher power structure of the empire. Snooker, a game related to but much more complex than pool, is very much of the lower middle classes. Frequently, it is played in social clubs to which one must apply and be accepted. The fees for such clubs are not large, considering the social classes to which they cater, but the notion of exclusivity, belonging, and class consciousness is present and prized nevertheless. There is also reference made to Beefeaters Gin and Wellingtons that suck the slop on Plunkett's pig farm (48.10), both of which refer in unsubtle fashion to Plunkett's position in service to the empire: a modern swine for Circe.

Walcott's practice of poetry has long been placed within a global historical tradition. In *Omeros*, he invokes the ancient world along-side modern society. He places local, cultural, and geographic markers throughout the text to mark the journey of his hero, Achille, and to iden-tify numerous settings as he charts a complex postcolonial reticulation amid the Atlantic world from the Caribbean, to Africa, to Europe, to North America, and then home again to St. Lucia. Although Walcott is celebrated for his artistry and sometimes critiqued for his global associa-tions, what consistently manifests in his poetry is a juxtaposition of the celebrated and commonplace. The pressured affiliations between high and low, local and global, obscure and popular culture that *Omeros* re-veals suggest the degree to which Walcott's technique is radically wide-ranging. While we might consider his appropriation of culture unusual in comparison to that of other writers, he deploys it in *Omeros* both to mark belonging and to suggest estrangement. The delight in reading Walcott's art and the tenacity necessary to appreciate the most obscure of his motifs require his audience to move beyond the easily evident and remember that, much as in "Forty Acres," his poem that celebrated the first election of President Barack Obama, the ruptured field ultimately becomes a dynamic body of regeneration.

INVITATION TO SCRUTINY

Omeros is a notoriously challenging work to grasp in its complexity, whether you are a general reader, a literary enthusiast, or even a special-ist. As the respected critic Edward Baugh has noted, "in its capacious-ness [*Omeros*] is inexhaustibly accommodating of scrutiny" (2006, 186). I suggest, however, that *Omeros* does not simply accommodate but requires and in fact invites close study from its readers. A central aspect in the study of Walcott and Caribbean literature is the examination of global cultural rhetorics and crosscultural perspectives even as the local is celebrated. Walcott's poetry reflects such multiple and open forma-tions of creativity, culture, and identity. His remarkable achievements become most evident when readers are open to the full scope of possible significance that each poetic detail, image, or passage possesses. We must explore his wildly innovative and dramatically challenging imaginative writing for its array of exponential meaning. Through such exploration, we encounter the stunning creativity of Walcott's imagination. Reading *Omeros* suggests both the pleasures of exponential connection and the demand for persistence that Walcott's work requires. For *Omeros* provides not the false "nostalgia" but the profound "revelation" that Walcott notes in "Isla Incognita" (2005, 51). Walcott reimagines the enduring myths of the New World not only as emblems of a traumatic past but also as powerful vessels that foster contemporary literary creativity. Walcott's ability to move beyond the boundaries of time, space, language, and culture, to reach back for the perfect analogy and to complicate any easy understanding that readers might initially venture toward, ensures both the rapture that readers experience and the endurance necessary to appreciate his modern, Caribbean-centered but broad Atlantic epic of wandering and return, exile and homecoming, *Omeros*.

❖ Book One

SUMMARY

The first book inaugurates the themes of loss, the quest to (re)discover home, the search for ancestors, the desire for progeny, and the overarching experiences of a wandering exile. The allusions range from the cultural specificity of St. Lucia to the broader Atlantic world, from the Middle Passage to perhaps the most widely understood of all of Walcott's allusions, the ancient Greek Homeric tradition. Although each allusion or representation of symbolic knowledge forms a textual potential for meaning, in fact many of Walcott's allusions in the opening book challenge the readers' basis for comprehension. We move from Caribbean English usage, for example, *maljo*, for "evil eye," to the myrmidons, the Greeks who fought alongside Odysseus at Troy, and then even to the cosmos, the stars and planetary system that aid sailors in navigation. The sea itself becomes a location in the poem. We are introduced to various means of voyaging across the sea, from the schooners of the Battle of the Saints to the pirogues of St. Lucia's local fisherman, the most famous of which is of course Achille's *In God We Troust*.

The poem opens with a scene of fisherman cutting down trees to fashion a canoe just outside of Gros Islet, a village on the western, Caribbean, side of the island near St. Lucia's northern coastal promontory. In this liminal zone on the beach between island and sea, we are introduced to Philoctete, a wounded figure trapped on the land because of his injury. In the remainder of the first book, the other major characters in the tale are established for the reader: Achille, a fisherman and the protagonist; Hector, another fisherman and the rival of Achille; Helen, a pregnant maidservant and the object of desire for virtually all the male characters; Major Plunkett, a minor British colonial settler; Maud Plunkett, his Irish wife; and Ma Kilman, a proprietress of a café/shop and an Obeah woman, a purveyor of cures. Achille and Hector sever their friendship over the desirable Helen. Although she is pregnant, possibly with Achille's heir, she leaves Achille and goes to live with Hector. This central incident introduces to the narrative the driving themes of inheritance and obscure progeny. Plunkett is revealed to be on a quest for a lost son as well. We also have a series of poetic personas or narrators who shift and merge but somehow remain distinctly deployed throughout the text: the first is Seven Seas, a blind seer who represents the global poetic unconscious; the second is the figure of Omeros, a modern vision of the ancient poet figure of the oral epic cycle, Homer; and the third and final narrative voice is that of Walcott himself, who enters the text at certain key points when he positions a highly autobiographical "I." The first book ends with Walcott's "I" encountering a shade of his father who "looks ahead" to a preordained rendezvous of paternal reunion, and Walcott's poetic destiny to give "voice" to his ancestors is foretold (76.3).

ANNOTATIONS

[page number.line number]

CHAPTER I

3.1 we cut down them canoes—Arawaks and Caribs, the original inhabitants of St. Lucia, crafted canoes from tree trunks. Each vessel was cut from a single trunk and carved until hollow. The interiors of the canoes were then carefully charred to seal and smooth the wood. The English word "canoe" originates with the Arawak *canoa*. Walcott's beginning of his tale with this act and this word is an homage to the inheritance of indigenous cultural practices and knowledge in St. Lucia. Physical evidence in the Caribbean and on St. Lucia suggests that the Arawaks arrived first on the archipelago, migrating north from South America. The Caribs, who followed the Arawak route north from South America,

BOOK ONE · 19

were in the Caribbean in general and in St. Lucia in particular in the late fifteenth century, when the Europeans arrived. The two groups, Caribs and Arawaks, were the first two peoples to fight over the island; the Caribs were victorious in both St. Lucia and the larger Caribbean.

3.2 Philoctete—the first character in the text whose name originates in Greek myth. Although Walcott reimagines these names, they somewhat recall the custom of European masters renaming African slaves with classical names in a manifestation of control, dominance, and mockery. In the ancient myth, Philoctetes, a commander of the Greek fleet, is known for his wound that causes him to be abandoned. Noted briefly in Homer, Philoctetes' saga gains in detail and transforms throughout classical drama and into modernity. In brief, he is a wounded and exiled man who must be restored in order for his people to achieve victory. Philoctetes lights the pyre upon which Hercules is burned alive; the gods give him Hercules' bow and arrow as a reward. On the journey to Troy, the fleet stops at the island of Tenedos to make a sacrifice to the gods. While on the island, Philoctetes is bitten by a snake. The wound gives off a terrible stench and Philoctetes is left in severe pain. Unable to tolerate either the stink of the wound or the cries of the man, the Greeks abandon him on the isle of Lemnos. Yet, the Greeks receive an omen that they will not take Troy without Philoctetes and his bow. His return to the Greeks is mentioned both in *The Iliad* and *The Odyssey*; Sophocles' (ca. 495/7–405/7 BCE) play, *Philoctetes*, is centered on Odysseus' and Neoptolemus' deceptive efforts to retrieve the bow and compel Philoctetes to aid the Greek forces. At Troy, Philoctetes famously kills Paris. Euripides (ca. 480–406 BCE), Aeschylus (ca. 525–455 BCE), and Sophocles all wrote plays entitled *Philoctetes*, but Sophocles' version is the only one that survives. Philoctetes also makes an appearance in Seneca's (ca. 4 BCE–65 CE) *Hercules Oetaeus*. Seamus Heaney's (1939–2013) *The Cure at Troy* is the most recent reimagination of Sophocles' play. Walcott's friendship with Heaney is well known. Heaney explores the wound of the abandoned figure but seeks the promise of a future informed by the past. Walcott's Philoctete has also been compared to the wounded Fisher King in T. S. Eliot's (1888–1965) *The Wasteland*. See notes 3.2, 6.1, 8.9, 14.5, 16.14–15, 17.5–6, 24.6, and 31.4.

3.4 *laurier-cannelles*—French for a Cinnamon Bay tree from the *Lauraceae* family. Cinnamon Bay is also a region on the island of St. John in the Virgin Islands.

3.15 white rum—the clear variety of rum made by distilling various fermented sugarcane products that are heated and combined with molasses. When distilled the rum is white or straw colored and contains alcohol levels of 40–75 percent or 80/150 proof. The drink was popular among enslaved subjects, troops, and early settlers of the Caribbean. Much more so than other forms of alcohol, rum is associated with sexual licentiousness and pleasure in the Caribbean. The consumption of rum was almost an epidemic at times and was widely condemned by religious leaders. Several varieties of rum are produced on the island by St. Lucia Distillers, including Bounty, Chairman's Reserve, and Admiral Rodney. They vary in color and expense, with Bounty having the lowest and Admiral Rodney the highest price points. While their business office is in Castries, the actual distillery is in the Roseau Valley, south of the capital, a location once known for its production of sugarcane. See note 63.17.

4.1 sea-almond—also called the Barbados almond, Demerara-almond, Indian almond, and West Indian almond. A type of tree (*Coccoloba uvifera*) it is originally from Malaysia and bears a rough-skinned fruit that when pounded reveals a consumable kernel or almond. Although the kernel resembles the larger almonds that are commercially available, it is much smaller.

4.4 conch—literally a type of mollusk of the *Strombidae* family, such as an oyster or mussel, but importantly the term also refers to large shells that are frequently used as wind instruments. The conch is critical in Caribbean slave rebellions as a method of communication and a calling forth for uprising, noted particularly in the Haitian Revolution. In Greek myth, the conch is the instrument played by the son and herald of Poseidon, Triton.

4.4 corolla—the leaves or petals, separate or combined, that form the linear, edge of a flower and are its most visible part. Also, the petals of a flowering plant, from the Latin *corona* or "crown."

4.8 La Sorcière—from the French term for "witch"; in St. Lucia, it is a mountain range on the eastern side of the island that forms a wall between the sea and the interior land mass. The term also refers to a road that runs along the coast until its reaches the town of Dennery.

4.9 ground-dove's mating call—the common ground dove (*Columbina passerina*); a nine-to-twelve-inch bird with rust and pink coloring that flies only for brief jaunts. It remains grounded, often in pairs, and has a mating call notable for its melancholy cooing. See notes 153.8 and 313.18.

4.26 akimbo—means "of the arms"; stance with hands on haunches and elbows away from the torso.

5.2 Auracs—(also Arawaks) original inhabitants of the island of St. Lucia. They named the island of St. Lucia "Iounalao," which means "where the iguana is found." See notes 92.5 and 92.15.

5.6 20 gommier—a gum tree or birch gum tree (*Pachyloba*); from the French for "gum tree." In St. Lucia it refers to a birch-gum tree specifically. A variety of the gommier can also be termed a gommier sang, which suggests the blood-red color of the bark. The linkage of the tree to the loss of a spirit or fallen figure evokes *The Iliad*—when Asios, Hector's uncle, is killed, he is compared to a falling oak tree used to build a ship.

5.21 tarpaulin—a heavy waterproof cloth usually made from a tarred canvas or thick plastic. It can also refer to a sailor's tarred or oilskin hat. An archaic use of the term refers to a sailor.

6.1 Achille—the central hero of *Omeros*, a fisherman. The figure of Achilles originates in Greek myth. He appears in both *The Iliad* and *The Odyssey* as well as in Sophocles' *Ajax* and Euripides' *Iphigenia at Aulis*. A great warrior, he is the son of Peleus, a mortal, and Thetis, a sea nymph; Achilles was dipped in the River Styx by Thetis, which makes him invulnerable except for one weak spot, his heel, the point from which his mother holds him. Achilles' central conflict is whether he should accept a long quiet life of anonymity or the short glorious life of a heroic warrior. Achilles chooses the latter and fights the great Trojan warrior, Hector, to avenge the death of his beloved comrade Patroclus. Although victorious over Hector, he falls to Paris' arrow that was shot into his one vulnerable point while he fought at Troy's famous Scaean Gates. Achilles appears in *The Odyssey* as a shade whom Odysseus encounters during his journey to the underworld; Achilles conveys to Odysseus both a pride in his son,

Neoptolemus, and a clear regret of his choice for a short but glorious life. Walcott's Achille incorporates aspects of the heroic deeds of the classical Achilles and the wandering of Odysseus while transforming the idealization of his Caribbean hero into a unique persona, highly reminiscent of Kamau Brathwaite's (1930–) figure of the New World negro in *The Arrivants*, who moves well beyond a straightforward reimagination. Achilles is also noted in Walcott's "Origins." Walcott's Achille has been compared to the questing knight in T. S. Eliot's (1888–1965) *The Wasteland*. See notes 8.4, 8.9, 10.25, 16.14–16, 24.6, 83.20, 146.15–16, 150.12, 175.13–14, 228.25, 296.2, 298.9, and 320.7–16.

6.7 cutlass—a short sword with a flat arched blade, like a machete, with which sailors were frequently armed.

6.8 sign of the cross—the phrase and practice originates with Roman Catholicism. It refers to the physical construction of tracing two lines intersecting at right angles on the body, from head to torso and then from shoulder to shoulder, to represent the figure of the Christian Messiah, Jesus, on the cross during the crucifixion.

6.13 The bearded elders endured the decimation—there were several historical decimations of people on St. Lucia. Large numbers of enslaved African subjects died on the Middle Passage from Africa to the Caribbean; those who survived the passage itself often died shortly thereafter as they endured the harsh conditions and cruelty of their lives as slaves. Before the arrival of African slavery on the island, however, early British and French attempts to gain control of St. Lucia virtually wiped out the Caribs through armed conflict and disease. Yet, in March 1660 a peace was negotiated between the British, French, and the remaining Caribs, who were forced to give up their claim to any of the Lesser Antilles in exchange for possession of St. Vincent and Dominica. This treaty effectively removed the Caribs from St. Lucia. It is also possible that this refers to one of the six hurricanes known to have devastated the region between 1756 and 1831. One of the hurricanes, in 1780, is thought to have killed a total of two thousand people from St. Vincent, St. Lucia, Barbados, and Martinique. Catastrophic earthquakes also shook the islands from 1839 to 1843, the worst of which, in 1843, killed six thousand people. See notes 81.19–20, 92.12–13, 121.6, and 225.2.

6.17 *bois-campêche*—a stick of campeachy wood also called logwood (*Haematoxylon campechianum*); a small and slow-growing tree, the roots of which can be boiled to make red dye.

6.18 *bois-flot*—flood wood, also a type of tree known as *Ochroma pyramidale* or balsa, the lightest weight wood in the world. This tree is quite common in the equatorial Americas, and in the Caribbean specifically. Its wood is often used for rafts because it floats readily.

6.18 *laurier-canelle*—see note 3.4.

6.19 thorns in the flesh—associated in Christianity with the crown of thorns on the head of Jesus; suggestive of extreme suffering as well as the potential for redemption.

6.20 Aurac's patois—also patwa; a local form of speech, generally French derived, on St. Lucia specifically, though it is also used to describe languages of the Anglophone Caribbean, such as Jamaican English. Arawakan belonged to a family of over eighty native languages that were in use from the Amazon to the Bahamas.

7.1 pygmies—originate in Greek myth. In *The Iliad*, they are dwarfs who fight off cranes to stop the birds from eating their harvest; the term now generally applies to inhabitants of Central Africa, though it can refer to anyone small in stature. However, its use is frequently derogatory with racist inflections, meaning "of limited capacity." For example, in Charlotte Brontë's (1816–1855) *Jane Eyre*, Rochester compares the intellect of his Caribbean wife, Bertha, to that of a pygmy.

7.21 adze—an axe-like tool with an arched blade used to cut wood.

7.24 gunwales—the upper frame along the periphery of a seagoing vessel onto which weapons are mounted.

8.1 pirogue—a specific type of canoe or open boat, the term originates in the Arawakan language with its root, the Carib, Arawak, and then Spanish *piragua*, meaning a long narrow canoe made from the hollowed trunk of a single tree or from the hollowed trunks of two trees fastened together. Generally smaller than the large indigenous canoes that held 50–100 people, historically pirogues were the principal mode of transportation between the towns of Castries, Soufrière, and Vieux Fort. In journeys that take several hours, the boats stay close to land to avoid being swept away by the strong ocean and sea currents. See note 3.1.

8.3 the swift—elegant, swallow-like bird, often black in color, notable for its rapid flight, from the family *Apodidae*. The white-collared swift (*Streptoprocne zonaris*) is common in the Caribbean, whereas the white-rumped swift (*Apus caffer*) is common in sub-Saharan Africa. Walcott's swift (*Cypseloides niger*), *l'hirondelle des Antilles*, pulls Achille's boat to Africa. Walcott gestures toward a play on the Greek hero's common description in *The Iliad* as "swift-footed Achilles." See notes 88.21, 239.16, and 242.15.

8.4 *In God We Troust*—Achille's boat, the name of which is a play on the phrase printed on U.S. currency, "In God We Trust," among other multiple signifiers of belief and doubt, difference and connection. The boat is towed by the swift across the Atlantic. Yet, both swift and boat will return like Achille to the waters and sands of St. Lucia. The name of the boat pays homage to Walcott's dear friend, Garth St. Omer's (1931–) early novel *A Room on the Hill*, which lists three boats: "God Will Provide," "Hope," and "In God We Trust." Walcott adds an "o" for Omer/Omeros to the name of Achille's boat. Walcott previously used the phrase without the "o" to refer to an American penny in *Another Life*. See notes 6.1, 8.9, 10.25, 16.14–16, 24.6, 83.20, 146.15–16, 150.12, 175.13–14, 228.25, 296.2, 298.9, and 320.7–16.

8.9 Hector—friend of Achille and secondary hero of *Omeros*, notable for his rivalry for Helen's attentions. The name comes from Greek mythology, whose Hector is not only a prince of Troy but also the greatest of its warriors. He plays a central role in Homer's *The Iliad*. Known as the "tamer of horses," he is both noble and brave in battle. It is Hector who kills Patroclus, Achilles' great friend; this murder inspires Achilles to return to battle for the Greeks. As his dying wish Hector asks Achilles to return his body to his father, Priam, for burial, but Achilles is still consumed with rage at the death of his friend. Rather than return the body to the Trojans, Achilles drags Hector's corpse around the battlefield and walls of Troy behind his chariot. The gods intervene, however, and prevent the body from being harmed. The next day Priam goes to the Greek camp to plead with Achilles for the release of his son's body. Achilles relents and returns the body. Hector and Helen are noted in Walcott's "Origins." Helen is also referenced in "Homecoming: Anse La Raye." See notes 16.14–15, 53.4, 96.1–2, and 130.3.

8.18 frond—a large leaf-like appendage formed by the union of stem and foliage in some flowerless plants.

9.4; 6 l'absinthe ... bitter bark—a notoriously dangerous alcoholic drink made from wormwood, the flowers of which contain a toxin, the terpene thujone. The "bitter bark" refers to the taste of thujone. The drink was popular among visual and literary artists in Europe in the nineteenth and twentieth centuries.

9.8 gunwales—see note 7.24.

CHAPTER II

9.10 Theophile—there are several possible embedded allusions for Theophile. The name potentially refers to Théophile Gautier (1811–1872), a nineteenth-century French writer, to Théophile Alexandre Steinlen (1859–1923), a French Art Nouveau painter, or to Theophilus (385–412), the Catholic patriarch of Alexandria who is known for his intellect and the unseemly exercise of power through brutality. Theophilus is noted for his contribution to the decline of polytheism in the Nile region, his intersection with the Origen (185–232) heresy, and the exile of St. John Chrysostom (347–407). Theophilus attacked Origenist monks, some of which fled to Constantinople seeking protection from St. John Chrysostom. In 402, Theophilus was summoned to Constantinople to answer the charges of the exiled monks. Showering the council and Chrysostom's enemies with money and gifts, Theophilus was able to form counter charges against Chrysostom, deflecting attention from himself.

9.11 Placide—a name of French origin. Placide-Louis Chapelle (1842–1905) was the Catholic archbishop of New Orleans (appointed in 1897) who began his studies in Mende, France. In 1898 in New Orleans, during the Spanish-American War, he was appointed as the Apostolic delegate to Cuba, the Philippines, and Puerto Rico. While in Manila he brokered the release of captive religious and political prisoners which got the attention of Pope Leo XIII (1810–1903), who wrote a pontifical brief praising Placide's work. He died in New Orleans in 1905 of yellow fever.

9.11 Pancreas—an organ that secretes insulin and regulates blood-sugar levels; the name is of Greek origin and literally means "all" (*pan*) "flesh" (*creas*). In modern Greek, *pankreas* means "sweetbread."

9.12 Chrysostom—Dio Chrysostom (ca. 40–120) is the renowned Greek historian and sophist born in a Roman province in what is now Turkey. Literally, Chrysostom means "golden-mouthed." Much of his work exists in fragments today, but significantly he is the author of "On Aeschylus and Sophocles and Euripedes; or, The Bow of Philoctetes." This work is the only ancient text that provides hints about the lost versions of Philoctetes that both Aeschylus and Euripedes composed. Without this treatment, Sophocles' version would appear alone and without a dramatic context in the ancient world. Dio Chrysostom is often confused with the later St. John Chrysostom (347–407), bishop of Constantinople. Born in Antioch, St. John Chrysostom entered a divided Catholic world and became a scholar in Greek and classical culture.

9.12 Maljo—Caribbean English word meaning "evil eye," derives from the French *mal* and *yeux*, or "bad eyes"; it can also literally refer to the grudge pea, which is planted to ward off theft.

9.15 bilge—an area where the bottom and sides of a ship meet. In double-hulled vessels, the bilge between the two hulls collects seepage that can then be pumped out into the open water.

9.20 sore on his shin—refers to the snakebite Philoctete received. See note 3.2.

9.21 anemone—a vibrantly colored creature from the order *Actiniaria* that is related to the jellyfish; the word comes from the Latin and Greek *anemōnē/anemos* for "wind." This soft-bodied invertebrate aquatic animal is most plentiful and visible when it inhabits warm waters. It often resembles a flower but can also sport horn or shell-like coverings. An anemone on land, from the family of the same name, *Anemone*, refers to a plant that bears delicate white flowers in spring as well as fall varieties that sport either pink or white blooms.

10.12 white rum—see note 3.15.

10.19 pirogues—see note 8.1.

10.23 manchineels—from the French *mancenille* and Spanish *manzanilla*; the *Hippomane mancinella* is a large evergreen, native to the Caribbean and Latin America, that can rise to forty feet. The tree commonly roots in swamps or marshy areas. Its canopy is wide. It is notorious because it contains a highly toxic compound in its fruit, sap, and leaves that poisons and blisters the skin.

10.25 myrmidons—faithful followers and servants. In *The Iliad*, they are the people from Phthia, subjects of Peleus (one-time husband to the sea nymph Thetis and father of Achilles); Greeks, transformed by Zeus from ants into people, who are led by Achilles. See notes 6.1, 8.4, 8.9, 16.14–16, 24.6, 83.20, 146.15–16, 150.12, 175.13–14, 228.25, 296.2, 298.9, and 320.7–16.

11.4 Praise Him—a Christian hymn dating from the mid-nineteenth century. The phrase is a common directive for believers in Jesus Christ. Walcott is using the phrase as a name of a boat; it is the first in a litany of named vessels and recalls Homer's catalogue of ships in *The Iliad*.

11.4 Morning Star—refers to a planet, commonly Venus, seen just before sunrise in the eastern sky. It is the second boat listed. See notes 114.10 and 314.12; 21.

11.4 St. Lucia—birthplace of Walcott and setting for the first two and last two books of *Omeros*. The island is located between Martinique to the north and St. Vincent to the south. French records indicate the island's name as "Sainte Alouzie" in 1624, but this name is most probably a derivative of the Spanish name "Santa Lucía." The British and French fought for the island over several centuries. The island changed hands between these two European powers at least fourteen times and gained the nickname of the "Helen of the West Indies" for launching so many ships and sailors into battle. During the French repossession of the island in 1763, there was a decade and a half of relative peace. It was during this period that the city of Carénage, now Castries, was settled. St. Lucia was not officially ceded to England until the Treaty of Paris in 1814. The center of the island is largely a protected area of rainforest, roughly nineteen thousand acres. Villages and towns are mainly located by the sea, on the island's periphery. The action of *Omeros* is at points organized geographically, journeying around the periphery of the island between the towns of Gros Islet, Dennery, Anse La Raye, Canaries, Vieux Fort, and the capital, Castries. St. Lucia is also the third of four boats named. The Roman Catholic Saint Lucia is sent to protect Dante in the *Inferno*. See notes 17.5–6, 24.6, and 34.20.

11.4 Light of My Eyes—an object of desire or adoration, sometimes spiritually inspired. It is also the name of the final boat.

11.9 conch-coloured—brightly colored. Conchs are a type of mollusk. Conch shells remain significant for their use in jewelry and art; conch meat is frequently consumed as a fried delicacy known as conch fritters. See note 4.4.

11.10 Seven Seas—the global poetic consciousness and a key narrator of the poem. The phrase evokes that which was used in several ancient cultures to refer to the known maritime world. It becomes a signifier for all the seas (and oceans) in the world. Seven Seas serves as an eternal if not overtly sacred guide with awareness of the poetic and cultural past(s) as well as their present manifestations and future potential. His mastery of language and knowledge of the earth suggest circularity and a fluid understanding of beginnings and endings. His name invokes Walcott's image of the sea as a liquid territory that serves as a repository. The sea encompasses the world; at various moments it takes, preserves, alters, and reveals all that it holds in an unremitting generative flow. Seven Seas' status as a blind seer evokes the blind prophet from Greek myth, Tiresias, as well as the poet Homer. See Walcott's poems "A Sea-Chantey" and "The Sea Is History."

11.21 pirogues—see note 8.1.

11.23 sea-almond—see note 4.1.

12.25 Omeros—title of the work, which invokes both the historical legacy of the Greek Homer and the new Eden of possibility that Derek Walcott (1931–) views in the Americas and in the Caribbean specifically. In Walcott's explanation, "Omeros" celebrates and incorporates the conch shell, the sea as mother, Caribbean English, and ossified bone. See notes 14.5, 14.10–12, 280.8, 283.17, 283.21, and 288.21.

13.6 shambling—an awkward walk or motion, disorganized and clumsy.

13.7 Cyclops—also Cyclopes; the mythical Greek one-eyed giants who live in a remote land without a government or laws. The term suggests myopia and limited perspective as well as a cyclone or hurricane. In *The Odyssey*, Odysseus and his men are imprisoned in a cave by Polyphemus, one of the giants. While imprisoned, several of Odysseus' men are eaten by Polyphemus. The rest of the men escape tied underneath sheep going to pasture after Odysseus blinds the giant. Polyphemus is the son of Poseidon, who after the blinding of his son swears to make Odysseus' return to Greece as difficult as possible. In Hesiod, there are three Cyclops (Brontes, Steropes, Arges) who are craftsmen of the divine order. According to this version of the myth, the Cyclops fashion thunder and lightening for Zeus because he freed their father, Uranus. Euripides (ca. 480–406 BCE) also wrote a play, *The Cyclops*, based on the myth. In the play, Euripides explores the version of the myth that appears in Homer.

13.9 scythed—a scythe is an instrument with a long slender blade that mows or reaps grasses with a broad motion.

13.12 the blind lighthouse—the expansive reach and struggle to focus of the injured Cyclops; also the Vigie lighthouse, built in 1914, which overlooks the sea and Castries Harbor. It has a visibility on a clear day of thirty miles. See note 13.7.

13.22 schooners—a small seagoing rigged vessel; they originally had two masts but now can have up to three or four. Schooners were an important vessel for Caribbean history, as many schooners transported slaves to the Caribbean from Africa. Walcott's long poem, "The Schooner Flight," describes a symbolic journey across the sea. See note 72.4–5.

14.5 Homer and Virg—Homer is the Greek poet to whom *The Iliad* and *The Odyssey* are attributed, though scholars chart the genesis of these epics within an ancient oral epic tradition and believe that they were only written down centuries after their initial creation. While it has been widely accepted that *The Iliad* and *The Odyssey* have been created by various different authors (with *The Iliad* being fashioned much earlier than *The Odyssey*), Homer represents a collation of centuries of poetic tradition in ancient Greece. See notes 12.25, 280.8, 283.17, 283.21, and 288.21.

Virg. is Virgil (also Vergil, 70–19 BCE) the Roman poet whose most famous work is *The Aeneid*, which focuses on Aeneas, a warrior who escapes the sack of Troy and who is the mythical founder of Rome. In an effort to link the Roman state with the achievements of the Greeks, Virgil creates a hero who must flee at the end of the Trojan War to give birth to a new progeny that will originate the glory of Rome. The work reflects an idealized vision of Roman history as well as a justification for the Roman Empire. At the time of his death, Virgil had not completed *The*

Aeneid. One of his dying wishes was to have the manuscript destroyed, but instead, several of his friends edited and subsequently published the text. Aeneas is noted in Walcott's "Origins." See note 95.12.

14.10–12 O . . . mer . . . Antillean . . . os—Walcott's brief yet multilayered explanation for his title. *O* is the invocation of the Conch shell. *Mer*, in French, suggests two different nouns: *la mère* means "mother," whereas *la mer* means "the sea." The Antilles is the French term for the Caribbean islands, and the Caribbean Sea in French is *la mer des Antilles*. *Os* is French for "bone." All of these French words have entered the St. Lucian vernacular. The reference to bone at the end of the stanza suggests an inheritance from pre-Columbian peoples and their practice of making flutes out of bone, the femur particularly. See notes 12.25, 14.5, 280.8, 283.17, 283.21, and 288.21.

14.18 Antigone—the daughter of Oedipus and Jocasta, most famous for Sophocles' (ca. 495/7–405/7 BCE) treatment of her life in his play *Antigone* as well as in *Oedipus at Colonus*. Euripides (ca. 480–406 BCE) and Aeschylus (ca. 525–455 BCE) also wrote plays that dealt with her life: *The Phoenician Women* and *Seven Against Thebes*, respectively. Sophocles' treatment focuses on the Theban War and the forbidding of the burial of her brother Polynices, who is seen as a traitor. Antigone defies the order and is condemned to death as a result. Antigone flouts the laws of the king, her uncle, Creon, a mortal, but adheres to the laws of the gods, the immortals, which govern burial rites.

15.11 lyre—an instrument with strings fixed between two supports; in ancient Greece, it often accompanied poetry and song and is associated with Apollo.

15.11 chiton—a commonly sleeveless garment worn in ancient Greece, though it also refers to a "sea cradle," a mollusk with a noticeable mantle, a form created by the body of the mollusk that lines its shell.

15.14 prow—also *proue*, from the French; the "forepart of a ship:, adjacent to the stern." In old French *prou* meant "good, valiant, brave, and worthy."

CHAPTER III

16.8–9 un homme fou—from the French; "a crazy man," a madman.

16.14–15 the face-off that Hector wanted—In book XXII of *The Il-iad*, Hector and Achilles meet in a fight that ultimately results in Hector's death. The duel between the two heroes is a particularly poignant one, since Hector is determined to fight despite being warned of the possible outcome. Hector fights and dies with honor rather than retreating in shame to safeguard his own life. Hector's internal deliberation concerns consequences that he would bear as the result of action or inaction; he is not primarily concerned with the effect his decision will have on the Troy. What is often noted about this heroic "duel" is the amount of help Achilles receives from the goddess Athena, because it is ultimately she, and not Achilles, who is responsible for Hector's demise. Apollo, Hector's supporter, abandons him to his fate. See notes 8.9 and 53.4.

17.5–6 The duel of these fisherman / was over a shadow and its name was Helen—Helen is the woman who works as a maid for colonial settlers that men desire and fight over in the narrative. The name "Helen" also refers to the ancient Greek Helen (ca. 480–406 BCE), the daughter of Zeus and Leda and the wife of Menelaus. Helen was abducted by Paris and taken to Troy. Homer's treatment of Helen in *The Iliad* is largely a compassionate one. However, some Greek playwrights take a much less sympathetic view of her character; Euripides (ca. 480–406 BCE), for example, in his play *The Trojan Women*, indicts her for adultery. She also has a more complicated role in *The Odyssey* because of her aid to the Greeks with their Trojan horse. Walcott's description of his Helen as a shadow is significant because it suggests the myth that it was not Helen who went back to Troy with Paris but her "shadow." This interpretation is based on a poem by Stesichorus (640–555 BCE) entitled "Palinodia." Euripides examines this tale in *The Trojan Women*. The modernist poet H.D. (Hilda Doolittle, 1886–1961) examines the life of Helen in her *Helen in Egypt*. Also of note here is the island of St. Lucia itself, which was known as the "Helen of the West Indies." Walcott uses the shadow of empire in his *Pantomime*. See notes 11.4, 24.6, 34.20.

17.7 Ma Kilman—a central female character in the narrative used to link St. Lucia with Africa. She is a healer and small businesswoman.

The name of her establishment, the No Pain Café, a tea room/bar/ shop/pharmacy, is significant because it is Ma Kilman who addresses Philoctete's enduring pain from a wound that resists healing throughout the poem. Ma Kilman relies on her inherited African wisdom for remedies that recall the struggle, resistance, and ultimate survival of her ancestors. Walcott previously used a figure named Ma Kilman in *Sea Grapes*, "Saint Lucie," where he transcribes and recreates a St. Lucian *conte*, or "folk song," whose third and fourth sections open with Ma Kilman, who is notable for having earned both the blessings and punishment of God for her charity and excess of religion. In the Caribbean, she serves as a paradigmatic Obeah woman/mother figure. The name "Kilman" also functions allegorically, if ironically, in *Omeros* given Ma's position as healer, and suggests Miss Kilman in Virginia Woolf's (1882–1941) *Mrs. Dalloway*, a woman who stands apart from conventional society in terms of gender and sexuality but who is drawn to spiritual practice. In Greek myth the figure who cures Philoctetes is a surgeon/ healer named Machaon, a son of Asclepius, the god of medicine. See notes 58.5 and 63.17.

17.13–14 No Pain Café—the establishment owned and operated by Ma Kilman where she serves refreshments and ministers to her customers. The primary model for the No Pain Café is the Keep Cool Café in Gros Islet, on the main road into the village just a few blocks off the Castries road. Walcott also used as a model the Gros Islet bar, Scotty's, where he would spend afternoons writing. Both of these establishments are just blocks from one another and continue to provide Gros Islet with vibrant public houses. See notes 17.5–6, 17.7, 24.6.

17.23 St. Omere—Garth St. Omer (1932–) and Dunstan St. Omer (1927–) are both St. Lucian–born artists who are friends of Walcott. Garth St. Omer is a novelist and cousin of Dunstan St. Omer, the painter whom Walcott met while at St. Mary's College. Walcott has written a poem "For Garth St. Omer." St. Omere suggests a play on the French term for the sea and mother, *la mer and la mère*, that relates to the narrator Seven Seas, who represents the innate global poetic consciousness, with knowledge of the past and present, of a Homeric poet. St. Omer is also a town in northern France, founded by a group of monks in the seventh century, and the location of a renowned Gothic Cathedral, Notre

Dame, built between the thirteenth and the fifteenth centuries. Dunstan St. Omer appears in Walcott's *Another Life* as Gregorias. See notes 8.4, 58.22–23, 98.3–5, and 120.15–16.

18.3 They were Greek to her. Or Old African Babble—Ma Kilman is unable to understand the language of her ancestors just as the milk-woman in James Joyce's *Ulysses* is unable to understand the Irish language of her ancestors.

18.15 acajou—French meaning "mahogany," though the *noix d'acajou* is a cashew nut; Ma Kilman has prepared a curative from acajou for Philoctete's wound.

18.20–21 I am blessed with this wound—a play on the French and St. Lucian Kwéyòl *blessé*, which means "wounded." See note 3.2.

19.6 Portuguese man-o'-war—British and French ships were referred to as "men-of-war." These ships played an important role in the struggle for control of the island between the British and the French during the colonial period. The Portuguese man-o'-war, a sea creature, is often mistaken for a jellyfish. It is in fact a hydrozoan, from the family *Physaliidae*, with a sack-like shape from which tentacles hang, endangering prey with poison. Their stings are painful but not often deadly in humans. They habitually travel in groups of up to a thousand and follow sea currents. See notes 43.18 and 65.15.

19.12 abattoir—the French term for "slaughterhouse."

19.25–26 senna . . . tepid tisanes—senna refers to a product of the cassia tree, which has a cinnamon-like bark. The bark is used as a spice and the leaves of the tree produce the senna, which has a laxative effect. Tisane, a tea made from herbs, also refers to dried herb and to ptisan, a drink made of barley water.

CHAPTER IV

20.7 estate with its windmill—refers to one of several windmills in the northern portion of St. Lucia. Windmills were used to generate energy and particularly to process sugarcane. Although most of the sugar mills in St. Lucia were not wind generated, a few notable exceptions exist: Morne Giraud, Gros Islet, estate of G. Purchase; Mount Pleas-

ant, Castries (no estate noted); and Cap Estate, Gros Islet, estate of
DeLongueville.

21.4 mole cricket—the common Puerto Rico mole cricket (*Scapter-
iscus vicinus*) is also known as *changa*. It is a nocturnal insect that has
strong front legs for digging and strong hind legs for jumping. Usually
found in moist soil, it has a mole-like appearance and burrows in the
earth; it feeds on roots and destroys crops.

21.20 Salope—from the French for "prostitute." In the Caribbean, it
can refer to a dirty, unwashed, street person, usually female.

22.12 haieing—a form of the French word, *haie*, literally a hurdle or
hedgerow, though the term is also used to refer to a line of bayonets. The
description of the cattle herdsman suggests a Homeric reference to the
oxen of the sun, the bold and ill-conceived slaughter of Helios' kine, for
which Odysseus' men paid with their lives.

**22.13–15 who set out to found no cities . . . they were the
ground**—homage to Aimé Césaire's (1913–2008) famous refusal of
conventional epic accomplishments in his *Notebook of a Return to the
Native Land.*

23.10 Lawrence—T. E. (Thomas Edward) Lawrence or Lawrence
of Arabia (1888–1935), born in Wales as the second illegitimate son
of an Anglo-Irish baronet father, Sir Thomas Robert Tighe Chapman
(1846–1919), and a Scottish governess, Sarah [Junor/Junner] Law-
rence (1861–1959), who had been in service to Lady Edith Sarah Ham-
ilton Chapman (1848–1930) and was educating the four daughters of
the Chapman family. Called Ned by his family, T. E. Lawrence, though
of limited professional options due to his birth, was Oxford educated,
spoke Arabic, and worked in the Middle East as an archaeologist for
the British Palestinian Exploration Committee before World War I.
During the war, he provided the British with critical knowledge of the
area; helped with the Arab Revolt led by Prince Faisal bin Hussein bin
Ali al-Hashimi (1883–1933), a member of the Hashemite dynasty and
descendant of the family of the Prophet Mohammed, against the Ot-
toman Turks (who supported the Germans); and became involved in
the taking of Aqaba (a location vital to protecting British interests and
the Suez Canal). After the war, he worked for the British, negotiating in
Paris the division of the Middle East between British, French, and Arab

interests, and privately published a memoir, *The Seven Pillars of Wisdom*, in 1926. His final publication was a translation of *The Odyssey* (1932) that is notable for Lawrence's archeological knowledge of the eastern Mediterranean world. See notes 31.13 and 262.3.

24.6 Helen—the central female character in the poem. She is the object of desire for Achille, Hector, and Plunkett. She works as a maid for the Plunketts and wears a yellow dress that she has gotten from Maud. Helen of Troy is a significant personage in Greek myth; the product of Zeus' rape of Leda when he took the form of a swan, Helen is the mortal wife of Menelaus, a Spartan ruler, who elopes with or is abducted by, depending on the interpretation, a Trojan prince, Paris. Renowned for her beauty, her face launches the "thousand ships" that fight the Trojan War. In *The Iliad*, during the sacking of Troy, she aids the Greek forces and after the war returns to Menelaus. Helen is referenced in Walcott's "Origins," "Homecoming: Anse La Raye," "Map of the New World," and *Another Life*. See notes 8.9, 11.4, 17.5–6, 34.20, 35.18, 36.21, 62.27, 153.1, and 298.9.

CHAPTER V

24.7 Major Plunkett—Major Denis Plunkett is primarily a representation of the settler or British colonial class on St. Lucia. Although in British service, many of his associations are more specifically Irish. He drinks Guinness and has an Irish wife, Maud. His name (like his wife's name, see below) is also linked to an Irish revolutionary, Joseph Mary Plunkett (1887–1916), who participated in the Easter Rising of 1916 and was one of the men who signed the *Proclamation of the Provisional Government of the Irish Republic to the People of Ireland*. The British crown executed the historical Plunkett in May 1916 for his participation in the Easter Rising. The father of Joseph Mary Plunkett was Count George Noble Plunkett (1851–1948), a Papal count, a title given for extraordinary service to the Roman Catholic Church. The elder Plunkett was the director of the National Museum on Kildare Street in Dublin (until he was forced to resign because of his son's involvement in the Easter Rising). He took over this leadership position at the museum from an Englishman, Lieutenant Colonel G. T. Plunkett of the Royal Engineers of Fitzwilliam Square, a former army man who was installed to run the Dublin Museum from the London central administrative office in South Kensington Museum, now the Victoria & Albert Museum. Colonel Plunkett had a son who served the empire as a lieutenant colonel in the 2nd Battalion King's African Rifles, Manchester Regiment, Arthur William Valentine Plunkett (1869/70–1903), who was killed in Somaliland. See notes 25.2, 26.9, 31.13, and 114.8–9.

24.9 Maud—the wife of Major Dennis Plunkett. Maud also refers to Maud Gonne (1866–1953), the famous stage actress and Irish revolutionary involved in the Easter Rising of 1916. She was reportedly a stunningly beautiful woman and the object of an adoring yet unrequited love of the Irish poet William Butler Yeats (1865–1939). Maud evokes Penelope in her attention to a textile that will be used as a funeral shroud. Unlike Penelope, however, Maud does not unravel her work. Rather, she embroiders fabric with birds that will cover her own casket. Penelope weaves a shroud for Odysseus' father, Laertes. Maud's association with avian images draws from Ovid's (43 BCE–17 CE) *Metamorphoses* and Ezra Pound's (1885–1972) *Canto IV*. Walcott links bird images with national identities in "The Season of Phantasmal Peace." See notes 24.6, 24.7, 25.4–5, 88.16–21, 199.1, and 200.5.

24.11 kraal—an enclosure for animals or a collection of huts surrounded with fencing to keep in animals. The term originates in South Africa and is originally Afrikaans, though it is related to the Portuguese, *curral*, for "pen."

24.12 raffia—a palm of the African genus *raphia*, which is a kind of tree that is found in Madagascar. It can also refer to the soft fiber made from the leaves of such a tree and used as twine in basketwork.

24.14 Martinique—an island that remains in French governance; part of the Windward Islands, immediately north of St. Lucia, and officially called *Département d'Outre-Mer de la Martinique*. Martinique is visible in outline on a clear day from the northern tip of St. Lucia. The capital of Martinique is Fort-de-France and the population of the island is around 433,000. The highest point on the island is the volcanic Mount Pelée. Columbus is believed to have landed on Martinique in 1502, but the Spanish ignored it. The French settled the island in 1635. Enslaved African subjects were brought to Martinique in 1664, and it was not until 1848 that slavery was abolished on the island. See notes 81.19–20, 92.12–13, 121.6, and 225.2.

25.2 the war—refers to World War II (1939–1945), during which Plunkett served in the British armed forces in their North African campaign. Walcott references this campaign in "Two Poems on the Passing of an Empire."

25.4–5 Glen-da-Lough . . . Wicklow—from the Irish *Gleann dá locha* or "glen of the two lakes," the location of medieval monastic ruins in County Wicklow, Ireland. Wicklow is the county south of Dublin known for its beautiful mountains. The ruins of a monastic community that was started by St. Kevin are now a tourist destination. This is the home of Maud Plunkett, to which she longs to return. See notes 197.1, 198.15, 199.1, 200.5, and 200.9.

25.8 Afrika Korps. / *Pro Rommel, pro mori*—Monty is shorthand for General Bernard Montgomery (1887–1976), the commander of British forces in Northern Africa during World War II. Rommel is German Field Marshal Erwin Rommel (1891–1944), commander of the German forces in Africa and nicknamed the "Desert Fox." The Afrika Korps is a reference to Rommel's two division tank corps that Adolf Hitler (1889–1945) sent to Africa to combat the British after the British defeated the Italians in several battles. *Pro* in Latin, when used in a phrase, means "in favor of." *Mori* is Latin for "death." The phrase "pro mori" evokes Wilfred Owen (1893–1918), the British poet of World War I who died just a week before peace and who wrote "Dulce et Decorum Est [Pro Patria Mori]" (It is Sweet and Fitting [to Die for One's Country]) a poem that take its title from an ode of the Roman poet Horace (65–8 BCE). Horace celebrates, whereas Owens condemns, such sacrifice. See notes 26.7, 26.22; 26, and 90.8.

25.14 *Pro honoris causa*—a Latin phrase, "*pro*" means "in favor of"; "*honoris causa*" means "for the sake of honor."

25.17 Victoria—the Queen of England (1819–1901) and Empress of India during Britain's apex of colonial power during the nineteenth century; a pub in the text has been named in her honor. See notes 26.9, 103.26–27, and 195.4.

25.20 the Raj—in general, "a dominion or rule." Specifically, it is often used to refer to British rule in India from 1757 to 1947.

25.23 pukka—of full measure or weight; "authentic, true, permanent, or excellent." It can also refer to a rare or obsolete copper coin. The term originates in Indian English and derives from the Hindi *pakka*, for "cooked, ripe, proper."

25.25–26 Luverly, Right-o . . . Ta—phrases that suggest upper-class British accents and education. Luverly is a phonetic spelling for lovely.

26.2–3 Cockney . . . Clods from Lancashire—A Cockney is conventionally an inhabitant of the East End of London, historically an impoverished area, though the term can also refer to a London dialect associated with the East End. A "clod" is a clumsy, awkward person or a dull, dim person. Lancashire is a county in northwest England.

26.7; 26 the war in the desert under Montgomery—the British North African campaign against the Germans and Italians in the desert during World War II. See notes 25.8, 26.22, 26.27, and 90.8.

26.9 pickled at the Victoria—the Victoria and Albert Museum in London, also known as the V&A. Its collections originated in the Great Exhibition of 1851 at The Crystal Palace. It underwent various reconceptualizations, and in 1857 it opened formally as the South Kensington Museum. It was finally renamed the Victoria & Albert Museum in 1899. Markers of heroism in the war become objects preserved or "pickled" for display in the V&A. See notes 25.17, 103.26–27, and 195.4.

26.11 Rover—a wanderer; an "obsolete term for a pirate ship" that now signifies a vehicle used for exploration and discovery, from the highly individualized space varieties sent to explore planets and moons to the mass-produced land vehicle commonly associated with administering colonial territories. The British car company, Rover, first produced its Land Rover in 1948 in response to a perceived need for military-style all-terrain vehicles.

26.22 Tobruk and Alameins—Tobruk is a Mediterranean city in Libya from which the Germans launched a relentless series of attacks against the British during World War II. El Alamein or Al Alamayn is also a city on the Mediterranean but further east in Egypt to which British forces at first retreated and then rebounded against the Germans. British General Bernard Montgomery (1887–1976) was victorious in the North African campaign and was ultimately named a viscount with the title Montgomery of Alameins. See notes 25.8, 26.7, 26.22; 26, and 90.8

26.27 Afrika Korps—See notes 25.8, 26.7, 26.22; 26, and 90.8

27.3 Tommies—British soldiers; the term originates from a common name used on sample bureaucratic forms that dates to the nineteenth century; however, it became a common usage during the world wars of the early twentieth century. A "tommy" is also a British slang term for a "tommy tank" or masturbation. See notes 102.6 and 251.18.

27.8 Messerschmitt's Gun—a weapon on a German fighter aircraft produced by the airplane design engineer Willy Messerschmitt (1898–1978). The ME-109 was the most renowned of his planes.

27.15 Kraut salute—a kraut is an informal and derogatory term for a German soldier during World War I and World War II; the term originated as an abbreviation for sauerkraut, a common German dish of pickled cabbage. The salute required of German forces under Adolf Hitler (1889–1945) was a raised right arm at a forty-five-degree angle.

27.23 Victoria—see notes 25.17, 26.9, 103.26–27, and 195.4.

28.21 Battle of the Saints—the conflict between the British and French navies on April 12, 1872. The battle involved the British taking up a position in Gros Islet Bay with thirty-six war ships. The French were convening in Fort Royal Bay, Martinique, with thirty-three ships under the command of Admiral François Joseph Paul, Comte de Grasse (1722–1788). The Comte de Grasse had helped the American colonists achieve victory in the American Revolution by keeping a British fleet from supplying General Charles Cornwallis (1738–1805), thereby forcing the British to surrender at Yorktown. At the time of the Battle of the Saints, the French were plotting with the Spanish to overtake Jamaica. Noticing the movements of the French fleet from his position in Gros Islet, Admiral Lord George Rodney (1719–1792) made the decision to engage the French fleet, gaining a decisive victory. See notes 31.26–27, 32.5, 32.6, 34.21, 43.1, 43.10, 79.18, 81.19–20, 84.1, 92.12–13, 99.21–100.5, and 100.9.

28.22 tea rose—the *rosa x odorata*, the leaves of which are noticeably fragrant, much like tea. The rose is a national symbol of Britain.

28.25 Seychelles—a nation comprised of approximately ninety islands in the Indian Ocean off the eastern coast of Africa and due north of Madagascar. These islands were initially colonized by the French, though the British took control of them in 1794; it was not until 1814 that British control was firmly established. The Seychelles are now an independent Commonwealth nation. See notes 90.7–8 and 227.27.

28.27 desert's white lily—a large fragrant flower (*Hesperocallis undulata*) common to the deserts of Mexico and the western United States, that resembles the Easter Lily, though the desert lily has cream petals or segments. The stems of these flowers can grow up to four feet.

29.5 raffia—see note 24.12.

30.3 Guinness—an Irish beer first produced in 1759 at St. James Gate Brewery in Dublin. Guinness was first shipped to the Caribbean in the 1820s. The present-day production, Guinness Extra Stout, was previously named Guinness East and West India Porter. See note 24.7.

30.4 Seychelles—see note 28.25, 90.7–8, and 227.27.

30.12 Upper Punjab—a northwestern region of the Indian subcontinent between the Indus and Yamuna Rivers; it was divided during the 1947 partition between India and Pakistan. The area was under Sikh control until 1849 when the British seized the region for their empire.

30.14 the Raj—see note 25.20.

30.18 Giza Pyramids—on the western bank of the Nile River in Northern Egypt on the Giza Plateau, opposite Cairo; the site is a large necropolis, a network of tombs, the most notable of which are the three Great Pyramids. See note 65.5.

30.19 Pitons—two mountains with volcanic peaks, Petit Piton and Gros Piton, on St. Lucia's southwestern shore that rise into view from the Caribbean Sea and dominate the island landscape. Gros Piton is southernmost of the two and overlooks Choiseul, whereas Petit Piton is a few miles to the north and overlooks Soufrière. The national flag, designed by renowned painter and friend of Walcott Dunstan St. Omer (1927–), bears a black triangle said to represent both the Pitons and the dominance of African cultures on the island. See notes 40.21, 59.13, 103.3, 227.10, and 289.8.

30.23 *Memento mori*—a Latin phrase referring to an object or "remembrance of death"; it is a warning or reminder of human mortality. It also refers to visual art, such as painting and sculpture, that captures the moment of death or an object representing death and decay such as a skull.

30.24 Remembrance Day—the day of armistice for World War I. The armistice was signed at 11:00 a.m. on November 11, 1918. In the United States, it has been referred to as Veteran's Day since 1954, while in France and Canada it is still referred to as Remembrance Day; in Great Britain it is called Remembrance Sunday. In Canada and Britain the day is commonly observed by the wearing of a red poppy, a token of remembrance for the dead. Walcott's play, *Remembrance,* evokes Remembrance Day and deals with the struggle between British and Caribbean cultures. See notes 257.12 and 262.1.

30.25 Trafalgar—refers to the Battle of Trafalgar in 1805 during the Napoleonic War that occurred off the southwest coast of Spain between the British, French, and Spanish. The British won the battle under the command of Admiral Horatio Nelson (1758–1805), who died from a wound suffered during the battle. Trafalgar Square in London is named after this battle. The northern side of the square contains a monument to Nelson. See notes 193.13, 193.21, 194.4, 194.9, and 195.4.

31.3 myrmidon—see note 10.25.

31.4 Troy—the ancient city that borders the Dardanelles, the strait between the Aegean Sea and the Sea of Marmara that provides the critical passage between Europe and Asia. In Asia Minor, it is the location of the great war of classical Greek myth portrayed in Homer's *The Iliad.* Founded in the Bronze Age, its location was re-discovered in the late nineteenth century in present-day Turkey. Walcott refers to Troy in "A Village Life" and *Another Life.* See notes 3.2, 6.1, 8.9, 14.5, 16.14–15, 17.5–6, and 24.6.

31.6 Pitons—see notes 30.19, 40.21, 59.13, 103.3, 227.10, and 289.8.

31.8 Gaul and Briton—Roman names for France and Britain, respectively.

31.13 Lawrence—the waiter at the club, but his name echoes the earlier Lawrence noted and compared to Plunkett. See note 23.10 and 262.3.

31.23–24 Gibraltar of the Caribbean—Because St. Lucia was such a desirable colonial possession over which many battles were fought between the British and the French, she was nicknamed the Gibraltar of the Caribbean. Gibraltar is a British colony located on the northwest end of the Rock of Gibraltar, which is part of the southern peninsula of Spain. The population is a mixture Spanish, Italian, Maltese, and Jewish descendents. English is the official language; however, like St. Lucia, the colony has undergone several changes of possession. The struggle for Gibraltar began in 711, when the Moors captured the area from Spain. The Spanish recaptured the land in 1309, maintained possession until 1333, but Spain did not gain complete control over the territory from the Moors until 1462. The British captured the land in 1704 and have maintained control ever since, despite the Spanish government's continued protest. Similar to St. Lucian history, the now British colony of Gibraltar had to endure attacks by the Spanish and the French, the first in 1704. The Spanish tried again in 1726 and then once more with the help of the French in a conflict that lasted from 1779 to 1783—both attempts were unsuccessful. See note 11.4.

31.26–27 her final peace was signed at Versailles—though many treaties have been signed at Versailles, the spectacular residence of the French monarchs prior to the French Revolution, the most salient of these are both the treaty after British victory over the French in the Battle of the Saints, signed in September 1783, and the treaty signed in June 1919 that concluded World War I between the Allies and Germany. The 1783 treaty, however, was not the ultimate end of the conflict over St. Lucia; in spite of the British victory, France still retained possession of St. Lucia. The Treaty of Paris in 1814 ended the conflict between the two rivals.

32.1 Lawrence—see notes 23.10 and 262.3.

32.4 Versailles—see note 31.26–27.

32.5 Admiral Rodney—Admiral Lord George Rodney (1719–1792) was the commander of the British naval fleet that participated in the Battle of the Saints. (See notes 28.621 and 11.190). Rodney served with merit in the Seven Years' War (1756–1763). He came to prominence at this time because of his capture of Martinique. After a brief stay in France because of financial debts, Rodney was recalled by the British government and sent back to the Caribbean. During his return voyage, Rodney's fleet stopped at Gibraltar to engage the Spanish navy that was attacking the British colony at Gibraltar off Cape St. Vincent. Rodney's victory over the Spanish Fleet secured Gibraltar for the British crown (also see note 37.702). Rodney is also the British officer who "won" St. Lucia for the British in 1763. After capturing Martinique in 1762, Rodney turned his attention to St. Lucia. With minimal resistance from the French on the island at the time, Rodney took the island for Britain, but in 1763 the Treaty of Paris was signed, giving control of the island back to France. In 1778, with another war between Britain and France beginning, it was Rodney who convinced the British government of the importance of St. Lucia. As a result of this action, Rodney set the stage for the Battle of the Saints in 1782. Rodney is named in the Middle Passage section of "The Schooner Flight." See notes 28.21, 32.6, 34.21, 39.21, 43.1, 43.10, 43.13, 79.18, 81.19–20, 81.21, 92.12–13, 99.21–100.5, and 100.9.

32.6 lion-headed island—Pigeon Island, a coastal promontory near Gros Islet in the north of St. Lucia, the silhouette of which resembles the profile of a lion. Now a national preserve, it was originally a separate island that was joined by an earthen causeway in the 1970s. The phrase also suggests the golden lion at the prow of the *Ville de Paris*, the ninety-gun ship that Admiral Rodney (1719–1792) captured from the Comte de Grasse (1722–1788) in April 1782. The defeat of the French during the Battle of the Saints gave the British control of St. Lucia. The lion is a common symbol of royal power for the French monarchy, though the prowess and mastery of the lion as a symbol of authority was common in the ancient world. See notes 28.21, 32.5, 34.21, 37.13, 39.21, 43.1, 43.10, 43.13, 79.18, 81.19–20, 81.21, 92.12–13, 99.21–100.5, and 100.9.

32.10 St. Peter's Day—June 29. The most well-known Peter, and the Roman Catholic saint for whom the day is named, is the apostle whose original name, Simon, was changed to Peter, *Petrus* in Latin, or "rock." Peter became an early leader of the church, the rock upon which Christianity was built. He was also thought to hold the keys to the kingdom of heaven. A lesser known St. Peter is St. Peter Gonzalez (1190–1246), who was a preacher known for passionate sermons that led many to convert to the Catholic faith. Gonzalez is the saint who was formerly known as St. Elmo. St. Elmo is often associated with "St. Elmo's fires," which are small electrical bursts that appear on the top of the masts of ships at sea during thunderstorms. Sailors once believed that these discharges were the souls of persons who had died at sea. During the classical period sailors referred to this phenomenon as "Helena." The third St. Peter of interest here is St. Peter Claver (1581–1654), another Spaniard. He arrived at Cartagena in the Caribbean in 1610 and became known over his four-decade stay as the "Apostle of the negro slaves." The Spanish were importing around a thousand enslaved Africans a month through Cartagena. After their arrival in the Caribbean, the slaves would be transferred from the island to the gold mines of Central and South America. Claver was the Catholic missionary to the slaves, who would greet them upon their arrival with food, drink, and conversion. The Catholic Church estimates that Claver converted somewhere around three hundred thousand enslaved Africans to Christianity. See note 196.24.

32.13 Aegean / Parthenon—the Aegean is the sea, the body of water that sits between Greece and Asia Minor. The name comes from Aegeus, the father of Theseus, who drowned himself in it out of despair over what he thought was the death of his son. The Parthenon is the temple that was built for Athena at the highest point in Athens. The name "Parthenon" signifies purity and a chamber of virgins. See notes 31.4, 177.9–11, 204.5, 230.13, 281.19, and 284.4.

32.16 *victor ludorum*—Latin for "victor of the games," the overall champion of a sports competition.

CHAPTER VI

33.3 centaurs—in Greek mythology the centaurs are half horse and half man. A group characterized by violence and intemperance, they often represent linked extremes of order and disorder, human and beast.

34.20 Menelaus—the younger brother of Agamemnon and the husband of Helen. Some records describe him as King of Sparta, while others make him share a throne with his brother Agamemnon at Argos. It is because of Paris' abduction of Helen that the Trojan War begins. In Book III of Homer's *The Iliad*, Paris and Menelaus meet in a duel to settle their dispute. Menelaus wins this duel but is prevented from killing Paris by Aphrodite. Throughout *The Iliad*, Menelaus is portrayed as an effective but kind warrior who often either defers or takes a back seat to his brother, Agamemnon. In *The Odyssey*, Menelaus is portrayed as happily at home with Helen, telling stories to the people of Sparta (the most notable of these stories is one wherein he recounts a trip to Egypt). After Homer, there are writings that advance the mythic story, adding details of Menelaus' life before and after that which is portrayed in the epics. Greek dramatists offer a less-than-sympathetic view of Menelaus, often portraying him as weak and in decline. See notes 17.5–6, 24.6, and 152.14–15.

34.21 Gros Îlet—St. Lucian Kwéyòl for Gros Islet, a village on the northwestern shore of St. Lucia. The village is southeast of Pigeon Island National Park. The inlet at this point is called Rodney Bay because it is where Admiral Rodney took up a position with his ships and attacked the French in the Battle of the Saints. Gros Islet remains a fishing village even today, though it is now sandwiched between the luxury resorts built on the causeway to Pigeon Island and the more local but still touristy Rodney Bay. Gros Islet is famed for its Friday night street party known as a "Jump Up." Much of the action in *Omeros* is set in and around this town. See notes 11.4, 17.13–14, 20.7, 28.21, 32.5, 32.6, 39.21, 43.1, 43.10, 43.13, 79.18, 81.19–20, 81.21, 92.12–13, 98.3–5, 99.21–100.5, 100.9, 105.13–14, and 109.18–21.

35.12 Troy—see notes 3.2, 6.1, 8.9, 14.5, 16.14–15, 17.5–6, 24.6, and 31.4.

35.16 Scamander—the river now known as the "Menderes," which flows from Mt. Ida to the Hellespont, the slim strait that divides Europe from Asia. This river in Turkey, now called the Küçük Menderes, was thought to be a source of fertility and generation in ancient myth. It feeds off of the smaller waterways in the Ida mountains and empties into the Dardanelles and subsequently the Aegean Sea. In *The Iliad*, the river god, Scamander, battles Achilles because of the number of Trojans that Achilles has killed. Scamander floods the plain of battle, attempting to drown Achilles, but Hera's intervention saves the Greek hero. She sends the fire of Hephaestus, with the aid of wind, against the waters of Scamander. See notes 31.4, 32.13, 204.5, and 281.19.

35.18 Agamemnon—son of Atreus and husband to Clytemnestra, the sister of Helen. In Homer he is the leader of the Greek invasion of Troy. He is valorous but easily dispirited. Achilles quarrels with Agamemnon over Briseis in *The Iliad*. *The Odyssey* tells the story of Agamemnon's return home, where his wife's lover, Aegisthus, kills him at a banquet. Agamemnon's wife Clytemnestra kills Cassandra, Agamemnon's mistress and the daughter of Priam, the king of Troy. In later treatments of the story, Clytemnestra is credited with killing both Cassandra and Agamemnon without any help from Aegisthus (for dramatic accounts of these murders, see Aeschylus' (ca. 525–455 BCE) *Agamemnon* or Euripides' (ca.480–406 BCE) *Iphigenia at Aulis*). Agamemnon is known for the sacrifice of his daughter, Iphigenia, for Artemis, the goddess of the hills and forest, after he boasted that he was a better hunter than she. Artemis was keeping Agamemnon and the Greek fleet from reaching Troy with unfavorable weather conditions. Iphigenia's murder placated the goddess, who then released the fleet. Walcott refers to Cassandra in "A Village Life." See notes 34.20 and 152.14–15.

35.20 swift's road—see notes 8.3, 88.21, 239.16, and 242.15.

35.24 Barrel of Beef—an island in the U.S. Virgin Islands, county of St. Thomas. It is a relatively small rock formation that rises roughly ten feet above sea level, approximately one and a half miles due west of Colombier Point, St. Bart's, or Saint-Barthélemy. An arid, rocky island, it is unsuited to plantation agriculture and mostly populated by the descendants of Europeans.

35.24 Seven Seas—see note 11.10.

36.6 golden moss of the reef fleeced the Argonauts—suggests the "golden fleece," guarded by a serpent, from the Greek myth of Jason and the Argonauts. Jason endeavors to reclaim his throne; to do so, he must retrieve the fleece. Jason represents a wandering hero in the ancient world a generation before Odysseus. His ship is the Argo.

36.21 passed her shadow mixed with those shadows—a reference to the version of Helen's story that contends that Paris actually brought her shadow back to Troy rather than her body. See notes 8.9, 11.4, 17.5–6, 24.6, 34.20, 35.18, 62.27, 153.1, and 298.9.

CHAPTER VII

37.11 Mohammedan melons—watermelons.

37.13 Etruscan lions—lions, now painted gold, are placed prominently on the four sides of the jewel-colored, tiled water fountain at the center of Castries Market. The Etruscans ruled Italy before the advent of Roman culture. They were rivals of the Greeks for dominance in the Mediterranean world during the sixth century before the Christian Era. Sculptures of lions, a common depiction in Etruscan art, were often placed on tombs to guard the passage into death. See notes 32.6, 39.21, 104.6, 120.6, 151.7–8, 194.5, and 230.11.

37.20 sapodilla—a three-inch red-brown fruit produced by a large evergreen tree (*Manilkara zapota*) or naseberry, whose wood is durable and whose sap produces chicle, a milky juice used to make chewing gum. The tree can also be called the chicle-gum tree or simply the chicle tree.

37.21 Conquistadores—literally "conquerors"; the term originates in the Spanish as *conquistar*, "to conquer." It specifically refers to the Spanish military men such as Hernando Cortés (1485–1547) and Francisco Pizarro (1475–1541) who took control of the Americas during the sixteenth century and defeated indigenous peoples. Walcott notes the conquistadores in his "Hurucan" and mentions both Cortés and Pizarro in "The Liberator."

39.21 the fort that ridged the lion-headed islet—Fort Rodney on the southern peak of Pigeon Island, which is now a peninsula, after the causeway was built from the mainland in the early 1970s. Built in 1778, Fort Rodney was instrumental in Admiral Rodney's actions in the Caribbean. He built up much of the martial architecture on the island. The fort was also critical for the Brigands' War in 1795 but had fallen out of use by the mid-nineteenth century. The canons atop the fort today are not original. The original arms were sold in 1861, during the time of the American Civil War. See notes 28.21, 32.5, 32.6, 34.21, 43.1, 43.10, 43.13, 79.18, 81.19–20, 81.21, 92.12–13, 99.21–100.5, and 100.9.

40.7 lee side—the side protected from the wind.

40.14 *In God We Troust*—see note 8.4.

41.21 where a barrier reef is vaulted by white horses—reefs surround St. Lucia from Anse-Chatanet Reef off of the south shore to the Coral Gardens at the base of Grand Piton; the Key Hole Pinnacles, four seamounts, or mountains of the sea formed through volcanic activity that remain underwater, are covered in coral and create a reef-like formation. The image suggests the force with which waves crash over a reef.

This force can be particularly strong in the north of St. Lucia, where the Atlantic meets the Caribbean Sea. The particular image seems drawn from the colony seal of Barbados, which pictures two horses vaulting in heavy seas over enormous waves.

42.4 bride-sleep that soothed Adam in paradise—from the book of Genesis; the slumber Adam underwent during which one of his ribs was removed to create Eve.

42.20 Morne—Morne Fortune, sometimes also Mourne, is a hill on the southern side of Castries. At its peak were various military barracks used by both the British and the French during their struggles for the island. The most notable building at the summit were the "iron barracks," which from 1829 to 1833 housed military officers. Designed to withstand the force of a hurricane, the barracks were characterized by the stone wall that surrounded them and the iron staircases and galleys that were built for every floor. The building was damaged during an earthquake in 1839. The old fort at the Morne is now the location of Sir Arthur Lewis Community College and the University of the West Indies Open Campus, which overlook Castries and whose more current buildings stand between the roadside and the old Colonial Governors' Graveyard. See notes 58.10, 223.3, and 314.27–315.1.

CHAPTER VIII

43.1 islet's museum—the Pigeon Island Museum, which is located in the colonial British mess hall that dates to 1808. The stone lower half of the building is the original mess and more recently housed a pub-style restaurant. The peach-colored upper or second level is a more recent addition. The museum focuses on colonial history and the Battle of the Saints, though the immediate pre-Columbian inhabitants of St. Lucia, the Caribs, are also represented. Pigeon Island is a nature preserve and national park at the northern edge of the island, just north of Gros Islet. Currently the museum is closed due to an apparent lack of funding. The ruins of the fortification that Rodney constructed remain visible on the island. See notes 11.4, 17.13–14, 20.7, 28.21, 32.5, 32.6, 34.21, 39.21, 43.10, 43.13, 79.18, 81.19–20, 81.21, 92.12–13, 98.3–5, 99.21–100.5, 100.9, and 109.18–21.

43.5 Cartagena—refers to two possible seaports. The one closer to St. Lucia is located on the Caribbean Sea in northwestern Columbia; it was founded in 1533 and was noted for its extreme profitability in trade for the Spanish crown. The more remote city of the same name is in southern Spain on the Mediterranean Sea. This original seaport was an important base for Spanish maritime endeavors. See note 32.10.

43.10 flagship of the Battle of the Saints—the Comte de Grasse's (1722–1788) flagship, the *Ville de Paris* (City of Paris). This three-level ship had ninety cannons and was completed in 1757. The original name for the ship was the *Impetueux* (Impetuous). After her service in the American Revolutionary War she sailed to the Caribbean to fight the British in the Battle of the Saints. After the French defeat in the battle, British Admiral Rodney assumed command of the ship. See notes 28.21, 31.26–27, 32.5, 32.6, 34.21, 39.21, 43.1, 43.10, 43.13, 79.18, 81.19–20, 81.21, 84.1, 92.12–13, 99.21–100.5, and 100.9.

43.13 the *Ville de Paris* sank—After British Admiral Rodney (1719–1792) took control of the ship *Ville de Paris* (City of Paris), its command was transferred to the fleet under the command of Admiral Graves (1725–1802), who was to sail the ship back to England. The ship sank off the coast of Newfoundland when the fleet was hit by a hurricane. In 1795 the British constructed a new ship, the HMS *Ville de Paris*, in her name. See notes 28.21, 32.5, 32.6, 34.21, 39.21, 43.1, 43.10, 79.18, 81.19–20, 81.21, 92.12–13, 99.21–100.5, and 100.9.

43.15 octopus-cyclops—an octopus, order of *Octopoda*, generally has two eyes that are notable for their skill and highly developed sight. They can rotate at acute angles and protrude from the body of this marine mollusk. The octopus has eight limbs and two hearts but no skeletal structure; this feature allows it to enter very small spaces. A cyclops is a creature with only one eye. See notes 13.7 and 155.25–26.

43.18 frigates—warships notable for their speed in the water. In the eighteenth century, they were usually "square-rigged," their sails at right angles to the length. See note 19.6.

43.21 galleon—a Spanish ship of at least two if not four decks with three or more masts used for both war and trade between the fifteenth century and the seventeenth century. They are notoriously slow moving and challenging to maneuver.

44.9 shallop—a small light boat maneuvered by sail or with oars for shallow waters.

44.25 fathom—six feet (1.83 meters), the unit of measurement used for the depth of any marine environment. The term originated in Old English, *fæthm*, for the measurement of the distance between a pair of outstretched arms. Shakespeare (1564–1616) famously used the fathom as a measurement for a paternal corpse in *The Tempest*, a play inspired by the shipwreck of the *Sea Venture* off Bermuda in 1609.

44.25 moidores, doubloons—"moidore" is a reference to a Portuguese gold coin that was used in England during the eighteenth century. In Portuguese, the phrase is *modea d'ouro*, meaning "money of gold." A doubloon is a Spanish gold coin. In the plural, as Walcott uses it here, it means "money." The Spanish word is *doblón*.

45.13 coins with the profiles of Iberian Kings—during the Bourbon dynasty, the coins that were produced in Spain were pressed with a portrait of the ruling monarch. This practice begins in 1700 and continues today. See note 191.21.

45.22–23 corpses that had perished in the crossing—a reference to the many enslaved Africans who died during the Middle Passage, from Africa to the New World. The sea holds the corpses and functions as a repository for history, ancestry, and memory. Unlike the Christian conception of the afterlife and descent as a Hell, there is no damnation associated with the sea and the ancestors who perished in it. In Haitian religious practices specifically and wider African Caribbean beliefs generally, the souls of the dead descend to an afterlife in the sea in a reunion with the ancestors. See notes 6.13, 130.8, 149.14–15, and 150.23.

46.7 Cyclops—see note 13.7.

46.16 whelk—or wilk, a sea snail of three to four inches; an edible creature with a striped black and white shell.

CHAPTER IX

47.13 hurricane season—June 1–November 30 annually in the Atlantic; the height of seasonal activity for storms is August through October, with the normal peak in early September. Walcott acknowledges the etymology of hurricane as Hourucan, the indigenous Caribbean god of the wind in "Hurucan" and *Another Life*. See notes 6.13, 43.13, 51.22, 54.20, 58.22, and 103.15.

48.6 ochre—a subtle yellow-orange pigment created using crushed minerals.

48.6 runnels—a small course of water; a brook or small stream.

48.8 gunwales—see note 7.24.

48.10 Wellingtons—long boots, generally waterproof, and often made of rubber; named for the Duke of Wellington (1769–1852), a British hero of the Napoleonic Wars. They are most often used for outdoor work such as farming and gardening.

49.1 lianas—climbing vines that grow in tropical climates.

49.6 Heron—a bird known for wading that has a long neck and legs. The plumage can be white, grey, or blue. The white heron is a smaller than the great blue heron. The white variety is common along the coasts of Florida, Mexico, and the Caribbean. The great blue (*Ardea herodias*) is often spotted in St. Lucia. See note 49.12.

49.7 heaven was breaking up in nations—in the book of *Genesis*, the descendants of Noah attempt to build a tower to reach the heavens. God, to punish those who presumed to reach heaven through worldly means, destroys the tower and the peoples are scattered with a variety of languages.

49.12 egrets—a white heron with a plume. Several types of egrets pass through St. Lucia, but the cattle egret (*Bubulcus ibis*) is a common presence near cattle herds and is known to breed on the island. See note 49.6.

49.15 termites singed their glazed wings—during termite mating season, in late spring, varieties of termites swarm and infest wooden structures. After mating, their carcasses blanket the ground and resemble piles of dead ants. Termites are also sometimes called flying ants. See note 62.4.

49.19 Ma Kilman's crowded shop—see notes 17.7; 17.13–14.

50.11 jackfish—a small fish, grey in color, similar in appearance to herring; also abbreviated as jack. It is noted for its taste as well as its boney structure. Generally a jackfish is a broad term that incorporates any number of fish species in the *Carangidae* family; they are common in tropical waters and are known for their slim bodies and forked fins. See note 223.11–12.

51.4 gunwale—see note 7.24.

51.22 Cyclone—another term for hurricane or typhoon. Atlantic storms are generally referred to as "hurricanes," whereas Pacific storms are usually referred to as "typhoons." These are all low-pressure systems over warm water with high-speed circular winds that are capable of enormous destruction. Winds produced in the most threatening systems can reach over 150 miles per hour. See notes 6.13, 43.13, 47.13, 54.20, 58.22, and 103.15.

52.1 jiggers—another name for chigoe, chiggoe, chiggers of the family *Trombiculidae*; fleas that infest sand. The females suck blood after inserting their feeding structures into the skin of a foot, causing itching and swelling that can result in the loss of toes if the mites are not removed.

52.14 Ma Kilman's shop—see notes 17.7; 17.13–14.

52.17 wreaths of the dead—see note 6.13.

52.21 Shango—the Yoruba deity of thunder. The worship of Shango is characterized by hymns, folk songs, drums, and gourd rattles, which are called *chac chac*. Shango drum ensembles, *Orisha*, were very popular in the capital of Trinidad, Port of Spain. Fearing that the drumming was inciting violence, the British attempted to ban the use of Shango drums in 1883. Walcott invokes Shango in his poem "Hurucan." See note 53.10.

52.22 Neptune Rock—the Roman god of the sea, who is also affiliated with freshwater. He carries a trident to destroy rock and master storms. The Greeks called him Poseidon.

52.22 Fête—French for a "celebration, festival, or party."

52.22–23 Erzulie / rattling her ra-ra—the African Caribbean goddess of love. She has three husbands—Damballa (god of serpents), Agwe (god of the sea), and Ogun (god of war). Erzulie is often depicted with tears streaming down her face that symbolize her lament for the shortness of life and the limits of love. She is often depicted as a water snake. See notes 52.23 and 52.24.

52.23 Ogun, the blacksmith—of Yoruban origin, the African Caribbean god of war and a warrior; one of the husbands of Erzulie (see note 52.22–23). As a blacksmith, or metallurgist, he is often associated with the saber or the machete and has a fondness for rum and tobacco.

52.24 Damballa—the African Caribbean snake god that lives near woods and streams. The patriarchal figure of devotion, he is also a god of fertility who is credited with giving birth to the *loa(s)*, or lesser god(s). Damballa is associated with the color of white, and in Haiti he is known as the *bon dieu* or "good god." See notes 96.22, 139.17, and 308.15.

52.24–25 zandoli / lizard—a species of ground lizard (*Zandoli terre*) that is indigenous to St. Lucia. It is often mistaken for a snake as its small legs are not easily seen. The Zandoli are brown, silver, and grey. They are known for their elusiveness.

52.27 seine—a partial play on the English word "insane," but Walcott's usage also refers to both a fishing net and the French river that share the name. In the Caribbean, a "seine" is a kind of fishing net with enormous lines and sizeable wings that can be operated from a boat or in shallow water from the shore. The River Seine flows through the cities of Troyes, Melun, and Paris before reaching its confluence in the English Channel. The river is of tremendous commercial importance to France and has been used by ships since the Roman occupation of Gaul.

53.2–3 fête—see note 52.22.

53.4 La Comète—French for "comet," the name of Hector's taxi. See note 8.9.

53.9 Ogun—see note 52.23.

53.9 Zeus—the chief god of Greek mythology. Zeus is the son of Cronus and Rhea; he begets mortals and immortals. He is the supreme god of the heavens and is often worshipped from mountain tops, the most important of which, Mount Olympus, is the one from which he rules. Zeus is often credited with causing rain and is associated with thunder and lightning. In Hesiod's (ca. 700 BCE) *Theogony*, Zeus is responsible for the current division of gods (where they are and what they are responsible for) after fighting the Giants and Typhon and castrating his father, Cronus. Thus Zeus is seen as the ruler of the world and responsible for everything that occurs. Concerned with law and order, he often punishes those who transgress the law. In one of the cults of Zeus (Melichios), he is, like Damballa, depicted as a large snake. See 52.24.

53.10 chac chac—a musical instrument made from small gourds that are dried, filled with rattling seeds, beads, or small rocks, and placed on sticks to shake by hand and produce sound, often in pairs, such as maracas. See note 52.21.

53.22 culverts—the side walls of a canal or a small waterway, habitually made of concrete; the term can also refer to a wall, commonly used for seating, that rises above the side of a roadway by several feet.

53.27 gunwales—see note 7.24.

54.4 fête—see note 52.22.

54.11 castanets—two shells attached to a finger and thumb and clicked together to create percussion in rhythm, often associated with Flamenco.

54.16 almond—see note 4.1.

CHAPTER X

54.20 torrents of mid-July—a reference to the period of July through October that is known in St. Lucia for its heat and tremendous rainfall. It is not unusual to experience strong winds and rain every day during this period, which coincides with hurricane season. See notes 6.13, 43.13, 47.13, 51.22, 58.22, and 103.15.

55.19 ginger tom—the informal expression for a Ginger Thomas, the bunches of cone-like yellow flowers of a thick shrub, the pods of which are also yellow and are commonly pointed upward like grasping fingers on the plant, which can grow to twenty feet.

56.5 crystal teardrop lamp—crystal, a glass of superior quality treated with lead, is cut into patterns to refract light. A signifier of middle- and upper-class social status for Irish women, it is commonly part of a marriage trousseau. Irish crystal manufacturers, such as Waterford, Tipperary, and Shannon, take their names from Irish geographic locations of their production, though Waterford, after declaring bankruptcy, has recently been bought and its production moved to continental Europe.

56.8 Seychelles—see note 28.25, 90.7–8, and 227.27.

56.10 monsoon—an extreme seasonal rainfall that accompanies heavy winds in the Indian Ocean and across Asia, often confused with a cyclone or hurricane. The winds change directions as a result of seasonal temperature differentials over the land; this pronounced difference initiates the rainy season. See notes 6.13, 43.13, 47.13, 51.22, 54.20, 58.22, and 103.15.

56.11 Bendemeer's stream—a poem by Thomas Moore (1770–1852) in his *Lalla Rookh: the Veiled Prophet of Khorassan*. See notes 56.16, 201.1, and 201.2.

56.16 *Airs From Erin*—a collection of songs from Erin, or Ireland. "Airs" generally refer to tunes or melodies suitable for a soprano. They can also refer to a traditional folk song that is usually played on the piano. Thomas Moore's (1779–1852) *Irish Melodies*, published in 1807 and 1835, is a collection of such songs; it includes an air titled "Erin, O Erin" that suggests Ireland will ultimately be freed from its enslavement. The collection is mentioned with some mockery in the opening section of James Joyce's (1882–1941) final story in *Dubliners*, "The Dead." The *Melodies*, particularly the note on St. Kevin, are also visible on background sheet music in the Irish painter, William Michael Harnett's (1848–1892) *Still Life—Violin and Music*, which hangs across from *The Gulf Stream* in the Metropolitan Museum of Art. See notes 56.11, 201.1, and 201.2.

57.7 Land Rover—see note 26.11.

57.17 bilharzia—a parasitic bloodworm that infects veins in the pelvic region in humans. It causes schistosomiasis, an infection transmitted through fecal contamination of water and often carried by snails. It is common in tropical regions across the globe.

58.1 La Sorcière / the sorceress mountain—see note 4.8.

58.5 *gardeuse*—French for "keeper" or "tender" in the feminine form (*une gardeuse d'enfants* is a baby-sitter); in the masculine form the term appears as *gardeur* (herdsman).

58.5 sybil—a female "prophet or fortune-teller" in the ancient Greek and Roman worlds. A prophetess, her toothless status suggests age. In Greek myth, the Cumaean Sybil refused to sleep with Apollo even after he awarded her a year of life for every grain of sand she grasped. Apollo did not give her youth to correspond to the extended duration of her life, so she became extremely aged. The Sybil of Cumae leads Aeneas through his journey to the underworld. Walcott links a Sybil with the Sphinx in *Midsummer*.

58.5 obeah—a religious system of belief originating in Africa and practiced in the Caribbean using material from nature, such as oils, earth, and bones, to ward off and/or exorcise the forces of evil. Through complex rituals the practitioner exercises agency in his/her use of natural elements to call on the loas or gods to achieve his/her cause.

58.7–9 Holy Communion . . . the wafers white leaf—the Catholic sacrament and ritual that performs and celebrates transubstantiation, when bread is transformed into the body of Christ, during the Mass. The bread takes the form of small, unleavened pale wafers made of simple grains. Protestant denominations vary in their acceptance and/or rejection of transubstantiation. See note 62.17.

58.10 Rover—see note 26.11.

58.10 Morne—Morne Fortune, a place from which the subjects of the following entries "Cul-de-Sac valley," "Roseau's old sugar factor," and "Anse La Raye" would have been visible. See notes 42.20, 223.3, and 314.27–315.1.

58.12 Cul-de-Sac valley—Cul-de-Sac Bay, which is located on the western side of St. Lucia, south of Castries. See second note 58.10.

58.22–23 Roseau's old sugar factory—Roseau is a valley and a town on the western coast of St. Lucia, just north of Massacre. The French started sugar cultivation on St. Lucia in 1765, in the area around Vieux Fort, at the southernmost tip of the island. The industry thrived, and over twenty plantations produced sugarcane until a hurricane in 1780. Although sugar production wavered until the mid-nineteenth century, by 1843 it had resumed its place as the chief export of the island. The cultivation of sugar is extremely labor intensive and dangerous. The transition from a tobacco economy, the harvest of which was relatively simple, to a sugar economy, the harvest of which was more perilous and required more intricate processes, was a catalyst in the Caribbean for a rapid increase in the African slave trade. Even today cane stalks are cut with a machete and taken to a mill that crushes the stalks, heats the extracted juices, filters them, and evaporates the sugar crystals from the remaining molasses. Roseau is an important valley for Walcott partially because his friend Dunstan St. Omer painted the mural at the Roseau Valley Roman Catholic church that Walcott has immortalized in his poetry. The mural is striking for its depiction of the St. Lucian peoples around the Holy Family, portrayed as figures of African descent. Walcott's "Saint Lucie" in *Sea Grapes* has a section dedicated to the "Altarpiece of the Roseau Valley Church," which celebrates St. Omer's depiction of everyday folk and the sacred. See notes 8.4, 58.22–23, 63.17, 98.3–5, and 120.15–16.

58.24 osiers—French for a "willow tree," which is known to thrive in water-logged environments. See notes 87.15; 18 and 92.26.

58.25 Anse La Raye—town on the western side of St. Lucia south of Castries and Massacre. A river and region of the island share the name. The town, well established by 1780, was one of the first settlements on the island. See note 59.13.

59.1 Rover—see note 26.11.

59.5 Canaries—a group of mountainous islands off of northwestern Africa in the Atlantic Ocean that are two Spanish provinces. They were an important base for the European colonization and the transatlantic slave trade.

59.13 the horns of the island were peaks split asunder—the two Pitons, pyramid-shaped mountains that have elevations of 3,000 (Petit Piton) and 3,300 (Gros Piton) feet. In French, the word "piton" can mean an "eye," a "hook," or a "peak." The Pitons are located on the Bay of Soufrière, the location of the Key Hole pinnacles, and are south of Anse La Raye. They dominate the landscape of St. Lucia from sea and land. See notes 30.19, 40.21, 59.13, 103.3, 227.10, and 289.8.

59.14 Soufrière—the French term for "sulfur mine"; the name of the volcano and a nearby town on St. Lucia's southwestern tip. The volcano provides hot springs and mineral waters that many believe have the power to cure ailments. There is also a volcano on Guadeloupe known as *La Grande Soufrière* that erupted in 1976 with no fatalities; a volcano of the same name on St. Vincent erupted in 1902, killed one thousand people, and destroyed a third of the island. See notes 60.7–8 and 289.8.

59.18 Malebolge—Italian for "evil bag," but can be used to refer to a "pool of filth" or a hellish place. It refers to the eighth circle of Hell in Dante's (1265–1321) *Inferno*, which holds Ulysses, who is captured in flame for his trickery. In Canto 18, the poets enter the "Eighth Circle," which is home to the "Fraudulent and the Malicious." The circle is constructed like an amphitheater subdivided into ten concentric circles. In each of these circles, the souls are tortured according to their particular sin, with Dante and Virgil (70–19 BCE) noting the "Panderers and the Seducers" as well as the "Flatterers," who are in "Bolgia" one and two, respectively. The "Panderers and the Seducers" are forced with lashes administered by horned demons on an endless brisk walk to symbolize how these sinners goaded people in life to serve them. The "Flatterers" are submerged in excrement as a symbol of their habitual practice of offering false compliments; their bodies exist in death in what their mouths expressed in life. The descent into the underworld, in Dante's case, the Christian Hell, serves as the epic convention of *katabasis*. Ezra Pound (1885–1972) depicts malebolge in *Cantos XIV* and *XV*. See note 137.7.

59.24 lime pits of Auschwitz—the German concentration camp in Poland where the Nazis murdered Jews and other prisoners. The camp was surrounded by lime, among other natural resources, which the Germans turned to their own purposes. Walcott's line also echoes the British poet Geoffrey Hill's (1932–) well-known untitled elegy for the dead in the camp that links Auschwitz with lime.

60.5 sulphur mine—see note 59.14.

60.6 hawsers—ropes used to moor sailing vessels; the term originates in Anglo-Norman *haucer* from the old French, *haucier*, "to hoist."

60.6 lianas—see note 49.1.

60.7–8 Messrs. Bennett & Ward, his countrymen / in 1836 Messrs. is the masculine plural form of the French word "*monsieur*" meaning "Mr." or "sir," which in the plural form would be "gentlemen." Walcott uses Henry H. Breen's (1805–1882) *St. Lucia: Historical, Statistical, and Descriptive* as a source for this pair but changes one name from Wood to Ward. According to Breen, two gentleman named Bennett and Wood (dates unknown) from Antigua came to St. Lucia to pursue the sulfur industry. The pair purchased a piece of land near Soufrière, where they built a base camp and established a mine in 1836. They were successful until sugar growers persuaded the legislative council to tax the sulfur. The tax made the export of sulfur unprofitable, and they left the island. The name "Wood," associated with Antigua, is infamous because of John Adams Wood (1783–1836), the final owner of Mary Prince (1788–c. 1830s). See note 99.16.

60.12–13 had one caught a fever / and yellow as that leaf—yellow fever, a viral ailment caused by the bite of a mosquito. In the nineteenth century the disease was rampant in the Caribbean. The incubation period ranges from three to five days, followed by fever, chills, headache, and vomiting. Three days after symptoms appear, they subside but subsequently return with a tragic intensity. The vomiting of blood, which is followed by delirium and coma, marks this "second" stage of the disease. In general, the illness causes inflammation, jaundice, high fever, and hemorrhages. Found in tropical climates, the illness was habitually fatal. Yellow Fever epidemics were common before the twentieth century and struck St. Lucia in 1842 and 1901. During the nineteenth century, the disease had an 85 percent mortality rate. See note 9.11.

61.10 amnesiac Atlantic—the sea is the realm of forgetfulness and in many Caribbean cultures is a location of reunion with ancestors in the afterlife. Walcott has described the sea as history and the past as well as a potential salve for the collective wounds of prior eras; the wound that Philoctete suffers serves as a symbol of this shared endurance of suffering. Walcott also associates amnesia with the maternal. See note 167.12.

61.20 going back to the bush—the journey to the central part of the island, a large rainforest in St. Lucia; more generally, it refers to the inland areas far from urban centers; in Guyana, for example, the bush is associated with the drive to find gold and other natural resources. The phrase also suggests the false hierarchies at the core of the ideology of colonization that assert the "civilization" of modernity and European norms against the "primitive" styles of humankind outside of Europe. Walcott uses the phrase to describe the choice Anton, a mixed-race character in *The Haitian Earth*, faces between his African and European roots.

62.4 rain flies—termites, also called flying ants, brown in color that can swarm in great numbers at twilight. See note 49.15.

62.12 monsoon—see note 56.10.

62.17 yellow chalices—a "yellow chalice" was discovered in Ardagh, Ireland, in 1868, that dates from the nineth or tenth centuries. In general, a chalice is a cup used during Catholic communion to hold the wine that is transubstantiated into the blood of Christ. See note 58.7–9.

62.18 morning glories—plants of the genera *Ipomoea* and *Convol-*

vulus that can produce a milky sap. The vines of the plants have funnel-shaped flowers. In fact, a morning glory can refer to a large number of species of vine, shrub, or tree with leaves and flowers that open in the morning and close in the evening.

62.18 Queen Anne—the daughter of James II (1633–1701) of England, Queen Anne (1665–1714) reigned as the final Stuart monarch. The Queen Anne's War, 1702–13, is the American term for the War of the Spanish Succession fought in Europe, 1701–14, the second of four wars in North America known collectively as the French and Indian Wars. As a result of the war, Britain gained control over St. Kitts.

62.18 Queen Anne's . . . lace—a wildflower; also called wild carrot (*Daucus carota*) or bird's nest, because of the shape of its flower, the seeds of which when ingested function as a contraceptive, preventing the implantation of a fertilized egg.

62.18 seraph—an "angel, a celestial being," a presence of sweetness and sublimity; in medieval Christian thought, the seraphim were the first in the order of angels. See note 159.5.

62.19 butterfly . . . blade—a type of pocket knife, the handle of which folds out in two wings and is pinned back in order to function or folded over to conceal the blade. It is also a term for a Ping-Pong racket. See note 203.21.

62.27 theft of the yellow frock—the dress that Helen was given or took from Maud. A girl wearing such a garment appears in Walcott's "A Lesson for This Sunday." See notes 8.9, 11.4, 17.5–6, 24.6, 34.20, 35.18, 36.21, 62.27, 153.1, and 298.9.

63.8 Before the snake. Without all the sin—from the book of Genesis. In Christian belief it refers to Eden before the "fall" of humankind into sin with Eve's temptation of Adam and the consumption of the apple from the tree of knowledge. See notes 12.25, 97.2, 181.3, 248.23–24, and 308.15.

CHAPTER XI

63.16 the Attic ideal—the ancient Greek, particularly Athenian, paradigm, from the high classical period of 450–400 BCE, in which Greek art achieved a remarkable and enduring unity of expression.

63.17 sea-grapes—a fruit, small, round, and purple, also called a seaside grape. Although the fruit hangs in clusters and thus resemble common grapes, the sea grape is produced by a tree (*Coccoloba uvifera*) rather than a vine. The term refers to both the type of tree and/or the group of berries that are produced. A sea grape tree can grow up to twenty-five feet. Walcott published a poem and a collection entitled *Sea Grapes* in 1976 in which the Caribbean is compared broadly to the ancient Mediterranean world. In one poem, Walcott alludes to Odysseus and Nausicaa, the famed ancient wanderer and the Phaenician princess who takes him in to her father's court where he is restored to well-being. See note 17.7.

63.21 swinish—piggish or otherwise coarse and disgusting.

64.4 a church that damned them to hell for contraceptives—the Catholic church's prohibition on contraception was codified with an encyclical *Humanae Vitae* (Of Human Life) by Pope Paul VI (1897–1978) in 1968.

64.7 Virgin Lamp—from the book of Matthew (25:1–13) in the New Testament. It refers to the lamps brought to a wedding by the ten virgins, half of whom brought oil for their lamps and half of whom did not. Those virgins who did not have oil were excluded from the wedding celebration. In Christian belief the lamp is a symbol for the soul, and the light of the lamp signifies preparation for the coming Messiah and eternal salvation.

64.19 history was Circe with her schoolteacher's wand—the Greek goddess, whose delights keep Odysseus by her side for a year. She has a beautiful singing voice. She is a master of men, an enchantress, and a goddess. She is sometimes confused with Calypso, who keeps Odysseus with her for a much longer period. Circe is perhaps the most famed sorceress in classical mythology; she is the daughter of Helios (the sun). In *The Odyssey* Circe transforms a group of Odysseus' men into swine. Despite the transformation, the men/pigs retain their human intelligence. Odysseus rescues his men by receiving some of the "moly" from Hermes. Odysseus and his men then stay with Circe for a year, after which she instructs them to go to the underworld to consult Tiresias. When the men return from the underworld, Circe gives them more detailed instructions on how to get home. Circe has reappeared throughout the centuries in a variety of artistic depictions. Ezra Pound (1885–1972) invokes Circe in his *Canto XXXIX*.

64.21 saint day processions—a celebration of an annual feast day devoted to a Christian saint. Frequently, the faithful will march in a parade to bring a statue of the particular saint to a holy site or a church named for that saint. The feast day for Saint Lucia (283–304), an early Christian martyr put to death by the Romans, was begun in Scandinavia as a festival of light as winter approached; it is celebrated annually on December 13. There are two important saints days in St. Lucia that are celebrated as flower festivals, the St. Rose of Lima, celebrated on August 30, and the St. Marguerite Mary of Alacoque (France), celebrated on October 17. These flower festivals have devotional societies that annually plan elaborate celebrations that incorporate songs and prayers for up to six months in advance of each festival.

64.27 Battle of the Saints—see notes 28.21, 31.26–27, 32.5, 32.6, 34.21, 43.1, 43.10, 81.19–20, 84.1, 92.12–13, 99.21–100.5, and 100.9.

65.5 ziggurat—a temple with several levels of terraces in a pyramid-like structure built by the Assyrians and Babylonians; a high tower. It also refers to a rectangular, stepped pyramid in ancient Mesopotamia; each level is slightly smaller than the last, an effect that creates small layers or floors. See notes 97.7, 100.6, and 151.9.

65.6 balsa—see note 6.18.

65.8 allamanda's bell—a yellow flower of about four inches, also called "yellow bell" or "buttercup," produced by a vine (*Allamanda cathartica*) that is sometimes considered poisonous but also has traditional medicinal applications for jaundice, malaria, and other ailments. Native to Brazil, it grows wild but can also be cultivated. This climbing evergreen vine is often cut into a form or shrub with yellow flowers. It thrives in tropical climates with generous sun exposure.

65.15 man-o-war's beak—the beak of a frigate bird, also called a cobbler, that commonly attacks other birds. Its wing-span of seven feet and ability to ascend quite high and to fly for a great distances makes it an imposing adversary for other birds. The man-o'-war bird or the magnificent frigate bird (*Fregata magnificens*) is a habitual resident of St. Lucia. These birds also breed on Frigate Island and Fous Island to a lesser extent. See notes 19.6 and 43.18.

66.4 cicada—a genus of insects (*Cicadidae*) with translucent wings. Some varieties are also called locusts. In the Caribbean, the cigale or rain-bird is a more common name for a variety that inhabits trees and produces its somewhat abrasive song at twilight. The male insects generally produce considerable noise from a membrane in their abdomens during mating season. The adults can grow up to two inches. They have multiple eyes and two pairs of wings. Several varieties are only occasional and appear in regular cycles.

66.15 Remembrance Day—see notes 30.24, 257.12, and 262.1.

67.7 In God We Troust—see note 8.4.

CHAPTER XII

67.10 bougainvillea—a tropical vine or shrub with vibrant flowers from the family *Nyctaginaceae*. These flowers with triangular petals range in color but are commonly shades of red and purple. The vine is habitually used to cover walls and fences.

67.11 printery—a printing shop. Walcott's childhood home in Castries was a lithographic press production site and office. The printery has since closed, and the house, on Chaussee Road, was acquired for the National Trust of St. Lucia to restore and preserve the building. While it is not yet restored, the lithographic sign has been removed and replaced with a plaque noting it as the Walcott family home.

67.17 negative—a printer's negative or plate that reverses the image or words that will be pressed onto paper.

68.21 Warwick. The Bard's county—is a reference by the poet to his father, Warwick Walcott (1897–1931), who died when the poet and his twin brother Roderick were just infants. Warwick was the son of a white Barbadian, Charles Walcott, who moved to St. Lucia to purchase land, and a local St. Lucian woman, Christina Wardrope (1866–1947). Warwick suffered a decline in the aftermath of surgery. He was well thought of and much liked in the community. Known to have a gift for painting and words, Warwick had worked as a clerk and registrar. Warwick is also a reference to the county of Shakespeare's (1564–1616) birth. The intersection of father and son evokes the intersection in Virgil's (70 BCE-!9 CE) *Aeneid* between Aeneas and his own father, Anchises, in the underworld. The encounter with an ancestral or paternal shade has also been compared to that of the dead king and young Prince Hamlet in Shakespeare's *Hamlet*, Stephen Dedalus' consideration of Shakespearean biography and progeny in the "Scylla and Charybdis" chapter in *Ulysses*, Seamus Heaney's (1939–2013) vision of James Joyce (1882–1941) in *Station Island*, the ghost in T. S. Eliot's (1888–1965) "Little Gidding" in *Four Quartets*, and Dante's (1265–1321) encounters with Brunetto Latini (1220–1294) in the *Inferno* as well as an ancestor, Cacciaguida, in the *Paradisio*. Walcott previously wrote of encountering his father's ghost in "Epitath for the Young" and *Another Life*. He invokes his grandfather's ghost in "Verandah." He links Warwick the father and Warwick the county in *Midsummer*, speculating that his father was named for the county.

68.24 Will—a reference to both William Shakespeare (1564–1616) and the desire to be a writer. See note 68.21.

68.26 Portia—the daughter figure of Shakespeare's (1564–1616) *The Merchant of Venice*. In the play Portia is courted by several men. While she had many suitors, she refused all who would not abide by the terms her father established. Each suitor had to guess which of three caskets, one gold, one silver, and one lead, contained her portrait. If the suitor guessed incorrectly, they were asked to leave at once and were sworn to never reveal which casket they had guessed and to never marry. See notes 72.9, 183.17, and 204.16.

68.27 Hamlet's old man's spread from an infected ear—In Shakespeare's (1564–1616) play *Hamlet*, Hamlet's father is murdered by his brother Claudius, who kills him by pouring poison into his ear. Soon after the murder, Claudius marries Hamlet's mother, Gertrude. See notes 68.21 and 138.24.

69.13 Grass Street with our Methodist chapel—Grass Street is located in Castries, several blocks southeast of Walcott Square and perpendicular to Chaussee Road. The Methodist chapel, the original wood-framed building and the now more imposing rebuilt Methodist church, were never on Grass Street. Rather the Castries Methodist chapel, now church, has always been on Chisel Street. In fact, Walcott notes this Chisel Street location clearly in "The Schooner Flight." Walcott's mother, Alix Walcott, taught and became an administrator at the Methodist school for many years. The Methodists are a minority of English-speaking Protestants on St. Lucia; the Roman Catholic French-based St. Lucian Kwéyòl-speaking majority constitutes roughly 80 percent of the population. The Methodists were known for education and antislavery work throughout the Caribbean. A Methodist chapel on Barbados was burned in protest of the group's antislavery work in the early nineteenth century. Walcott was raised as a Methodist, though he attended the elite Roman Catholic St. Mary's College, the only secondary school in the world to have produced two Nobel Prize winners: Walcott for literature and Arthur Lewis (1915–1991) for economics. Grass Street is noted in chapter VIII of Walcott's "Tales of the Islands." See notes 167.12 and 187.11.

70.3 Angelus—a ritualized though short devotional prayer that is recited three times a day in the Roman Catholic Church at the sound of a bell (morning, noon, and evening). The devotion consists of reciting the Hail Mary three times to mark the Annunciation, when the archangel Gabriel appeared to Mary to convey that she would be the mother of God. See notes 120.15–16.

70.6 dried Easter palm—fronds from palm trees that are distributed to the Christian faithful on Palm Sunday, the Sunday before Easter Sunday. The palm is frequently maintained in the family home as a sign of devotion and is also sometimes plaited into a cross. See note 70.21.

70.7–8 Veni Creator—"Veni Creator Spiritus," a Christian hymn. The hymn is commonly played when in devotion to or asking for guidance from the Holy Spirit.

70.9 poui flowers—flowers that can be on either the pink poui tree (*Tabebuia pentaphylla*) or the yellow poui tree (*Tabebuia serratifolia*); both varieties are decorative hardwoods that provide ample shade and are very common in Trinidad.

70.11 pith helmets—lightweight head coverings with a rounded brim made from plant stems (*parenchyma*) that are used to protect the wearer from sunlight; they are strongly associated with colonial officers of the British Empire.

70.11 Angelus—see note 70.3.

70.21 cabbage palms—a variety of palm trees (*Roystonea oleracea*) also called mountain cabbage and palmiste that are indigenous to the southeastern United States and the Caribbean; these trees can reach heights of over one hundred feet and have crowns that grow in clusters with edible fronds that are often used in the Christian ritual for Palm Sunday. See note 70.6.

CHAPTER XIII

71.7 Speaker—the chair of a legislative body or assembly who maintains order; initially in the British House of Commons, the Speaker held the chair to address the monarch.

71.11 *The World's Great Classics*—published by the New York publisher The Colonial Press between 1899 and 1902. Timothy Dwight (1828–1916), the president of Yale University, and Julian Hawthorne (1846–1934), the son of the well-known American novelist, Nathaniel Hawthorne (1804–1864), edited the series. They published *A History of English Literature*, *Orations of American Orators*, *Oriental Literature*, and *Sacred Books of the East*.

71.12 chamberlain—a servant of lofty rank in a court or aristocratic house; also a treasurer.

72.4–5 Not a nation or a people—echoes Walcott's "The Schooner Flight" when Shabine, the narrator, considers his own identity. Seamus Heaney (1939–2013) compared Shabine to Ulysses in *The Government of the Tongue*. See note 13.22.

72.9 Shylock—the controversial Jewish title character in Shakespeare's *The Merchant of Venice* who demands a pound of flesh as compensation. His depiction can be viewed variously as an exploitation, promulgation, or questioning of Jewish stereotypes. See notes 68.26, 183.17, and 204.16.

72.10 an Adventist—a follower of one of several branches of Christianity founded during the nineteenth century by William Miller (1782–1849), who believed that the second coming of Christ was imminent. Miller gave two dates for Christ's return. The first was sometime during 1843 and the second was April 12, 1844. The false predictions caused a division within the faith. Upon his death, Miller is believed to have had around fifty thousand adherents. Today there are at least six different types of Adventists: The Evangelical Adventists, The Seventh Day Adventists, Advent Christians, Life and Advent Union, Church of God, and the Churches of God in Christ Jesus. All the different divisions believe that the second coming or advent of Jesus is near.

72.11 Garvey—Marcus Garvey (1887–1940), activist and organizer, born in Jamaica. He quickly became interested in social reform, and in 1907 he organized the first printer's union strike in Jamaica. In 1914, he organized the Universal Negro Improvement Association and the African Communities League, which were headquartered in New York. Garvey toured the United States advocating black nationalism and his plans to build an African nation. Garvey was imprisoned and deported to Jamaica in 1927. Once in Jamaica he continued to campaign for such rights as minimum-wage laws and self-government. He left for England in 1940, where he died. Walcott refers to Garvey in *Another Life*. See notes 72.12 and 110.7.

72.12 braided tricorne—a hat with its brim folded up on three sides; often associated with revolutionary figures in the late eighteenth and early nineteenth centuries. Marcus Garvey would commonly wear a tricorne in parades. See note 72.11.

72.12 epaulettes—decorations on the shoulders of military uniforms, usually fringed and often gold in color. Marcus Garvey would commonly wear such decorative features in his formal dress for parades. See note 72.11.

72.15 Shylock silver—see notes 68.26 and 72.9.

72.16–17 Bridge Street—a major commercial thoroughfare in Castries with a police station, customs house, several banks, and the post office; it runs one block west of Walcott Square and south of the bay. See notes 72.17; 23.

72.17; 23 liner as white ... white liner—a commercial vessel that takes passengers or commodities on a regular route. The commercial ships that dock in Castries would have historically been processed at the end of Jeremie Street, just west of Bridge Street, the location of the Customs House. However, a large mooring dedicated to cruise ships has been built across Port Castries Harbor at Point Seraphine with a collection of duty-free shops to entice tourists, thus replacing the plantation commodities for the most part with those based on St. Lucia's marketing as a paradise. The selling of the island to tourists is a recurring concern for Walcott. See notes 72.16–17 and 122.12.

72.20 which marries your heart to your right hand—Walcott uses the marriage of a hand in his poem "Jean Rhys" to discuss her devotion to the page.

73.17 phosphorous—a chemical compound, though the term suggests the bringing forth of light and/or an item or thing that inherently manifests light.

73.24 torchon—French for "loofah"; a dried plant rough in texture commonly used for cleaning, though the term can also refer to cloth,.

74.6 hawsers—see note 60.6.

74.16 pith helmets—see note 70.11.

74.18 anthracite—a hard luminous kind of coal, dark grey in color, consisting of relatively pure carbon.

75.12 ancestral rhyme—alludes to Aubrey de Vere's (1814–1902) "The Bard Ethell," which was included in *A Book of Irish Verse*, a collection of poetry compiled and published by William Butler Yeats (1865–1939) in 1895. The collection was part of the Irish Celtic Revival, a movement to assert Irish independence from British cultural and political dominance.

75.19 hills of infernal anthracite—see note 74.18.

76.5 fob-watch—a pocket watch; the fob refers to the pocket in the front of a pair of pants or a vest. These were fashionable until the early twentieth century, when wrist watches became popular.

❖ Book Two

SUMMARY

The second book centers on the historical past. Major Plunkett, a figure identified with modern, twentieth-century history, fought with General Montgomery during the North African campaign in World War II. References to the campaign and Africa abound. They range from the specter of T. E. Lawrence to the solidity of Tripoli, Amiens, and Tobruk. Sea voyages and the sinking of ships preoccupy several characters. Plunkett is intrigued with the vessel named the *Marlborough* on which his ancestor and (imagined) son is drowned. Yet, it is the son in this poetic paradigm in search of a lost father, namely, Achille's quest to encounter Afolabe, that drives the beginning of the sea journey in *Omeros*. History is being revised incessantly, much like the endless ocean tides that Walcott charts.

The second book opens with an acknowledgement of the Dutch ascent in the Northern Antilles. Although the Dutch imperial endeavor in the Caribbean is not commonly associated with St. Lucia, this book foregrounds their limited presence on the island. The Dutch briefly established a fort on the southern tip of St. Lucia in the early seventeenth century. However, they ceded this outpost after Carib raids made maintaining the fort untenable. Walcott introduces the imagined specter of Major Plunkett's lost son as an actual historical personage. This imagined Plunkett from the past emerges riding in a carriage within an agricultural ideal, a farmer's landscape, in the Dutch countryside. He becomes a minor officer, and his vessel is the *Marlborough*. This quest for paternal inheritance and progeny is a preoccupation throughout the narrative. We encounter the history of the island of St. Lucia as a colonial outpost. The Caribbean plays a significant role in the American Revolution. The seafaring vessels are contrasted with the toil on the island of Achille's ancestor, Achilles, who is renamed. The Battle of the Saints looms just as Walcott returns the narrative to the twentieth century. The contemporary Plunkett considers museums that encapsulate the glories of empire even as they mock such attempts alongside museums of wax. The Major's wife, Maud, is pictured stitching birds onto fabric that will become her funeral shroud. Maud's ethereal figure of bodily decay and impossible fecundity is contrasted with the highly embodied, pregnant Helen. Helen is the future of gestational possibility for the island after which she is named. The question of the sale of the body, the island, and the future remains just as the relationship between Achille and Hector and Helen emerges as problematic. Achille determines to find home. The quotidian affairs of St. Lucian politics manifest in the Professor or Statics who is running for office. This is the only sustained section of St. Lucian Kwéyòl in the work. The final movement to the historical past in Book Two emerges as Achille ventures to his ancestral home, Africa, courtesy of the sea swift. His transatlantic journey, a middle passage in reverse, has begun. The open ocean greets him.

ANNOTATIONS

CHAPTER XIV

77.3 The Dutch Road—The Dutch attempted (like the British and French) to establish settlements on St. Lucia. Although they were unsuccessful in controlling the island, they did leave a legacy in its cultural history. On the southern tip of the island, the Dutch fleetingly instituted an outpost or fort as a location for obtaining wood and water for their sea vessels in the earliest part of the seventeenth century. However, Carib raids successfully drove the Dutch off of the island. Scholars suggest that the Dutch settlement was near to Moule Chic and that the aptly named town of Vieux Fort, French for "Old Fort," also on the southern tip of St. Lucia, is itself named for this early Dutch fort. Ruins of the fort have long since been reclaimed by wind and water. There are numerous unnamed or only informally named roads in St. Lucia. Yet, none is termed the Dutch Road. Thus, while the actual road(s) are in fact multiple in their signifier(s), metaphorically the meaning expands beyond any actual road into multiple cultural possibilities. Walcott himself has Dutch ancestry. See notes 77.14–15.

77.14 Lowland reaches—the topography of St. Lucia varies between highlands and lowlands. This distinction between the two areas was made because lands at higher elevations were considered nonarable and relatively worthless, whereas lowlands were considered comparatively easy to cultivate and therefore more valuable. See note 153.8.

77.14–15 Dutch . . . Northern Antilles—now known as the Netherlands Antilles, an autonomous region located in the West Indies that is divided into two groups. The first group of islands is Bonaire and Curaçao, located off the coast of Venezuela. The second group is located east of Puerto Rico and includes Saba and St. Eustatius as well as the southern half of Sint Maarten and Willemstad. The capital of the Netherlands Antilles is Curaçao. The Dutch attempted but failed to establish a settlement on St. Lucia. See note 77.3.

78.2 flambent Flemish—from the French, the verb *flamber* means "to blaze" or "to inflame." It also suggests the color red, as in a flush from too much drink. Flemish is the language, Dutch in origin, of northern Belgium. The term also refers to the people of northern Belgium.

78.5 The Hague—governmental center of the Netherlands (Amsterdam is the constitutional capital). The Hague is the location of the International Court of Justice, the Dutch Supreme Court and Legislature, as well as foreign embassies. It is also now the headquarters of the European Union.

79.1 black-mapped, creamy cattle—cattle farming has been long established on St. Lucia, though such farming for the harvesting of meat is much less common today than it was. The black and cream mottled cattle to which this line refers are sometimes pictured in Walcott's paintings of the island, particularly in some works shown at the June Kelly Gallery in New York and appearing as illustrations in *Tiepolo's Hound*. Dairy cows are a common feature of the St. Lucian landscape.

79.8 blue Delft plate—Dutch pottery was originated in the seventeenth century in the Dutch town of Delft. The technique requires a dark bulk of clay that is then coated with a type of white enamel to create the appearance of porcelain, in imitation of imported Chinese and Japanese porcelain that had recently arrived in the Netherlands via the trade routes of the Dutch East India Company. Delft pottery and tiles traditionally had designs such as landscapes and coats of arms and were cheaper to create and sell than their imported counterparts.

79.12 The Hague—see note 78.5.

79.16 St. Eustatius—an island, once part of the Netherland Antilles, in the Leeward Islands. After British and French attempts to capture the island failed, the Dutch settled Oranjestad, the island's capital, in 1632, after which the island was briefly named Nieuw Zeeland. During the American Revolution, the island was a center for the arms supply and trade with the rebellious colonies and was the first government to formally acknowledge American independence in 1776. During the eighteenth century the island was a favorite of pirates, making it a leading trade center of the West Indies. The island is also affectionately known as Statia. In 2010, the Netherland Antilles dissolved and the island (like Bonaire and Saba) became a municipality within the governmental structure of the Netherlands. See notes 77.14–15, 80.10–11, and 81.19–20.

79.18 Plymouth to serve with Rodney—Plymouth is a port city on the coast of England southwest of London from which the English Navy sailed to confront the Spanish Armada in 1588. It was also a critical port from which the English embarked and conquered territory in the Americas. For the reference to Rodney, see notes 28.21, 32.5, 32.6, 34.21, 39.21, 43.1, 43.10, 43.13, 81.19–20, 81.21, 92.12–13, 99.21–100.5, and 100.9.

79.18 a florin—a monetary unit. The term originates in the thirteenth century in Florence and derives from the Italian word *fiorino* and *fiore*, or "flower." The name is suggestive of the lily design that initially appeared on the coin. The term has also been used in Britain and the Netherlands. In Walcott's context, the term suggests the guilder, a Dutch unit of money.

79.24 *The Marlborough*—a ship that takes its name from a series of British vessels. The first British sailing ship with this name was a three-masted warship that was built in 1767 and wrecked in 1800 off the coast of France. Another British ship with the name "Marlborough" made several trips between England and New Zealand between 1876 and 1890; the ship mysteriously disappeared during a voyage from London to Lyttleton, New Zealand, in 1890. In 1919 the ship was found with the remains of the crew on board near Cape Horn, South America. These ships were named for John Churchill, 1st Duke of Marlborough (1650–1722), a famed general known for aligning himself against the Catholic James II (1633–1701) and with the Protestant William of Orange or William III (1650–1702).

80.1 St. Eustatius—see notes 77.14–15, 79.16, 80.10–11, and 81.19–20.

80.10–11 The merchantmen / sold guns—the arms traders notable for their commerce and supply of the American Revolution on St. Eustatius. See notes 77.14–15, 79.16, and 81.19–20.

80.16 Martinique—see notes 24.14, 81.19–20, 92.12–13, 121.6, and 225.2.

80.23 the Night Watch—the Rembrandt (1606–1669) painting from 1642 also known as the "Company of Frans Banning Cocq and Willem van Ruytenburch" that is now at the Rijksmuseum in Amsterdam. It is a martial image that depicts a group of civic guards about to embark on a mission. Yet, significantly, the canvas has been cut from its original shape, most noticeably on the left. This creates a movement from the margins to the center for the two highlighted figures that now seem surrounded in darkness.

81.6 Night Watch—see note 80.23.

81.19–20 after the Dutch defeat on the islet facing Martinique—indicates the defeat in 1781 of Dutch forces and the capture of St. Eustatius by Admiral George Rodney that was followed in 1782 by the Battle of the Saints. This battle provided the British with a remarkable victory. The "islet" or small island is Pigeon Island on the northern coast of St. Lucia where a museum once chronicled Admiral Rodney's victory. See notes 24.14, 28.21, 32.5, 32.6, 34.21, 39.21, 43.1, 43.10, 43.13, 79.16, 79.18, 80.10–11, 81.19–20, 81.21, 92.12–13, 99.21–100.5, 100.9, 121.6, and 225.2.

81.21 Rodney was building a fort—the late eighteenth-century British military base that Admiral Rodney built on Pigeon Island is known as Fort Rodney. Walcott invokes the fort in the first chapter of

Another Life. See notes 28.21, 32.5, 32.6, 34.21, 39.21, 43.1, 43.10, 43.13, 79.18, 81.19–20, 92.12–13, 99.21–100.5, and 100.9.

81.23 poinciana—small trees or shrubs with orange or vermilion flowers (*Delonix regia*) the plant was named after a governor named de Poincy. The tree is also commonly called the Royal Poinciana, Flamboyant, or Flame tree for its vibrant coloring.

81.24 bandoliers—(bandolier) an over-the-shoulder cross-body belt that was often part of a ceremonial military uniform. The belt would often serve as a repository for bullets and other necessary martial gear. See notes 93.15–16.

82.9–10 white noise / of the sea lace—white noise is a repetitive yet unobtrusive sound that is used to mask nuisance noise. Sea lace refers to the poem of that same name in Marie Tudor Garland's (1870–1937) collection *The Marriage Feast* (1920). Sea lace refers to the white, foam traces a wave leaves on the sand that is then remade when the next wave crashes upon the shore (the term also sometimes signifies seaweed washed ashore). Garland is notable not only for her poetry but also for her friendship with the painter, Georgia O'Keeffe (1887–1986). O'Keeffe resided as Garland's guest in the summer of 1930 on Garland's New Mexico ranch, the H&M, and painted its arid topography in such works as *Black Mesa Landscape, New Mexico, Out Back of Marie's II* (1930).

83.20 Afolabe "Achilles"—Afolabi, with an *i* rather than *e* at the end, is a masculine name of Yoruba origin that means "born into wealth." Achilles refers to the Greek war hero who was vulnerable in only one spot, his heel. Achilles is also the main character in Homer's *The Iliad.* See notes 6.1, 8.4, 8.9, 10.25, 16.14–16, 24.6, 146.15–16, 150.12, 175.13–14, 228.25, 296.2, 298.9, and 320.7–16.

CHAPTER XV

84.1 "Les Saintes"—many Caribbean islands are named after Christian Saints. To do so was thought by Europeans to be a means of paying homage to God for their ventures. St. Vincent and St. Lucia are prime examples of this naming practice. There is also a specific group of islands lying between Guadeloupe and the Dominican Republic, encompassing an area about a half mile wide from east to west, so named "Les Saintes" because they were supposedly "discovered" on All Saints' Day, November 1. The Battle of the Saints also indicates a contest between Caribbean islands used as proxy locations for European powers. See notes 28.21, 31.26–27, 32.5, 32.6, 34.21, 43.1, 43.10, 81.19–20, 92.12–13, 99.21–100.5, and 100.9.

84.3; 5; 11 *The Marlborough*—see note 79.24.

85.17 *The Marlborough*—see note 79.24.

85.18 gommier—see notes 5.6; 20.

85.24 *Ville de Paris*—see notes 28.21, 32.5, 32.6, 34.21, 39.21, 43.1, 43.10, 81.19–20, 81.21, 92.12–13, 99.21–100.5, and 100.9.

86.16 *Ville de Paris*—see notes 28.21, 32.5, 32.6, 34.21, 39.21, 43.1, 43.10, 81.19–20, 81.21, 92.12–13, 99.21–100.5, and 100.9.

86.19 casks and demijohns—cask is a barrel of any size, whereas a demijohn is a large bottle usually surrounded with a protective layer of wicker. These storage vessels would have been common aboard ship, particularly those on transatlantic voyages, which would have been outfitted with such stores for the long and difficult crossing.

CHAPTER XVI

87.3 Somme's—the largest battle on the Western Front during World War I in which thousands of British soldiers lost their lives on just the first day. The battle lasted from July 1 to November 18, 1916. The total loss of life was around 420,000 British, 200,000 French, and 500,000 Germans. It has become both a cry for the remembrance of those lost and a warning of the high human costs and dangers inherent in war. The Somme in noted with memories of blood and of gas in Walcott's *Midsummer*.

87.5 Bloemfontein—city that served as the capital of the Orange Free State (1846) and as the epicenter of law in South Africa. The city now also functions as a transportation and manufacturing heart in the country. The British took control of the city in 1900. The city was the site of the negotiations (1909–1920) that led to the formation of the Union of South Africa.

87.6 the War Office—the administrative structure and body within the British government led by the secretary of war.

87.9 snooker-ball—a ball used in snooker, a game similar to pool or billiards, in which opponents use a white cue ball to pocket the other balls (in snooker, there are 15 red and 6 colored) in a set order. Snooker is considered more challenging that either 8 ball or 9 ball in pool or billiards. Snooker is commonly associated with the working classes in Britain, but it also occupies a unique, somewhat exclusive position because of the private clubs that players commonly join upon paying dues. See note 266.15.

87.10 hunched as a raven—a large and sleek black bird (*Corvus corax*) considered an ill omen and even a harbinger of death with its rasping call. Edgar Allan Poe's (1809–1849) famed lyric poem, "The Raven," is well known for its refrain, "nevermore," a cry the bird appears almost proud of as his ability to repeat the word as a warning of loss.

87.12 Agincourt to Zouave—the Battle of Agincourt was fought in northern France on October 25, 1415, as part of the Hundred Years' War. Notoriously, a British force of six thousand defeated the French forces, who outnumbered the British considerably. The British victory at Agincourt allowed them to take over much of France. The battle is the focus of William Shakespeare's (1564–1616) *Henry V*. The final act of *Henry V* provides a moving negotiation between Henry and the French Princess. A zouave is a member of a body of light infantry in the French army. The term "zouave" derives from the Arabic, *zwawa*, originally a tribal designation among the Berbers for the Kabyle people. It was from this group that Algerian French light infantry soldiers were originally formed in 1831; they were known for their vibrant uniforms and intricate footwork. A papal zouave refers to a corps of French soldiers that defended the Pope in Rome (1860–1871). In the American Civil War, Union troops that modeled their uniforms and drilling steps on these Algerian French units were also called zouaves. In Walcott's most recent play, *O Starry Starry Night*, which details a relationship between two painters (Paul Gauguin and Vincent van Gogh) and a prostitute in France, a zouave enters in the second act. The soldier's overtures are rejected by the ailing prostitute who has found solace in the island "paradise" Gauguin has promised her. See note 183.17.

87.13 blue blood—signifies noble birth and aristocracy in English but derives from the Spanish *sangre azul*, which Castilian families used to signify the privilege of their relatively pale skin, whose veins supposedly were visible to the naked eye. People who claimed *sangre azul* wished to be seen as distinct from both Jewish and Moorish peoples.

87.14–15 Why a claymore / with a draped tartan—a claymore is a Scottish two-sided blade noted for its style, which mimics the braiding of a basket. A tartan refers to any number of unique plaids worn in Scotland and particularly among the Highlanders to distinguish their specific clans.

87.15: 18 willow—a tree, commonly called a weeping willow; there is a similarly shaped tree called a Casuarina (*Casuarina equisetifolia*) in the Caribbean. When used as a surname or placed on a coat of arms, the willow suggests one who lives by rivers and/or willows. See notes 58.24 and 92.26.

87.20 Madame Tussaud—Marie Tussaud, nee Marie Grosholtz, (1761–1850), the French wax modeler and royalist who survived the Terror after the French Revolution and eventually moved to London, where she opened her famous Madame Tussaud's Museum of Wax Figures. This museum remains in London yet has expanded to include several global branches today. See note 178.6.

88.5 trunions, bore—or trunnion; supports a cannon or other large arms with a cylindrical prop on either side. A bore refers to the hollow diameter of a circular container or barrel.

88.10 Bond's Ornithology—James Bond (1900–1989), American ornithologist. Bond published extensively on avian life in the Caribbean. *The Birds of the West Indies* (1936) is his most famous work. Bond spent several weeks collecting on St. Lucia in 1927 and 1929. The author and bird-watcher Ian Fleming (1908–1964) borrowed Bond's name for Fleming's James Bond series of British spy novels. Fleming resided in part in Jamaica and set some of his fiction in the Caribbean.

88.16–21 mockingbirds … widgeon—see individual entries below.

Mockingbirds—a variety known as the tropical mockingbird (*Mimus gilvus*) emigrated to the Lesser Antilles after land was opened for cultivation. Clear land and dry scrub are ideal conditions for the bird. See note 152.10.

Finches—the St. Lucia black finch (*Melanospiza richardsoni*) was spotted by Bond during his work on St. Lucia in the late 1920s. Previous to Bond's record, the bird had eluded observers for forty years. See note 313.22.

Wrens—the St. Lucia house wren (*Troglodytes aedon*) was seen by Bond during his work on St. Lucia in the late 1920s. Previous to Bond's record, the bird had been thought extinct.

Nightjars—the rufous nightjar (*Caprimulgus rufus*) has a local version on St. Lucia, known both for becoming inactive and for the size of its wings.

Kingfishers—the belted kingfishers (*Ceryle alcyon*) migrate to St. Lucia in the fall. Their arrival mostly occurs in October, but some early visitors can be seen in late summer.

Hawks—the red-tailed hawk (*Buteo jamaicensis*) is an occasional winter dweller on St. Lucia. The broad-winged hawk (*Buteo platypterus*) lives in St. Lucia throughout the year.

Hummingbirds—the purple-throated Carib hummingbird (*Eulampis jugularis*) and the Antillean crested hummingbird (*Orthorhynchus cristatus*) reproduce on St. Lucia for half the year.

Plover—three varieties of plover, the black-bellied plover (*Pluvialis squatarola*), the American golden plover (*Pluvialis dominicus*), and the semipalmated plover (*Charadrius semipalmatus*) journey to St. Lucia in the early fall months.

Ospreys—the osprey (*Panion haliaetus*) rarely resides in St. Lucia for the winter but is drawn intermittently by abundant waterways and plentiful fish.

Falcons—the peregrine falcon (*Falco peregrinus*) is rare in St. Lucia but can be seen occasionally in its sporadic winter residence. Yet, these falcons habitually fly to and briefly tarry on the island in the spring. See note 313.25.

Wild Ducks—the masked duck (*Oxyura dominica*) makes an infrequent summer sojourn on St. Lucia. See note 218.9.

Migrating Teal—the green-winged teal (*Anas crecca*) is an irregular winter guest on St. Lucia. The blue-winged teal (*Anas discors*) is similarly rare but not unheard of on the island.

Pipers—multiple varieties of sandpipers pass through St. Lucia on their migratory patterns. The semipalmated sandpiper (*Calidris pusilla*) is the most common on St. Lucia during the fall journey from North America to South America. In spring the migration reverses, though spring sightings of them are much less common on St. Lucia. See note 185.13.

Wild Waterfowl—a common collective name for swimming birds such as geese and swans, none of which are common on St. Lucia but all of which are common in Ireland. This appears to be the only type of bird in Maud's avian embroidery that is exclusively Irish rather than commonly residing on or migrating through St. Lucia.

Widgeon—the American widgeon (*Anas americana*) appears in St. Lucia as a very rare winter guest.

88.21 Cypseloides Niger, l'hirondelle des Antilles—Latin and French for the black swift (also called on St. Lucia the *Hirondelle morne*), a summer inhabitant of St. Lucia that leaves the island by early fall, though it has been designated a winter itinerant on the island; it is known for reproducing on the larger islands in the Caribbean. See notes 8.3, 239.16, and 242.15

89.6; 19 curlew—a shorebird, the long-billed curlew (*Numenius americanus*) was once spotted, without confirming evidence, on St. Lucia.

89.15 aureole—a radiant ring, commonly of light, that suggests a sacredness of person or location.

89.18; 21 swift—see notes 8.3, 88.21, 239.16, and 242.15.

89.22 silver jubilee—a twenty-fifth anniversary. Jubilee is usually used for more public, rather than private, anniversaries, dates of independence for former colonies or a period of rule rather than a wedding anniversary. Jubilee derives from the Latin, *jubiliare*, "to exclaim for happiness, with delight." Silver signifies twenty-five years, whereas gold signifies fifty years.

90.1–2 whimsical cartographers aligned the islands / as differently—the eighteenth-century French hydrographic engineer and mapmaker Jacques Nicolas Bellin (1703–1772) famously drew St. Lucia on its side, with the north/south axis of the island drawn horizontally rather than vertically on his 1758 map of the island. Bellin mistakes the Atlantic, or eastern, coast of the island for its northern coast, and the Caribbean, or western, coast for its southern coast.

90.7–8 Singapore to the Seychelles—both former island colonies of the British Empire until the second half of the twentieth century. Singapore is an island city-state that comprises Singapore Island and sixty smaller islands in the Malay Peninsula. The English East India Company took over Singapore in 1819, and a formal Anglo-Dutch treaty in 1824 ratified this assertion of might, despite previous Dutch associations and prerogatives to the area. In 1959, Singapore became self-governing to a degree, but it was not until 1971 that all British forces left the islands. The Seychelles comprise approximately 115 islands in the Indian Ocean. The English East India Company landed on the islands in 1609. There was a dispute for many years between the English and French for these islands, but the Treaty of Paris in 1814 granted the Seychelles to the English until the Seychelles achieved independence in 1976. See notes 28.25 and 227.27.

90.8 Eighth Army outfit—a cohesive group on a military expedition, the supplying of such a unit, and the attire worn by soldiers in the British Eighth Army, which fought campaigns in North Africa and Italy. They rose to fame under General Montgomery (1887–1976) for pushing back Rommel's (1891–1944) German forces, the Afrika Korps, from Egypt into their final humiliating surrender in Tunisia. See notes 25.8, 26.7, 26.22; 26, and 90.8.

90.13 first musket-shot that divided concord—the shot that began the American Revolution in April 1775 in the Massachusetts colony. It remains unclear which side actually fired first. The British sent troops from Boston to Concord to confiscate weapons. On the way, the British troops encountered resistance from colonials at Lexington Green. The clash on the way to Concord ultimately became known as the Battle of Lexington and Concord. British troops took more than twice the casualties than the Americans did as the Redcoats returned to Boston. This early victory spurred large numbers of American colonial volunteers in the burgeoning resistance. See notes 208.10 and 209.24.

90.14 Sind—the province of Sind or Sindh in southeastern Pakistan; once part of India before partition and the British Empire, a critical location for the arrival of Islam in South Asia. The most populous city in the area is Karachi. Walcott also used the word that evokes this location in the British Empire as a play on "sinned" in *Another Life*.

90.21 egret—see note 49.12.

CHAPTER XVII

91.10 man-o'-war bird—see notes 19.6, 43.18, and 65.15.

91.12 the museum—the islet's museum or the Pigeon Island Museum. See notes 43.1 and 81.19–20.

92.5 Iounalo—also louanala; indigenous name for St. Lucia that means "where the iguana is found." See notes 5.2 and 92.15.

92.12–13 de Grasse leaving Martinique—the French Admiral de Grasse sailed for Martinique on November 5 and arrived on November 25, 1781. On April 8, 1782, de Grasse was confronted by British Admiral Rodney off the coast of Martinique. This attack ultimately led to the Battle of the Saints on April 12. De Grasse's flagship *Ville de Paris* surrendered some time in the evening and de Grasse was taken to Jamaica as a prisoner. De Grasse is noted in the Middle Passage section of "The Schooner Flight." See notes 24.14, 28.21, 32.5, 32.6, 34.21, 39.21, 43.1, 43.10, 43.13, 79.18, 81.19–20, 81.21, 99.21–100.5, 100.9, 121.6, and 225.2.

92.15 Hewannora—"land of the iguana," etymologically related to "louanalao," the indigenous name for St. Lucia. Hewannora is also now the name of the international airport on the island. See notes 5.2 and 92.5.

92.19–20 lizard / with an Aruac name—see notes 3.1, 5.2, 52.24, 92.5, 92.15, 162.14, and 164.16.

92.26 casuarina—akin to a willow, a tree native to Australia and parts of the South Pacific; from the family *Casuarinaceae*, with delicate foliage, giving it the look of a slight evergreen. It exhibits ideal growth in tropical locations with high winds. See notes 58.24 and 87.15; 18.

93.4 Ordnance—military provisions, particularly those discharged during war. An ordnance datum serves to gauge a sea level to which all heights are compared in an ordnance survey. The ordnance survey was an official extent of Great Britain and Ireland that generated highly detailed maps and renamed indigenous Irish locations in the English language. The mapping of Britain was begun in 1791; Ireland followed and was fully mapped by the mid-nineteenth century. The desire for state-endorsed and authorized cartographs arose from the competitive maritime endeavors of European imperial powers. Ruling the sea was critical to the expansion and supply of colonial territories.

93.6–7 *Georgius Rex* / . . . Wrecks—King George III or George William Frederick of Hanover (1738–1820), British monarch, who lost his American colonies and descended into madness in later life. The King was intellectually challenged as a child and grew increasingly unstable as an adult. He was king during the American, French, and Haitian Revolutions. See notes 103.25 and 257.17.

93.10 Military Hospital—during World War II, the U.S. military built a hospital in Vieux Fort. It was part of a large military logistical build up of the southern part of the island that was negotiated between the United States and Britain. It remained in use until a fire in 2009. Rebuilding efforts continue. See notes 77.3 and 108.5.

93.14 yellow fever—see notes 9.11 and 60.12–13.

93.15–16 dry bandolier / of the immortelle—an immortelle is an orange-flowered tree also known as the "mother of the cocoa," as it is used to safeguard the other cocoas from the sun. There are a large variety of flowers also called "everlasting" from the family *Asteraceae* that are indigenous to the Mediterranean but cultivated widely in tropical zones. They have tiny, fragile petals; these plants preserve their hue and structure even when desiccated, making them ideal for flower arranging. See note 81.24.

94.4 Aetat xix—from the Latin "aetatis" or "at the age of" nineteen.

CHAPTER XVIII

95.4 George the third's hearth—see notes 93.6–7, 103.26–27, and 257.17.

95.12 From arms and men—from the opening line of Virgil's (70–19 BCE) *The Aeneid*, an epic written to celebrate Rome and claim ancestry with the Greek world through their rivals, the Trojans. The Irish playwright George Bernard Shaw (1856–1950) also uses Virgil's words

"Arms and the Man" as a title for a play in 1894 that is openly critical of militarism. See note 14.5.

95.22 ziggurat—see note 65.5.

96.1–2 Homeric repetition of details—the Homeric epic cycle is known for repeated phrases and epithets. The Homeric epics emerge from a tradition of oral literature, and such repeated phrasing was used to aid memory and provide key phrases for both the performer(s) and audience(s). See notes 12.25, 14.5, 130.3, 280.7, 283.17, 283.21, and 288.21.

96.9 Circe—see note 64.19.

96.22 bracelet coiled like a snake—snake jewelry, including bracelets, was a common talisman for health and fertility in the ancient world. Snakes are associated with the Greek (and later Roman) god of medicine, Asclepius, who is mentioned in *The Iliad* for his skill as a physician. Asclepius is often figured as holding a staff with a snake twisted around it. He was noted for curing the infirm while they dreamed. His son, Machaon, is the physician who heals Philoctetes. See notes 17.7, 52.24, 139.17, and 308.15.

97.2 a second Eden with its golden apple—the Caribbean is identified as a second Eden, the Judeo-Christian garden of innocence, in Walcott's essay, "The Muse of History." Paris, the Trojan Prince in Greek myth, awards Aphrodite, the goddess of love, a golden apple in his famous Judgment of three goddesses because she has promised him the most beautiful woman in the world, Helen. See notes 12.25, 63.8, 181.3, 248.23–24, and 308.15.

97.7 Judith—a book of the Roman Catholic Bible, though it is not included in either the Hebrew Torah or the King James Bible. The widow Judith uses her physical attributes to overpower Holofernes, an Assyrian general. After he has become sufficiently debilitated, she decapitates him. She returns victorious to her people with his head as evidence of her triumph. See notes 65.5, 100.6, and 151.9.

97.12 Susanna—from the apocryphal section of the book of Daniel. Susanna was a resident of Babylon who was married to a Jewish man. Falsely accused of adultery and facing death, Susanna is saved by Daniel from execution. He examines the testimony of her accusers, two elders, and he highlights troubling contradictions within their testimony. The two false accusers are then sentenced to death.

98.1 scabrous—from the Latin *scaber*, or "coarse," it means having a rugged surface or being offensive and lewd. It is related to scabies, the skin disease carried by mites that commonly erupts when people live in close quarters.

98.3–5 tower / of a Norman church . . . French in their power— the Roman Catholic church of St. Joseph the Worker in Gros Islet is constructed in the Norman style, with thick walls, high windows, and an adjacent tower. The tower holds the bell that is rung for Mass. The church is notable for its depiction of the Blessed Virgin Mary, which was painted during the 1950s by Dunstan St. Omer. (Unlike his mural at Roseau Church, which was commissioned after Vatican II and St. Lucian Independence and thus reflects a vision of the Holy Family as St. Lucian, this mural of the Blessed Virgin Mary in the church in Gros Islet, directly behind her statue to the right of the altar, has a European physiognomy. St. Omer did include St. Lucians of African descent among the coteries of Mary's adoring followers). The Gros Islet church was constructed after the original church was largely destroyed in the earthquake in 1906 that devastated the area. The new church was completed in 1931. The style of architecture that Walcott terms Norman actually reflects the practical choice to use reinforced concrete and to rest the roof on the remaining pillars and walls of the original church that had withstood the earthquake. The front of the Gros Islet church is similar in style to both the Roman Catholic cathedral in Castries and the Roman Catholic church in Choiseul. The Gros Islet church in the center of the village is directly in front of the Gros Islet cemetery, which houses remains in typical aboveground monuments in the French style, common for modern St. Lucian burial practices. The rear of the tower and church are visible from the cemetery. Just across the street from the cemetery and close to a village school is the local cricket pitch. A modern cricket stadium is in the hills far above Gros Islet, but the church cemetery and local field are directly across from one another. It is not uncommon to see a match on the field and gravediggers preparing for a burial across the street at the same time. This church is named as the location of an important commission for Gregorias/St. Omer in *Another Life*. See notes 17.23, 24.6, and 34.21.

98.7 sea grapes—see notes 17.7 and 63.17.

98.20 midden . . . of domestic trash—recalls a line from James Joyce's (1882–1941) *Ulysses* when Stephen Dedalus considers the cycle of life and death on the beach in the "Proteus" chapter (*Ulysses* 3.150). See notes 199.26, 200.11, 200.12, 201.7, 201.11, 201.12–14, 201.16, 209.18, and 297.17.

98.22 calabash—the gourd of the calabash tree (*Crescentia cujete*) often used for food preparation, personal ornamentation, ritual performance, and domestic decoration. The tree can reach thirty feet and is indigenous to the Caribbean. The tree bears a fruit with white pulp and large seeds in the form of large gourds that are hollowed out and used as vessels.

99.4 from Carthage from Pompeii . . . antipodal Troy—all ancient cities that were sites of destruction. The founding by Phoenicians and ultimate end of Carthage in 146 BCE at the end of the Punic Wars is famously portrayed in *The Aeneid*; the ruins of the city are on the outskirts of Tunis, Tunisia. The eruption of Mt. Vesuvius brought about the entombment with ash of Pompeii in 79 BCE. Because of the volcanic matter that preserved the ancient city, it is remarkably conserved even today. The ruins of ancient Troy are in present-day Hisarlik, Turkey, but the life of the famed city of *The Iliad* ranged from 3000 BCE until the Roman sack of what was by then called Ilion in 85 CE. The Romans then rebuilt the city because of their claim of Trojan ancestry, but it was ultimately eclipsed in size and fame by Constantinople (now Istanbul), a city that remains a critical nexus between Europe and Asia. See notes 3.2, 6.1, 8.9, 14.5, 16.14–15, 17.5–6, 24.6, 31.4, and 191.11.

99.9 Gros Îlet—see notes 11.4, 17.13–14, 20.7, 28.21, 32.5, 32.6, 39.21, 43.1, 43.10, 43.13, 79.18, 81.19–20, 81.21, 92.12–13, 98.3–5, 99.21–100.5, 100.9, 105.13–14, and 109.18–21.

CHAPTER XIX

99.16 Breen's encomium—refers to Henry H. Breen (1805–1882) and his book *St. Lucia: Historical, Statistical, and Descriptive* (1844), which provides a history of St. Lucia. The history is very much a colonial-era narrative with all of the assumptions of a nineteenth-century writer of

British imperial history. However, the account does provide detailed information on the infrastructure of St. Lucia in the mid-nineteenth century. See note 60.7–8.

99.21–100.5 When we consider . . . on the seas secured—This is a direct quotation from Breen's *St. Lucia: Historical, Statistical, and Descriptive* (72–73). The excerpt celebrates the victory of Admiral Rodney's (1718–1792) vessels against the Comte de Grasse (1722–1788) in a naval engagement in 1782 that ultimately led to the Battle of the Saints. See notes 28.21, 32.5, 32.6, 34.21, 39.21, 43.1, 43.10, 43.13, 79.18, 81.19–20, 81.21, 92.12–13, 99.16, and 100.9.

100.5 yellow allamandas—see note 65.8.

100.6 fleur-de-lys—(also fleur-de-lis) or the "Lily of France," an elegant swirl-covered emblem and symbol of the French Monarchy in particular; also commonly understood to represent the Roman Catholic Trinity and the Virgin Mary. The origins of the symbol reach back to ancient Assyria. See notes 65.5, 97.7, and 151.9.

100.9–10 April 12 *Ville de Paris* struck her colours to Rodney—the ship *Ville de Paris* that was captured by the British Admiral Rodney at the naval Battle of the Saints in 1782 between the British and the French. Her colors would have been the flag of the French King Louis XVI (1774–1792), not the tricolor flag of the French Revolution. See notes 28.21, 32.5, 32.6, 34.21, 39.21, 43.1, 43.10, 43.13, 79.18, 81.19–20, 81.21, 92.12–13, 99.16, and 99.21–100.5.

100.11 Paris give the golden apple—the Judgment of Paris. Paris, the Trojan prince, son of Priam and Hecuba, is asked by Zeus to choose the most beautiful of three goddesses. Paris gives the winner a golden apple. All three attempt to sway him with a reward: Hera with kingship, Athena with martial power, and Aphrodite with the most beautiful woman in the world. He opts for the most beautiful woman. He takes Helen, the wife of Menelaus, to Troy, thus setting in motion the Trojan War. Some accounts suggest that Helen went willingly with the Trojan prince. See notes 6.1, 17.5–6, and 24.6.

100.25 Enfield—the Lee-Enfield rifle was the conventional armament given to soldiers in the British army in the early twentieth century, particularly during both world wars. It is noted for its swift fire. Enfield is also a borough of London.

101.1 Armistices—from the Latin *arma,* or "arm," with *stitium,* to "cease" or "the period of peace after war." See note 30.24.

101.3-4 Mortimer and Glendower and Tumbly and Scott—Edmund Mortimer, 5th Earl of March (1391–1425), was thought to have a right to the throne as an heir to King Richard II (1367–1400). Owen Glendower (1354–1416), a Welsh prince, attempted to establish Welsh independence. Both men were famously transformed into characters by William Shakespeare (1564–1616). Shakespeare dramatizes the alliance of Mortimer and the famed Glendower in *Henry IV: Part 1,* a tragedy that deals with rights of succession in the late fourteenth- and early fifteenth-century English court. Tumbly and Scott are Major Plunkett's companions (without evident historical analogues) who fought with him in the North African campaign.

102.6 Rover—see note 26.11.

102.6 young Neds and Toms—from British slang, a Ned is a ruffian, lout, or small-time criminal, or someone who is merely foolish. A Tom is a male representative of the common people, an ordinary guy. A Tommy refers to a soldier. See notes 27.3 and 251.18.

102.11 Scott's cry and Tumbly's—see note 101.3–4.

102.15 palms swayed like poplars along the Dutch marshes—the cabbage palm (*Roystonea oleracea*) is indigenous to the Caribbean, although other kinds of tropical palms have been introduced for decorous cultivation. A poplar tree (genus *Populus*) is a general term for over thirty types of large trees with round, lush canopies that thrive in colder but mild zones. The Dutch marshes can refer to any of the marsh areas in the Netherlands. The country is protected by a series of water management systems. Due to its low, flat landscape, and its position between the strong air currents between Iceland and the southwest of Europe, it is extremely windy—hence, the Dutch facility with using windmills to harness energy. See note 70.21.

102.18 Cyclops eye—see note 13.7.

102.21 Able semen—a pun on able-bodied seaman, a higher rank with more skill and charge than ordinary seaman, the basic rating in the British navy. The distinction between these two types of sailors emerged in the seventeenth century.

103.3 the island's breasts—the two volcanic peaks of St. Lucia,

Gros Piton and Petit Piton, which are conical in shape. They are a dramatic and striking feature on the island landscape. Ezra Pound (1885–1972) compared mountains to the breasts of the earth goddess, Tellus Helena, in his *Canto LXXVI*. See notes 30.19, 40.21, 59.13, 103.3, 227.10, and 289.8.

103.15 slanted monsoon—the wet season largely coincides with hurricane/cyclone season and usually occurs in summer and fall. The winds of such a storm can drive the rainfall sideways. See notes 6.13, 43.13, 47.13, 51.22, 54.20, and 58.22.

103.26–27 Royal House of Hanover to Kaiser Wilhelm—British royal house of German origin. The Hanoverian British monarchs begin in 1714 with George I (1660–1727) and end in 1901 with the death of Victoria (1819–1901). Kaiser Wilhelm II (1859–1941) was the son of Victoria. See notes 93.6–7 and 257.17.

104.1 "A few make history. The rest are witnesses"—the title of Major Plunkett's history essay or thesis on the Roman Empire.

104.2 Beethoven's clouds—Ludwig van Beethoven (1770–1827) was German by birth but later resided in Vienna. A famed composer, pianist, and conductor who grew deaf, he continued his remarkable creative endeavors despite his loss of hearing. Fred Hoyle's (1915–2001) 1957 novel, *The Black Cloud*, uses Beethoven's Hammerklavier Sonata as an evocation of the speed and complexity of human thought, music, and art. Hoyle coined the phrase "the big bang" as a description for the origin of the universe.

104.2 Herman Hesse—German novelist and poet (1877–1962) who renounced his German citizenship and adopted Swiss citizenship after the outbreak of World War I. He won the Nobel Prize for Literature in 1946. His Nobel lecture highlights the multiplicity of his family and ethnic history; he is a son of a Baltic German Estonian father and a mother who was French Swiss and Swabian. His mother resided in India for some time. His works often highlight the alienation and solitude inherent in modernity.

CHAPTER XX

104.6 iron market—Castries Central Market, located on Jeremie Street, is built on and adjacent to the Iron Market, built in 1894. The building has survived the fires of Castries; thus the iron market remains in use today. The market is the center of life surrounding the harbor in downtown Castries and bordering the district close to Walcott Square and the cathedral. Local and imported goods are for sale. It is a vibrant social and commercial space filled with vendors of merchandise and purveyors of food. See notes 37.13 and 120.6; 9.

104.10 son of a barber—George William Odlum (1934–2003), St. Lucian politician and head of the Progressive Labour Party (PLP), he served as foreign minister and as deputy prime minister. He was the son of a barber. The PLP is an offshoot from the left but is more center than the St. Lucia Labour Party (SLP).

104.10 Compton—John George Melvin Compton (1925–2007), St. Lucian politician and head of the United Workers' Party (UWP); he was prime minister in 1979, 1982–96, and 2006–7.

104.11 Maljo—also spelled maldjo; here, a political candidate. See note 9.12.

105.6 No Pain Café—see notes 17.7 and 17.13–14.

105.7 Seven Seas—see note 11.10.

105.13–14 charter yachts . . . F. Didier—Cuthbert Didier (dates not available) was a former manager of the Rodney Bay Marina and now the director of yachting with the St. Lucia Ministry of Tourism.

105.18–19 Professor / Static—person who the crowd calls Maljo, see note 9.12.

106.19 toothless sibyl—See note 58.5.

106.21 MacArthur's vow as he left: "Moi shall return"—a localized political statement that brings together the colloquial expression in the French/St. Lucian Kwéyòl *moi*, or "me/I," with a famous statement of return made by U.S. General Douglas MacArthur (1880–1964) on leaving the Philippines.

106.22–23 Pope / in his bulletproof jeep—after the assassination attempt on Pope John Paul II (1920–2005) in 1981, the Pope traveled in a bulletproof vehicle that had a protruding bulletproof and reinforced glass area in which the Pope could sit or stand in view of the crowds. Pope Francis (1936–), the current pope, has chosen more open forms of transportation.

107.4–6 quittez moin dire z'autres! . . . **ces mamailles-la, pas blague**—St. Lucian Kwéyòl, "let me tell you, . . . these children there, no joking (or lie)." Suggests lines from the St. Lucian folk singer, Sensenne's (Marie Seltipha Descartes, nee Charlery 1914–2010) work, who is later referenced in Walcott's Nobel lecture and a poem, "Homecoming" in *The Bounty*. See note 318.19.

107.8 Titanic—an enormous British ship, built in Belfast, and initially referred to as "unsinkable"; it hit an iceberg on its maiden voyage across the Atlantic and sank on April 15, 1912, with 1,517 people lost to the sea. The casualties in steerage were considerably greater proportionally than those in the upper-class decks.

107.14 tends ça moin dire z'autres—St. Lucian Kwéyòl, an abbreviation of "wait, that's what I tell you."

107.18 The United Force—a political party in Guyana that advocates conservative positions. It seems to oppose in sentiment, if not in actuality, the United Love Party. See notes 107.20–21.

107.20–21 LP and WWPP / and United Love can give you the answers—a gibe at the political parties that have vied for power in St. Lucia. The left-of-center St. Lucia Labour Party (SLP) rivals that right, conservative United Workers' Party (UWP). United Love suggests the liberal socialist Progressive Labour Party (PLP). See notes 104.10.

108.5 from Vieuxfort to Cap—Vieux Fort is a town on the south side of St. Lucia. The area is now the location of the island's international airport. The opposite end of the island on the far north is called Cap Estate. However, there is also a Cap Moule a Chic, a promontory with stunning views of Vieux Fort. See notes 77.3 and 93.10.

108.16 Ces Mamailles-la, nous kai—St. Lucian Kwéyòl, "these children, be real."

108.17 Gros Îlet—see notes 11.4, 17.13–14, 20.7, 28.21, 32.5, 32.6, 39.21, 43.1, 43.10, 43.13, 79.18, 81.19–20, 81.21, 92.12–13, 98.3–5, 99.21–100.5, 100.9, 105.13–14, and 109.18–21.

108.17; 21 United Force—see notes 107.18 and 107.20–21.

109.1 fête—see note 52.22.

CHAPTER XXI

109.16 Atlantic City—a seaside resort town in the southeast part of New Jersey that has legalized gambling. While considered a posh resort in the early twentieth century, the city has fallen on hard times with overwhelming poverty beyond the boardwalk and closing casino hotels.

109.18–21 the dull week, as it dies, exploded with . . . vendors— the Friday night street party in Gros Islet village that is termed a "Jump Up." Several blocks are off limits to traffic during this weekly celebration that brings food, music, dancing, and overall good cheer to the village locals and visitors. See note 34.21.

110.4 Gros Îlet—see notes 11.4, 17.13–14, 20.7, 28.21, 32.5, 32.6, 39.21, 43.1, 43.10, 43.13, 79.18, 81.19–20, 81.21, 92.12–13, 98.3–5, 99.21–100.5, 100.9, 105.13–14, and 109.18–21.

110.5 United Force—see notes 107.18 and 107.20–21.

110.7 Keep Cool, No Pain Café—the Keep Cool is an actual rum shop in Gros Islet village that is the model for Walcott's fictional version, the No Pain Café. Marcus Garvey's (1887–1940) poem, "Keep Cool," urges his audience to refrain from despair in the face of struggle. See notes 17.7, 17.13–14, and 72.11.

110.9 seraphic white—see notes 62.18 and 159.5.

111.27 Soul Brothers—a popular South African band that formed in 1974 with three members and now comprises thirteen musicians. This is also the name of a Ray Charles (1930–2004) and Milt Jackson (1923–1999) album from 1958.

112.22 *Dominus illuminatio mea*—Latin, "the lord is my light," from Psalm 27.

112.24 howdah'd—howdah, a raised board device constructed for traveling in relative comfort on the back of an elephant.

113.1 Gurkas, Anzacs, Mounties—soldiers from colonies who served the British and/or Commonwealth. A Gurkha is a Nepalese soldier serving in the British army. An Anzac is a soldier in the Australian and New Zealand Army Corps in its original usage, though the term now describes any soldier from those nations. A Mountie serves in the Royal Canadian Mounted Police.

113.2 Eden's Suez—refers to British Prime Minister Anthony Eden

(1897–1977), who held office from 1955 to 1957 during the Egyptian nationalization of the Suez Canal. See note 23.10.

113.3 Alexandria—one of the major cities of Egypt at the mouth of the Nile on the northern coast, renowned for its library that was destroyed in the third century CE; it was the center of knowledge and cosmopolitanism in the ancient Mediterranean world. See note 9.10.

113.4 muezzin's prayers—an official of a mosque who is responsible for calling the faithful to prayer five times daily.

113.6 Himalayan hill stations—numerous hill stations dot the Himalayas; the British constructed such stations (at Darjeeling, for example) as retreats high in the hills for the relief (from the hot and humid climate) of their colonial officers, functionaries, and dependents. These stations then became seasonal centers of commerce and government.

113.14 *Dominus illuminatio mea*—see note 112.22.

114.7 Bear nor Plough—refers to the constellations, noted in *The Iliad* on the famed description of Achilles' shield, Ursa Major, which means "great bear," and the linked plough constellation, which comprises the tail end of the bear in Ursa Major. These constellations are also noted by Virgil in *The Aeneid*. See notes 114.8–9.

114.8–9 Ursa or Plunkett Major, / or the Archer aiming—Ursa refers to the constellation Ursa Major, which has the shape of a bear. Archer refers to the constellation for Sagittarius that has the shape of an archer with a bow and arrow. See notes 24.7 and 114.7.

114.10 Venus, nor even find / the pierced holes of Pisces—Venus is a planet, the Roman goddess of love and beauty, the daughter of Jupiter, and the lover of Mars and Vulcan. Pisces rests on the track of the sun through the sky; he is depicted as two fishes. See notes 11.4 and 314.12; 21.

CHAPTER XXII

117.9 atavistic—a tendency to regress into inherited, expected form.

117.12 Icarian future—a poor or doomed future. Dionysius gave Icarius the "gift of the vine." Icarius shares his good fortune by imparting wine to local farmers, who believe their inebriation is in fact poisoning. They murder Icarius in revenge for the harm he has caused. Icarius is also the father of Penelope. The adjective may also refer to the son of Daedalus, Icarus, who flies too close to the sun with wax wings as he attempts to escape from the labyrinth of the Minotaur. Beyond Greek myth, a second possibility is that it is a reference to Étienne Cabet (1788–1856), a French utopian leader; his followers were known as Icarians. Cabet's *Voyage en Icarie* (1840) described a society in which an elected government regulated all aspects of existence except the personal/familial. Cabet and some of his followers tried to found utopian communities in the United States, all of which failed.

117.20–21 Bon Dieu!/Déjà—French and St. Lucian Kwéyòl, "Good God!/Already."

118.8–9 the swaying virgin not to forget her / at the hour of our death—the final lines of the Catholic prayer, Hail Mary.

118.20 Vieuxfort—see notes 77.3, 93.10, and 108.5.

118.26 camerades—unusual spelling of the French *camarades*, a group of military men or compatriots, that changes one vowel, an a to an e, and thus places the French word for "sea/mother," la *mer/e*, in the middle of the word.

119.7–8 of old London journals The Sphere, The Tatler, The / Illustrated London News—*The Sphere: An Illustrated Newspaper for the Home* was published from 1900 to 1964. *The Tatler*, begun by Richard Steele (1672–1729), appeared briefly from 1709 to 1711. *The Illustrated London News* began publishing weekly in 1842, went to monthly publication in 1971, and more recently just biannual publication. It is one of the earliest illustrated papers. Walcott references *The Illustrated London News* in *Another Life* and uses it as a prop in *Remembrance* as a relic of empire.

120.3 their seine—see note 52.27.

120.6 the coal market—located in Castries, the coal station was in operation through the mid-nineteenth century and until the early to mid-twentieth century. St. Lucia was a hub for the Caribbean coal industry. The coaling station was critical for the British navy as well as for commercial vessels. Coal was imported from England, off loaded and stored in Castries Harbor just south of the Iron Market area, and then loaded onto ships as needed for fuel. The work was gender stratified. Men loaded and unloaded the enormous baskets with coal, whereas women carried these baskets filled with upward of one hundred pounds of coal on their heads up and down planks to and from the various ships. Castries served as a coaling station because of its deep harbor and position on the shipping routes between North America and South America. After World War II, the coaling station was put out of service because the technology for propelling ships changed. Coal was no longer needed on such an enormous scale. During World War II, German submarines sank two Allied ships in Castries Harbor because St. Lucia's harbor and fueling station were seen as critical for the British navy. Walcott refers to the coaling station in Castries, and his Grandmother's work therein, in "The Glory Trumpeter." See notes 37.13 and 104.6.

CHAPTER XXIII

120.9 coaling-station—see note 120.6.

120.13 carillon—French, "bells or chimes," particularly those in use in churches.

120.15–16 The Church of Immaculate Conception / was numbering the Angelus—The Roman Catholic Cathedral of the Immaculate Conception in Castries, St. Lucia, is on the east side of Derek Walcott Square. Built between 1894 and 1931, it stands on the location of several previous churches that were destroyed by fire. The cathedral is one of the largest churches in the West Indies. Dunstan St. Omer (1927–) painted the interior; much like his work in the Roseau Valley Roman Catholic church, the saints and the Trinity are all pictured as African in origin. The Angelus is a short devotion marked by church bells. See note 70.3.

120.18 Georgian library—the central library of St. Lucia, which is in Castries. It was originally built in 1924 as a Carnegie library. Destroyed by the Castries fire of 1948, it was reconstructed in 1958 and renovated as recently as 1994. It is located on Derek Walcott Square across from the cathedral.

120.20–21 a dozen halos of sound down through the ages / confirmed the apostles—a reference to the number of Christ's apostles, twelve.

121.5 Pompeii—see note 99.4.

121.6 ash of the Angelus—see notes 70.3 and 120.5–6.

121.6 St. Pierre—formerly the primary port and largest town in Martinique; it was destroyed by a devastating volcanic eruption in 1902. Estimates suggest that thirty thousand people lost their lives. The sole survivor was an inmate in a fortified cellar in the *cachot de Cyparis*. There is now a museum in the area that memorializes the eruption. The town was also known because the French impressionist, Paul Gauguin (1848–1903), depicted St. Pierre in some of the works he created during his brief sojourn on Martinique in the 1890s. The Centre d'Art Musée Paul Gauguin is located close to St. Pierre today. Walcott refers to Gauguin in *Another Life* and *Midsummer*. He also appears as a character in the play *O Starry Starry Night*. See notes 24.14, 81.19–20, 92.12–13, and 225.2.

121.13 carillon—see note 120.13.

121.23–24 morning-glory . . . sea grapes—see notes 17.7, 62.18, and 63.17.

122.1 *memento mori*—see notes 25.8 and 30.23.

122.12 A liner grew from the Vigie promontory—peninsula in St. Lucia located on the northwestern side of the island, opposite of Castries proper. It is the location of the George Charles Airport and the Point Seraphine Cruise Ship terminal. See notes 72.17; 23.

122.16–17 Portugal / to Southampton, then Dublin—European locations from the country of Portugal, a critical location for the development of European imperialism and the transatlantic slave trade, to Southampton, a prominent port city on the southern coast of Britain, also a critical location for the British Empire and the transatlantic slave trade, and finally to the capital of Ireland. Dublin represents an early location of British imperialism (the Anglo-Norman invasion of 1159 and onward) and the first colony to escape the empire in the twentieth century, with the establishment of the Irish Free State in 1922. See notes 24.7, 155.25–26, 189.3, 191.21, 200.11, 200.12, 201.7, 201.11, and 201.16.

123.11 allamanda—see note 65.8.

123.14 Land Rover—see note 26.11.

CHAPTER XXIV

126.23 l'hirondelle des Antilles—see notes 8.3, 88.21, 239.16, and 242.15.

127.7 the Trades—the winds that flow west across the Atlantic generally at latitudes that maintain such consistency that mariners called them "Trade winds" because they allowed for a reliable progression of commerce across the ocean. See notes 6.13, 45.22–23, 122.16–17, 129.14–15, 149.14–15, and 190.11.

127.17 gommier—see notes 5.6; 20.

127.21 Habal—the father of Jules in Walcott's *Sea at Dauphin.*

127.21 Winston James—Winston James (dates not available), the scholar who has written on the Caribbean in general and on the Caribbean diaspora in Britain/Claude McKay in particular.

127.22 Toujours Sou—French, for "always soused, or drunk."

127.24 white rum or l'absinthe—see notes 3.15 and 9.4; 6.

127.24 Herald Chastenet—Anse Chastanet is both a reef well-known for snorkeling and fishing and a large resort just north of Soufrière.

129.1 Oui, Bon Dieu!—French and St. Lucian Kwéyòl, "Yes, Good God!"

129.14–15 Senegal / or the Guinea coast—Senegal is a country in sub-Saharan Africa on the Atlantic coast, a center of the slave trade and home to Gorée Island, the last stop for many enslaved African subjects before they were forced to board ships for the ocean voyage. The Guinea coast refers to an enormous land and marine zone in West Africa that rests between the Tropic of Cancer and the equator. The Gulf of Guinea has long been divided according to the commodities it produced and sold at market from the Gold Coast to the Slave Coast. See notes 149.6, 150.1–2, 184.1, and 224.15.

130.3 my tamer of horses—in *The Iliad*, Hector, the rival of Achilles and great hero of Troy, is called the tamer of horses. It is perhaps his most well-known epithet. In Greek myth, Poseidon, the god of the sea, is the father of the winged horse, Pegasus, as well as many other horses. See notes 8.9, 16.14–15, 53.4, and 96.1–2.

130.5 Ithaca—a Greek island. In *The Odyssey*, it is Odysseus' home kingdom to which he returns. See notes 153.1, 194.15, 203.11, and 232.21.

130.8 the triangular trade—refers to the transatlantic slave trade, the course traveled by European ships originating in coastal ports of Europe, going south to West Africa to load their ships with enslaved African subjects, and then traveling across the Atlantic to the Caribbean as well as North America and South America (The Middle Passage) to condemn them and their progeny into bondage. The profits from the sale of the enslaved Africans would then be taken to Europe. See notes 6.13, 45.22–23, 122.16–17, 129.14–15, 149.14–15, 150.23, and 189.3.

130.19 pirogue—see note 8.1.

❖ Book Three

SUMMARY

The third book in *Omeros* opens in the realm of history. Achille, with the forceful tug of the sea swift, the mythic bird who guides his Atlantic journey, meets his ancestor Afolabe in the African coast. Allusions to snake gods, river gods, African geography, spiritual beliefs, and memory permeate these pages. The encounter of the lost son, Achille, in search of the abstracted and unknown father, Afolabe, aided by the sea swift, that mythic bird, powerfully reenacts the paradigm of the Christian Trinity. Even if Achille remains an obscure progeny for the African grandfather, Walcott ends the chapter by entering the text with an autobiographic presence when he is called "Warwick's son" (166.23). The ancestors' forgetting and the rupture between generations are now placed on the maternal figure; Walcott ends with "mother's amnesia" (167.12).

The third book begins in Africa. Achille's journey across the open ocean, via the swift whose wings form a cross, has brought him to the land of his ancestors. There, a river formed as a snake becomes a symbol of power as it evokes Damballa, the snake and river loa. Achille meets Afolabe, his symbolic figure of paternal inheritance, who both forgets and remembers him. A sense of loss, of lamentation, memory, and potential for reconnection becomes evident as Achille encounters several centuries of forced displacement, enslavement, and final emancipation for his African forebears. Their survival emerges as a testament to endurance and strength amid extreme pain and nearly unimaginable loss. Achille acknowledges the splitting of his paternal figures, half with Africa and half with Europe, even as his absence is noted in St. Lucia. Philoctete inquires of Seven Seas, the blind seer, where his friend has gone. Seven

Seas reassures Philoctete that Achille is not drowned or lost at sea, as some fear and report, but is on a quest for his "name and soul" (154.6). Achille's journey examines the idea of the root. The links between the indigenous peoples of the Caribbean and those of North America are highlighted through allusions to the music of Bob Marley and to the juxtaposition of American Indians and West Indians, both peoples forcefully displaced. The third book ends with Walcott emerging clearly as the narrative voice. His own quest for origins takes him to Castries, St. Lucia, and the Marian Home for the aged. His mother, Alix Walcott, is introduced as being humbled by unrelenting time as she struggles for memory at the end of her life's journey.

ANNOTATIONS

CHAPTER XXV

133.1 Mangroves—several types of these tree varieties grow in the West Indies (and other tropical zones) alongside or in water, particularly in swamps or marshlands. The root systems of these trees are exposed in low tide and covered in high tide.

133.9–10 the endless river unreeled / those images that flickered into real mirages—the Congo River serves as Africa's largest system of passable river water, though the Nile proper is actually longer. The Congo has an extensive aquatic network that reaches over a broad arc in central West Africa and exhausts into the Atlantic Ocean. The journey on such a mythic river has captured the imagination of writers from Joseph Conrad (1857–1924), in *Heart of Darkness* (1899), to V. S. Naipaul (1932–), in *The Bend in the River* (1979). See notes 52.24, 134.24, 135.10–12, and 139.17.

133.13 hippopotami—plural of hippopotamus, a large four-toed mammal of sub-Saharan Africa that is at home in water. Its name derives from the Greek for "river horse." It is the second largest land animal in Africa after the elephant; the hippopotamus is commonly spotted on riversides and in marshy areas.

134.18 the swift whose wings is the sign of my crucifixion—see notes 8.3, 88.21, 239.16, and 242.15.

134.24 the river- and the tree-god—suggestive of several possible African river and tree gods. Nyaminyami is the Zambezi river god. Oshun is the Yoruba goddess of the river. The Igbo have no less than three river deities: Idemili, Urashi, and Ava. Osiris is the Egyptian tree and fertility god. See notes 52.24, 133.9–10, 135.10–12, and 139.17.

135.10–12 its old snake skin . . . this branch of the Congo—the description by Joseph Conrad, Józef Teodor Konrad Korzeniowski (1857–1924), of the Congo River in *Heart of Darkness*. See notes 52.24, 133.9–10, 134.24, and 139.17.

135.19–20 One half with the midshipman / by a Dutch canal—Walcott's familial history is famously of both Dutch and African origin. A midshipman is a rank for young naval personnel. Canals were introduced to the area that is now the Netherlands by the Romans in order to manage and drain the lowland of its excess water. During the seventeenth through the twentieth centuries, the Dutch canal system became increasingly important not only for water management but also for trade. See notes 68.21, 77.3, 77.14, and 77.14–15.

137.2 Afolabe—see note 83.20.

137.7 What does the name mean? I have forgotten—dialogue between Achille and Afolabe in Africa evokes the intersection between Aeneas with his own father, Anchises, in the underworld. See notes 6.1 and 83.20.

138.24 a shadow. And you, nameless son, are only the ghost—a reversal of William Shakespeare's (1564–1616) *Hamlet*, a father-son relationship characterized by haunting in which it is the father who appears as the ghost. Afolabe's and Achille's encounter evokes those in the novels of Amos Tutuola (1920–1997) such as *My Life in the Bush of Ghosts* that focus on the Yoruban underworld. See notes 68.21 and 68.27.

CHAPTER XXVI

139.11 the ritual of the kola nut. Drain gourds of palm-wine—the kola nut is central to Igbo communal practices in southeastern Nigeria. It is harvested from the evergreen trees of the cocoa family (*Sterculiaceae*). The nuts contain caffeine and are used in both Africa and the

Caribbean for various therapeutic and curative endeavors. The novel *The Palm-Wine Drinkard*, by Amos Tutuola (1920–1997), is based on Yoruba practices. It charts a young man's journey from intoxication to wisdom. The wine itself is made from fermented palm tree sap. See note 98.22.

139.13 balaphons whine—a balafon, also called a marimba, resembles a xylophone. It originated in West Africa and is commonly constructed of hollowed-out shea trees. The instruments are strategically positioned to amplify their sound.

139.17 the serpent god—Legba, Ellegua, Damballah are all African Caribbean gods that are represented as snakes; there is also a strong tradition of serpent deities in Africa. Nyaminyami is Zambezi river god who appears with the head of a fish and the body of a snake. See notes 52.24, 133.9–10, 134.24, and 135.10–12.

139.20 albino god—the Christian savior, Jesus Christ; the God commonly represented as European despite being of Middle Eastern Jewish origin.

140.10 huge yams, to find that heaven—suggestive of a critical passage in Ralph Ellison's (1914–1994) *Invisible Man* when the protagonist embraces his African heritage and history by embracing one of the most important crops in Africa. The yam is a critical commodity in West Africa and is frequently used in ritual celebrations. See note 237.14.

141.21–22 brewed a beer / which they fermented from a familiar bark—Mbege is a fermented banana beer to which Msesewe, a derivative of cinchona bark, is added. Cinchona is commonly used to make quinine, a key ingredient in tonic water and bitters and notable for its antimalarial properties.

142.1 flat keels of whales—the whale shark (*Rhincodon typus*), a massive creature that can reach close to sixty feet, is harmless to humans but inhabits the Caribbean Sea and other temperate waters across the globe. It has several prominent crests, called "keels," that are often visible when the whale shark feeds while swimming close to the surface, using its mouth to strain plankton from the water. See notes 184.9, 184.20, and 303.3.

142.7 anemones—see note 9.21.

142.11 aeons—an immeasurable aspect of temporal history; an evocation of the eternal. In geology, aeons comprise many eras or ages and are the most expansive characteristic of measurement.

142.15 ingots—a lump of metal, commonly used for weight, portion, and conveyance; the mold in which the hot liquefied metal is poured.

142.16 privateers—sailors on an armed seacraft under private command that is allowed by a government to attack rival vessels, usually viable profit-making ones. Common through the nineteenth century, they were sometimes challenging to discern; sanctioned privateers were similar to yet distinct from pirates, corsairs, or buccaneers, who possessed no such imprimatur. See note 156.2.

143.1 Barrel of Beef—see note 35.24.

143.8–9 mitre . . . calabash—a mitre or miter is a headdress worn by bishops in several faiths. It resembles two pointed linked shields arranged back to front and often has two fabric tails hanging in the back. Bartolomé Mitre (1821–1906) was the president of Argentina as well as a writer, poet, and translator of Dante. For Saint-Barthélemy, see note 35.24. For calabash, see note 98.22.

143.11 fifes and tambours—a fife is a petite flute that is commonly paired with the drum in martial music and usually has six holes; associated with infantry soldiers, it is also considered a folk instrument. A tambour[ine] is a small drum, held and shaken by one hand while touched rhythmically with the other.

143.18 divining rods—the material deployed in dowsing, using a forked figure to discern sought-after elements such as water in the practice of necromancy.

143.19 chac-chac and ra-ra—Ra-ra refers to a rhythmical music in Caribbean (and particularly Haitian) street fairs, the reverberation of which stems from maracas or chac-chac (as well as other instruments). See note 53.10.

CHAPTER XXVII

144.7–8 Then war came—the capture and enslavement of Africans. See notes 122.6–7, 129.14–15, 130.8, and 189.3.

144.16 baboon cries—a rather low, deep, almost raspy cry.

145.5 the slavers waiting up the coast—The European slavers, or slave traders, would stay in port along the western coast of Africa and venture to the interior to steal, trap, and purchase Africans who either were free or already enslaved as captives of war. The Slave Coast extended from the Volta River to the Niger Delta (now Togo, Benin, and Nigeria). See notes 129.14–15, 130.8, and 189.3.

145.10–146.6 the chain of men . . . when a swivel of dust rose—these lines reappear in a slightly altered form on pages 215.16–216.6.

145.14 the thorn barrier—at the edge of African tropical zones where the land turns to desert, thorn copses and scrub prevail; these areas can be taxing to navigate. They are filled with acacia, myrrh, boscia, and balanite trees. The balanite specifically is famed for its spines and thorns.

146.14 liana—see note 49.1.

146.15–16 and then Achille died again—the loss of ancestry and the forgotten progeny represent death. The death of Achilles is not represented in *The Iliad*, but his funeral is mentioned in *The Odyssey*. Hector believed he was slaying Achilles when he killed Patroclus, who was wearing Achilles' armor. Achilles himself fell to Paris' arrow, which was guided by Apollo. See notes 6.1, 8.4, 8.9, 10.25, 16.14–16, 24.6, 83.20, 150.12, 175.13–14, 228.25, 296.2, 298.9, and 320.7–16.

146.18 griot's hymn—West African historian, bard, and troubadour. Griots are the keepers of narrative, and they are charged with the oral transmission of their people's history. These positions are inherited.

147.8 manchineel—see note 10.23.

148.6 ocelot—a carnivorous spotted cat common in Latin America that hunts at night; commonly black and tan in coloring, though sometimes yellow and grey. See note 151.7.

CHAPTER XXVIII

149.6 the Bight of Benin, from the margin of Guinea—the Bight of Benin refers to a bay off the West African coast that outspreads eastward for several hundred miles from Cape St. Paul to a channel of the Niger

River. The bay is within the Gulf of Guinea. The area was a center of the slave trade. See notes 122.16–17, 129.14–15, 130.8, 145.5, 150.1–2, 184.1, and 189.3.

149.9 the river-gods—see note 134.24.

149.14–15 the ribbed corpses / floated, riding, to the white sand they remembered—the palm frond and its ribs serve as a metaphor for the enslaved African subjects who were cast overboard during the Middle Passage. See notes 45.22–23, 130.8, and 150.23.

150.1–2 Ashanti one way, the Mandingo another, the Ibo another—The Ashanti or Asante are a West African people in southern Ghana, Côte d'Ivoire, Togo. Their social order is systematized matrilineally and they are renowned farmers. Mandingo or Malinke are a West African people who live in the upper Niger River Valley (Guinea, the Ivory Coast, Mali, Senegal, Gambia, and Guinea-Bissau). Famed warriors, they have a system of patrilineal nobility. The Ibo or Igbo reside in Nigeria. They are traditionally farmers with communal land holdings. Igbo women often fill leadership roles in their governmental and civic structures. See notes 129.14–15, 184.1, and 224.15.

150.12 the shield held up to Hector–in *The Iliad*, Achilles' shield is detailed at the culmination of Book XVIII; it was constructed exquisitely with elaborate scenes by the blacksmith and god of fire, Hephaestus. It represents not only Achilles but also the Greek world. W. H. Auden (1907–1973) published *The Shield of Achilles* in 1955. Walcott refers to the famed shield in "Crusoe's Island." See notes 8.9, 16.14–15, 53.4, and 114.7.

150.13 the hammerer's art—refers to a smith or blacksmith; this profession entails using a hammer to strike metal into a certain shape or form. See note 150.12.

150.18 foetid—fetid, a foul smell.

150.23–24 each carried / the nameless freight of himself to the other world—the Middle Passage. See notes 45.22–23, 130.8, and 149.14–15.

151.7–8 russet lions . . . where ocelots—a russet lion is a reddish-brown cat and an ocelot is a spotted cat; both native to Latin America. See notes 32.6, 37.13, 148.6, 194.5, and 230.11.

151.9 Assyria—located near the upper Tigris River, in present-day northern Iraq and southern Turkey, this early kingdom grows out of the city of Ashur (also spelled Assur). The Assyrians were known for being phenomenal fighters with prowess in battle and a high amount of malevolence. See notes 65.5, 97.7, and 100.6.

151.10 Thracian phalanx—Thrace is both an ancient and modern area of Greece, though its limits have altered considerably with the passage of time. A phalanx is a strategic formation for infantry soldiers. The most famous use of the formation in the ancient world was by Alexander the Great (356–323 BCE), who used it to overthrow the Persian Empire and reach India.

151.12 barracoons—a "barrack or depot"; a holding area or prison where enslaved subjects or those awaiting forced transportation would be held; from the Catalan *barraca* or "hut."

152.6 never . . . again—a phrase popularized after the Holocaust by the American Israeli rabbi and activist Meir [Martin David] Kahane (1932–1990) in his *Never Again!: A Program for Survival.*

CHAPTER XXIX

152.10 nightingale's full throttle—the Eurasian nightingale (*Luscinia megarhynchos*) is known for its delightful song. John Keats' (1795–1821) "Ode to a Nightingale" conceptualizes the song of the nightingale as an eternal melody that can provide respite from the pain of contemporary life. In the Caribbean, mockingbirds are often called nightingales. See notes 88.16–21 and 313.24.

152.14–15 Agamemnon, but the low fingered O of an Aruac flute—Agamemnon is a character in some Greek tragedies as well as the epic poems *The Iliad* and *The Odyssey*. He was a commander in the Trojan War. After returning home, he is killed by his wife because he sacrificed their daughter. His son, Orestes, commits matricide to avenge his father's death. This is famously dramatized in Aeschylus' (525/524–456/455 BCE) *The Oresteia*. The "O" refers to the *os*, or "bone," from which the indigenous peoples in the Amazon made flutes. See notes 3.1, 5.2, 34.20, 35.18, 92.5, 92.15, 162.14, and 164.16.

153.1 Penelope—Daughter of Icarius of Sparta and the nymph Periboeia; cousin to Helen. Penelope was married to Odysseus. In Homer's account, she is well known for being a faithful and clever wife. She successfully thwarted the attentions and schemes of the suitors who were pressuring her to marry in Odysseus' continued absence (and presumed death). She wove and dismantled a shroud for Odysseus' father, Laertes, for several years as a stalling tactic. The mother of Telemachus, she is a model of Greek womanhood. Walcott refers to Penelope in *Another Life* and "Lampfall." Walcott's depiction of Penelope in *The Odyssey: a Stage Version* is striking for her criticism of violence, particularly of the masculine, heroic codes that demand it. See notes 130.5, 194.15, 201.16, and 232.21.

153.8 ground dove—the common ground dove (*Columbina passerina*) is an arriviste in St. Lucia from Latin America. It propagates in spring and summer. It is especially drawn to parched areas, coastal regions, and gardens. See notes 4.9 and 313.18.

154.12 blind saint—Saint Lucy or Santa Lucia (d. 304 CE), virgin and martyr, is the patron saint of the blind; *lucia* derives from the Latin *lux* for "light," and *luce* in Italian means "light." She is associated with sight because of her martyrdom during which her eyes were gouged. She was frequently represented as carrying her eyes during the Middle Ages. Her feast day is December 13. See notes 11.4 and 64.21.

154.20 split trotters, with my curved tusks—a trotter is a springy, light-footed creature; the term is particularly used when the feet of such animals are eaten as food. A tusk is a extended piercing tooth, especially one that distends from a closed mouth. In elephants, it is a protruding upper tooth and is prized by ivory hunters. Although the trade in ivory is now illegal, an underground market remains.

155.9 then Circe embraced her swine—see note 64.19.

155.14 the submerged archipelago—suggestive of the myth of Atlantis; an island said to be west of the Strait of Gibraltar. The tale originated with the ancient Greeks but has endured throughout the ages. It occupies a peculiar position in the Western imagination as an island civilization lost to the sea.

155.19 manumission—emancipation from enslavement. Laws granting freedom to enslaved subjects vary across time and place. In the British Caribbean, the legal abolition of slavery was followed by an apprenticeship system, which functionally was slavery under another name.

155.21–23 a Jesuit mission // burned in Veracruz—in 1767, the Spanish king, Charles III (1716–1788), barred the Jesuits (the Society of Jesus, a Roman Catholic religious order of priests founded by Saint Ignatius of Loyola [1491–1556] in Paris in 1534) from all Spanish territories; they were thought too powerful in the undertakings of the colonies. Resistance to the ejection of the Jesuits was met with viciousness and the burning of the assets of any who dared to contest the ban. Villa Rica de la Vera Cruz (Veracruz) is a city in Mexico founded by Hernán Cortés, marqués del Valle de Oaxaca (1485–1547), the Spanish conquistador who conquered the Aztec Empire.

155.23–25 a Sephardic merchant, bag locked in one elbow, / crouched by a Lisbon dock . . . reborn in the New World—Jacob-Abraham-Camille Pissarro was a Sephardic Jewish merchant of Portuguese descent who emigrated to St. Thomas in the West Indies where his son, the renowned impressionist painter Camille Pissarro (1830–1903), was born. Camille Pissarro is referenced in *Another Life* and is a central figure in *Tiepolo's Hound*.

155.25–26 Lima, Curaçao . . . the Pyrenees—Lima is the capital city of Peru. Founded by the Spanish in the sixteenth century, it rests just eight miles from the Pacific and its attendant port city of Callao. Present-day Lima is a sprawling metropolis that has earned the nickname "the octopus." Curaçao is West Indian island in the Lesser Antilles, north of Venezuela; it is also a self-ruling state within the Netherlands. The Pyrenees refers to the mountains in southwestern Europe that run between the Atlantic and the Mediterranean, a striking geographic feature that serves as a national border between France and Spain. The small principality of Andorra rests among these mountains. Due to this dominant geographic mountain boundary, both Spain and Portugal necessarily developed powerful maritime cultures with colonies across the ocean. See notes 77.14–15 and 204.6.

155.27 an ape behind bars, to Napoleon's orders—a reference to Toussaint Louverture or L'Ouverture (1743–1803). Born as an enslaved subject, he became a dynamic leader of the Haitian Revolution. He gained control over Hispaniola and ended slavery. Napoleon Bonaparte (1769–1821) saw Louverture as a significant impediment to returning Haiti to France as its most profitable colony. Louverture was taken as a prisoner to Fort-de-Joux, located in the French Alps, where he was imprisoned and ultimately died. Walcott's *Haitian Trilogy* depicts Toussaint Louverture amid the revolution and wider Caribbean history. See note 172.16.

156.2 Port Royal—a city in Jamaica that largely fell into the sea during an earthquake in 1692. With only one-third of the city still on land, most survivors crossed the bay on which the remaining port stood to resettle and found Kingston, the present capital city. During the seventeenth century, Port Royal was a famously debauched and corrupt city, home to privateers and buccaneers who frequently raided ships flying enemy flags. A museum at Fort Charles in Port Royal remains open today.

156.3 Victoria—see notes 25.17, 26.9, 103.26–27, and 195.4.

156.4 Wilberforce—William Wilberforce (1759–1833), a member of the British Parliament. After his conversion to Evangelicalism, he worked relentlessly to end the slave trade and was a founding member of the Anti-Slavery Society. Wilberforce achieved success in 1807 when the British Parliament abolished the slave trade. Despite the abolition of the trade, tragically slavery endured. Wilberforce then worked to end slavery in the British Empire. He died on July 29, 1833, mere days after the Slavery Abolition Act was passed in the lower House of Parliament. See notes 122.16–17, 129.14–15, 130.8, and 189.3.

156.4 Saul—Saul (ca. 1021–1000 BCE), the first king of Israel in the Old Testament book of Samuel. In the New Testament, Saul of Tarsus (4 BCE–62/64 CE) initially persecuted Christians but on his way to Damascus he encountered a vision. Thereafter he became an apostle, renamed Paul, and ultimately the Christian St. Paul.

156.7 Darwin—Charles Darwin (1809–1882) was a British naturalist who published *On The Origin of Species* in 1859. His theories of natural selection and evolution were revolutionary in scientific discourse.

156.8 Madrasi climbed the hull—Madrasi refers to people from Madras, a southern province in India on the Bay of Bengal. Indian indentured laborers were brought to the Caribbean from the late 1840s (after the emancipation of enslaved African subjects) until the early decades of the twentieth century. The Indian workers were used as substitute cheap labor. See notes 156.10–11, 221.9, and 322.6.

156.9 Calcutta and Bombay—Calcutta is the Anglicized colonial name for Kolkata, a city in Bengal, a state of India that once served as the British colonial capital. Bombay is the former colonial-era name of Mumbai, a city of islands joined by land bridges and once submerged, now reclaimed, territory. Both cities were critical ports for Indian emigration. See notes 156.8, 156.10–11, and 221.9.

156.10–11 Fatel Rozack—Fath Al Razak, "Victory of Allah the Provider"; the sailing vessel that carried the first Indian indentured laborers to Trinidad and Tobago in 1845. This day is now a national holiday in Trinidad and Tobago May 30, known as Indian Arrival Day. See notes 156.8, 156.9, and 221.9.

156.12 Cape of Good Hope—also known as Cape Province; a coastal promontory on the far southern tip of Africa. Bartolomeu Dias (1450–1500), the Portuguese explorer, first navigated this promontory in 1488 and was followed by his countryman Vasco da Gama (1460–1524) in 1497. In fact, Dias died when his ship sank in the waters off the Cape of Good Hope in 1500. It is a critical passage from the Indian Ocean to the Atlantic Ocean. The waters are notoriously treacherous to sail and dangerous to swim. High surf, crashing waves, and great white sharks predominate in this meeting point of two oceans.

CHAPTER XXX

157.5 Trade—transatlantic slave trade and the Trade winds. See notes 122.16–17, 127.7, 129.14–15, 130.8, and 189.3.

157.7 Mackerel running—a fish that thrives globally. The common variety in the Caribbean is the Atlantic mackerel (*Scomber scombrus*), a fish of approximately twelve inches with a greenish-blue body with wavy vertical markings. It runs, or moves, in large groups or schools.

157.14–15 mako . . . albacore—mako has a variety of meanings in Caribbean English, ranging from a meddlesome individual to an object of exceptional size. It is also a kind of shark, the mako, or the mackerel shark (*Isuridae*). These can grow to thirteen feet in length. A kingfish, also known as the king-mackerel (*S. cavalla*) is a long, very large round-bodied fish with a lustrous, dark-gray and silvery coloring that grows to over five feet. An albacore (*Thunnus alalunga*) is a long-finned tuna. The albacore is mostly blue but also sports greenish, white, and silver hues and reaches almost nine feet in length. The meat of the albacore is prized.

158.13 herring-gulls—a sizeable gull with dusky wing ends (*L. argentatus*) from the North that is considered an itinerant species on St. Lucia.

158.20 frigate—see notes 19.6 and 43.18.

159.5 seraphic space whose cumuli—Cumulus are dense, pillowy, bright-white clouds that have well defined but rounded tops and flat bottoms. They usually indicate fair weather. For seraphic, see note 62.18.

159.22 Homeros—see notes 12.25, 14.5, 280.8, 283.21, and 288.21.

160.1 Barrel of Beef—see note 35.24.

160.8 Every bird is my brother—the Holy Spirit in the Roman Catholic Trinity is represented as a bird.

CHAPTER XXXI

161.4 blockorama—an open-air party with several steel percussion bands, commonly held as a fundraising affair.

161.6–7 he washed the canoe, of a Marley reggae . . . "Buffalo Soldier" . . . "heart of America"—lyrics from a Bob Marley (1945–1981) song, "Buffalo Soldier." Buffalo Soldiers were members of African American cavalry units that served on the Western American frontier from 1867 to 1896 and were noted for their restraint and discipline. Initially these men provided security to stagecoaches and livestock on the frontier. After the Red River War (1874–75), an uprising of American Indian warriors, the Buffalo Soldiers were primarily used to engage American Indians, such as the Apache nation, who resisted their forced relocation onto reservations. See notes 3.1, 161.11.164.16, 164.21, 174.15, 179.19, and 181.21.

161.11 buffalo, a black rider—Buffalo or the American bison dominated the landscape east of the Rocky Mountains and provided a critical life source for the Plains Indians. The slaughter of the American buffalo in the late nineteenth century was part of a campaign by the U.S. government to force the American Indian nations onto reservations. While the buffalo numbered up to 50 million when the Europeans first landed in the Americas, by the end of the nineteenth century, only about one thousand remained. See notes 161.6–7, 164.16, 164.21, 174.15, 179.19, and 181.21

161.16 pennons—a triangular flag from medieval heraldry often sported by knights; a long, narrow or tailed flag used in contemporary military decoration. These pointed flags frequently were used on the end of a lance or at the top of a mast. In the Middle Ages, knights used them to signify rank, provide warning of approach, and indicate the reach of their weapons.

161.20 scull—an oar used to propel a rowing vessel and/or the vessel itself.

162.5 Winchester—a repeating weapon named for its manufacturer, Oliver Fisher Winchester (1810–1880), who enhanced the design of the rifle in his Winchester Repeating Arms Company.

162.14 pomme-Arac—see Walcott's "Saint Lucie," where he engages in an etymology for the word, a union of *pomme*, meaning "apple" or "potato," and a gesture of indigeneity for Aruac or Arac. See notes 3.1, 5.2, 92.5, 92.15.

164.5 totem—a natural object (common in the Northwestern United States, western Canada, and the Pacific Islands) created by indigenous artists as an emblem. A totem frequently represented a revered spirit or protector. It also could refer to "totem pole," which holds aloft an image of this object, incised into a cut or fallen tree trunk, in a vertical symbolic narrative.

164.6 oleander—oleander (*Nerium oleander*) is a flowering plant with dull green leaves and pink, red, and/or white flowers; also an evergreen shrub with groups of small flowers. It is poisonous if ingested, particularly its milky juice, and can cause inflammation and prickliness to the skin from mere touch.

164.11 mole crickets—see note 21.4.

164.16 Aruac to Sioux—Aruacs are the native inhabitants of St. Lucia. The Sioux are a community of American Indian peoples (primarily comprising three language groups and peoples: the Santee, Teton, and Yankton) in North America that were dispossessed of their land by European settlers and later engaged in wars with the U.S. government. Their warrior culture is closely tied to the supernatural. Buffalo and bear are important animals in their sacred practices. Walcott engages with North American indigenous cultures in his poems "Elegy," "Over Colorado," and "Forest of Europe," his play, "The Ghost Dance," and in an essay on Robert Frost, "The Road Taken." See notes 3.1, 5.2, 92.5, 92.15, 161.6–7. 161.11. 162.14, 164.21, 174.15, 175.12, 176.3, 176.6, 179.19, 180.18, 181.16–17, 181.21, 182.10, and 182.15.

164.21 Ghost Dancer—In the final decade of the nineteenth century, the Ghost Dance religion gathered a wide following among the Sioux. This spiritual practice foretold a North America rid of all Europeans, the resurgence of the buffalo, a coming messiah, and a final assemblage with the ancestors and fallen warriors in death. This spiritual movement was integrated into many American Indian belief systems. The dance was a critical turning point in American Indian resistance but was used by the American government as a excuse to further suppress and kill American Indians. It was often misinterpreted by outsiders as a war dance or a call for uprising. It reportedly played a part in increasing hostility and led to the massacre at Wounded Knee. Walcott wrote a play, "The Ghost Dance," (1989) in which he examined the consequences of Sioux efforts to rid North America of Europeans; these efforts sadly resulted in hastening the end of Sioux resistance against the U.S. government and its appropriation of their land. See notes 161.6–7, 161.11.164.16, 174.15, 175.12, 176.3, 176.6, 179.19, 180.18, 181.16–17, 181.21, 182.10, and 182.15.

164.24 Sybils—see note 58.5.

CHAPTER XXXII

165.6 Marian Home—a home for the elderly in Castries, St. Lucia, affiliated with the Roman Catholic Church.

166.6 allamanda's bells—see note 65.8.

166.6–7 bougainvillea—See note 67.10.

166.18 Derek, Roddy, and Pam—Derek Walcott (1930–), his twin brother, Roderick (1930–2000), a well-known theater director, set designer, playwright, and painter, and his sister, Pamela Walcott St. Hill (1928–2010), a mother of three who lived in Barbados. See note 68.21.

166.23 Warwick's son—see note 68.21.

167.12 my mother's amnesia—Alix Walcott (1894–1990) was Derek Walcott's mother. She was the daughter of a Dutch father, Johannes van Romondt (dates not available), and a woman from St. Maarten, Caroline Maarlin (dates not available). Alix immigrated to St. Lucia as a young girl, and she became a teacher in the Methodist Infant School. As an English-speaking Protestant, she was part of an exclusive cultural minority on the island, although the family had little money. Alix lost her memory as she grew old; she resided in Castries in a Roman Catholic home for the aged until her death. See notes 61.10, 68.21, 69.13, and 187.11.

❖ Book Four

SUMMARY

The fourth, central, book of *Omeros* is the shortest in the work. It opens with a stark departure and the circular image of a carousel bordering Long Island Sound. The movement to the United States suggests a vortex out of which the author struggles and with which he grapples. The first person narrator of the poem—based on Walcott himself—takes the foreground in this journey from St. Lucia to Boston, Massachusetts. The author is also revealed to be on a quest for home, though here, in New England, he lives in exile. The rupture of his displacement is mirrored in the book with its departure from the convention of the three-line poetic form, to which the poet has been somewhat faithful heretofore. In this search for home, the poet switches to couplets that suggest the earliest American poets of the Puritan tradition and even the couplets of *The New England Primer*, which overtly links language and geography with sacred instruction. This home in poetic couplets is transformed utterly with the invocation of manifest destiny, that perverse delusion of virgin land that brought the settler juggernaut to the West of the continent and forcefully displaced American Indians. The struggle that Walcott endures in America is couched with recognition of the loss and destruction of indigenous cultures, particularly that of the Sioux. The Sioux nation, Sitting Bull, their famed leader, and Catherine Weldon, a well-meaning activist for indigenous rights, play a significant part in the imagination of America for Walcott. (Weldon narrates a section: poem II of chapter XXXV). Walcott joins the fate of the Sioux nation with that of African Americans, in their struggle for civil rights and against the history of lynching, and of Caribbean peoples, who also struggle to achieve emancipation and equality. Achille emerges in this juxtaposition as a manifestation of the desire to find an ancestral home, brought across the Atlantic courtesy of Winslow Homer's *The Gulf Stream*. The swift circles a new vortex, "the skyscrapers of Boston" (188.6).

Book four serves as the core of the narrative journey. In this book, Walcott's protagonist, now an autobiographical "I," enters the United States via Long Island in a quest for New World indigeneity. The African cultures dislocated through forced movement to the Caribbean and the wider Americas have long manifested a sense of displaced indigeneity and of longing for both return and restoration. If Achille's journey to Africa suggests that return is not an entirely fulfilling option, then the first-person narrator's restoration or homecoming in the New World becomes the endeavor amid the journey. Yet, the quest for belonging, of finding that rightful and authentic place for our voyager(s), rests not in North America.

ANNOTATIONS

CHAPTER XXXIII

169.3 carousel—a carousel (or roundabout; also merry-go-round) derives from an ancient Middle Eastern game of contest on horseback between opposing teams. Such games were introduced to Europe with the homecoming of European Crusaders. The mechanical carousel is largely a product of the nineteenth century; its golden age in Europe and America emerged with a swift period of industrialization. The carousel evokes nostalgia for an agrarian, gentle pastime of jaunting or galloping on horseback. Carousels dot Long Island Sound from New London to New Haven, Connecticut. They are prominent features of coastal resorts and served as popular diversions from everyday life. Ocean Beach Park in New London, Connecticut, houses a carousel and is close to Lyman Allyn Art Museum and Fort Griswold, the site of American defense against the British in the Battle of Groton Heights. The Lighthouse Point Park Carousel in New Haven, Connecticut, dates to 1911.

169.3 Long Island Sound—a large body of water (ninety miles in length and between three and twenty miles in width) that extends off of the Atlantic Ocean and serves as an element of the Intracoastal Waterway. Located between Long Island to the south and Connecticut to the north, it supports a somewhat limited commercial fishing industry focused on shellfish. The Sound provides a backdrop for F. Scott Fitzgerald's (1896–1940), *The Great Gatsby*, which is set in the wealthy enclaves amid the north shore of Long Island. See note 169.7.

169.6 loon—a diver; any one of five species of aquatic diving birds from the *Gaviidae* family. They spend the majority of their lives in water and can journey to depths of two hundred feet below the surface; they have webbed toes, and regulate their dives with the control of their air sacs. They are common in North America.

169.7 New London—the city of New London, Connecticut, is the home of the U.S. Coast Guard Academy. A port, it is also one of the critical stops for ferries that travel from Long Island to the New England coast. The county of New London is the southern and easternmost county in Connecticut; it borders the state of Rhode Island and the Long Island Sound. It was an important location for the whaling industry in the nineteenth century. The Pequot and Mohegan controlled the area before European colonization. See note 169.3.

170.12 Mayakovsky's clouds—Vladimir Vladimirovich Mayakovsky (1893–1930), the Russian (and then Soviet) poet of the revolution. His work, "A Cloud in Trousers," focuses on a troubling desire and was published before the revolution. Mayakovsky is referenced in *Another Life*.

170.19 Brookline—a seven-square-mile town and Boston, Massachusetts, suburb where Walcott lived while he was teaching at Boston University. The town is considered a well-off, desirable location and is the birthplace of the U.S. president John Fitzgerald Kennedy (1917–1963).

170.24 bedragonned—a variation of bedraggled, which means "disheveled" and/or "filthy," and a play on the word "dragon," a mythological creature. In the West, the dragon is generally considered a foul force; yet in the East (and particularly in China) it often represents magnanimity. The dragon was a symbol of the Chinese imperial family.

171.1 Jap soldier on his Pacific island—the island nation of Japan is located in the western Pacific; a sizeable chain of isles off the coast of

the Asian continent. Japanese soldiers were in loyal service of the Impe-
rial Japanese Army during World War II. These soldiers were deployed
on islands in the campaign to win the Pacific theater during the war.
After the end of the war, tales of forgotten Japanese soldiers on isolated
island outposts captured the public imagination.

171.20 oarlocks—a notch or device on a boat's brim to ensure the
oar remains in place and does not fall into the water.

171.27 Marie Celeste—Mary Celeste; a ship that sailed from New
York Harbor and was found without her crew near the Azores in De-
cember 1872. The final entry in the captain's log was dated in late No-
vember but gave no indication of any issues. There are inconsistent tales
related to the ghost ship, none of which have yielded any absolute de-
termination. The infamy of the ship is due to Sir Arthur Conan Doyle's
(1859–1930) story, "J. Habakuk Jephson's Statement," which was based
on the Mary Celeste case and was published in *Cornhill Magazine*. In
Doyle's narrative, an African slave murders the European captain and
crew and then sails for Africa. Sister Maria Celeste (1600–1634) was
Galileo's (1564–1642) daughter. The young nun and her esteemed fa-
ther produced a voluminous correspondence. See note 172.16.

172.16 Vallombrosa—Italian for "shady village"; a village located in
Tuscany in northern Italy just southeast of Florence that is surrounded
by a dense chestnut and beech tree forest. The poet Dante Alighieri
(1265–1821) visited the Benedictine Abbey of Vallombrosa. Galileo
(1564–1642) was a student at the monastery's school at Vallombrosa
before he enrolled at the University of Pisa. John Milton (1608–1674)
uses Vallombrosa in a famous epic simile in *Paradise Lost*, Book 1: the
poet compares the enormity of Satan's shield to the image of the moon
when viewed through the telescope of the monastery's famed student,
Galileo. The monastery was raided several times in its history. The Bene-
dictines established residence at the monastery again after World War II.
See notes 155.27 and 171.27.

172.21 home. Yet I was lost—a well-known juxtaposition of the
seeming incongruity of being lost and home from Seamus Heaney's
(1939–2013) "The Tollund Man."

173.1–174.14 House of umbrage . . . becoming home—these
rhyming couplets are a dramatic switch from the three-line stanzas used

heretofore. They evoke the rhymes of the *New England Primer*, a volume first published in Boston in the late seventeenth century, and those of Emily Dickinson (1830–1886). Walcott's repetition of "house" is striking as it transforms finally into a home. However, the displacement throughout these lines suggests a fleeting if not impossible domestic sanctuary.

173.12 wrinkled clouds with Onan's stain—the story of Onan in the book of Genesis deals with issues of progeny and intimate relations; in one account Onan is condemned for masturbation, and in another he refuses to sleep with his sister-in-law, thus declining the opportunity, troubling as it is, to produce progeny. His stain is a marker of his sins of disobedience and of wasting the opportunity for and seeds of procreation.

173.18 rites of genuflecting verse—a verse that is meant as a ceremonial or sacred act on metaphorical bended knee to show respect or worship; common in the Roman Catholic sacred practices. See note 236.11.

CHAPTER XXXIV

174.15 The Crow horseman—the "horse culture" of the Crow American Indians, also called the Absaroka or Apsarokee. They followed the migrations of their subsistence animals (buffalo primarily) for food, shelter, and clothing. The Crow ultimately lived in the Yellowstone River valley in Montana. In the eighteenth century, they developed a specialty in raiding for and managing horses. The Crow were known for having the most horses of any of the indigenous peoples. Horses and buffalo became central to their sacred practices. Due to incursions on their land from the Blackfoot and Dakota Sioux, who were themselves fleeing the movement of European settlers and the American government into the western frontier, the Crow allied themselves with the American government in the Plains Wars. See note 161.6–7. 161.11.164.16, 176.3, 176.6, 179.19, 180.18, 181.16–17, 181.21, 182.10, and 182.15.

174.16–17 Colorado's palomino mountains—Palomino is a 12,230-foot mountain located in Mineral County, Colorado. A palomino is a horse, yellow in body color, with a white silver tail and mane.

175.2 Crow horseman—see note 174.15.

175.10 Manifest Destiny—the idea that originated in the mid-nineteenth century from a phrase used in 1845 by John Louis O'Sullivan, a Boston journalist, in the *United States Magazine and Democratic Review*. The ideology of manifest destiny justified the westward expansion of the United States well beyond the Mississippi River and the Louisiana Territory. This catchphrase became a marker of dramatic territorial seizure. Such blatant territorial appropriations rested on the perverse colonial and imperial delusion of empty, virgin land. American expansionism in the mid- to late nineteenth century was of extreme concern to the indigenous peoples of the Americas, who were forcibly displaced from their lands, and even for peoples of the Caribbean, who feared there would be no limit to such territorial gains. Peoples who resided on land that the American government sought were forcibly removed.

175.12 the Sioux in the snow—refers to the massacre at Wounded Knee in December 1890, when the U.S. Calvary murdered two hundred disarmed Sioux men, women, and children. This was the final battle of the American government's campaign to subdue the American Indian nations. After the massacre, a blizzard set in, and all the dead were left on the battlefield, freezing as they fell slaughtered. The Sioux dead remained in the snow all winter and were buried only during the following spring thaw. See notes 164.16, 176.3, 176.6, 180.18, 181.16–17, 182.10, and 182.15.

175.13–14 Achille's hallucination—a journey undertaken following Achille's sunstroke when he follows the swift, returns to Africa, and encounters his ancestors; this voyage evokes a journey to the underworld. See notes 6.1, 8.4, 8.9, 10.25, 16.14–16, 24.6, 83.20, 146.15–16, 150.12, 228.25, 296.2, 298.9, and 320.7–16.

175.18 the spike for the Union Pacific—the "golden spike" that was driven into the track on May 10, 1869, thereby joining the railroads of the Central Pacific, which originated in Sacramento, California, and of the Union Pacific, which began in Omaha, Nebraska. There is now a Golden Spike National Historic park in Utah with a monument that encases the "golden" point at the site that united the American transcontinental railroad system.

176.3 Parkin farm—a farm in the Dakota Territory that is significant as a location in the destruction of the Sioux and the site of the incident that caused the death of Catherine Weldon's only child, a son, Christie (dates not available, though he was reported to be twelve or thirteen at the time of his passing). He stepped on a metal object on the farm and contracted an infection, likely tetanus, that killed him. Weldon accompanied her sick boy on a desperate journey to seek medical attention at a hospital when the boy succumbed to his infection. See notes 164.16, 164.21, 175.12, 176.6, 180.18, 181.16–17, 182.10, and 182.15.

176.6 Catherine Weldon—a New York woman who was a member of the National Indian Defense Association. Born Catherine Schlotter in Switzerland (date of birth unknown), she emigrated to the United States, married, and had a son. She seems to have been trained in painting in the fashion typical of middle-class women of the era. After being widowed and gaining an interest in the rights of indigenous peoples, Weldon settled with her son in the Dakota Territory in 1889. Weldon helped Sitting Bull (1831–1890) fight against U.S. government seizures of land. Sitting Bull named her "Woman Walking Ahead." She was also called derisively, by the American authorities who sought to undermine her cause, Sitting Bull's "white squaw." Weldon served as a secretary, read written documents, and wrote letters on behalf of Sitting Bull. She also painted him. Weldon often clashed with the U.S. government, which eventually forced Weldon to leave the territory. Weldon returned to New York but longed to go back to the Plains. During the "Ghost Dance" movement of 1890, Weldon spoke out against the belief in the power of the dance. She believed the American authorities would use the dance as a pretext to attack the Sioux. Although much about her life remains unknown, Weldon returned to New York ultimately, died there, and was buried in Greenwood Cemetery in Brooklyn in 1921. Walcott portrays Catherine Weldon in his play, "The Ghost Dance," the first production of which was in 1989, though it was not published until 1995. See notes 164.16, 164.21, 175.12, 176.3, 180.18, 181.16–17, 182.10, and 182.15.

177.1 Indian summer—a late fall occurrence of unseasonably lovely warm weather, usually in the Eastern United States. In Britain, this phenomenon is termed an Old Wives' summer.

CHAPTER XXXV

177.4 the Trail of Tears—the involuntary ejection of southeastern American Indians (Choctaw, Chickasaw, Creek, Seminole, and Cherokee) from their lands during the 1830s. The tragic journey dislocated roughly one hundred thousand people and killed an estimated fifteen thousand people. Although the damage of removal was widespread, the nation most associated with the traumatic journey was the Cherokee. The Cherokee starting point is located in northeastern Georgia around the New Echota State Park and in southeastern Tennessee around the Red Clay State Park. What were termed "moving points," or official points of departure/removal, varied. One water route began in Ross's Landing in Chattanooga, Tennessee; a land starting point included Rattlesnake Springs, Tennessee, located about ten miles north of Red Clay State Park. The motivation for this dislocation was unbridled avarice stemming from an unearthing of gold on Cherokee land in 1829. The Indian Removal Act of 1830 quickly granted permission to President Andrew Jackson (1767–1845) to force the indigenous peoples westward beyond the Mississippi River. The "trail" ended in Oklahoma, which was then simply designated "Indian Territory." Walcott invokes the Trail of Tears in "Forest of Europe." See notes 177.8–9, 177.16, 177.20, and 178.6.

177.8–9 Choctaws. Creeks—The Choctaws are American Indians who lived in the southeast Gulf zones of Mississippi, Alabama, and Louisiana as well as the Atlantic territory of Georgia. The Choctaw's culture was similar to that of their rivals, and sometimes enemies, the Creek. Agronomy was central to the Choctaw way of life, and they were esteemed in the area for their agricultural prowess. The Choctaw formed a union with the French rather than with the English. After being forced out of Alabama and Mississippi, they lived in Oklahoma. The Creek originally lived in both Alabama and Georgia. They also had an economy that was systematized around corn and squash. The Creek cooperated with the English instead of the French, yet in the 1830s they were also ultimately forced west of the Mississippi to Oklahoma. See notes 177.4 and 177.20.

177.9–11 I thought of the Greek revival / carried past the names of towns with columned porches / and how Greek it was—Greek

Revival architecture was most common in the United States in the early nineteenth century, just before the American Civil War. In such a building the gabled roof has a markedly low pitch with striking columns; the porch in the front of the structure can vary in length, spanning either the entryway or the entire front façade. The style achieved prominence due to its associations with antiquity as well as perhaps its presumed immutable ideologies, which incorporated both democracy and slavery. There was also interest in the new nation, after the revolution and the War of 1812, of breaking with British paradigms, such as Georgian (in the United States, Federal) styles. The Greek Revival style reimagined fifth-century-BCE architecture such as the Parthenon. While some plantation houses in the South adopted the style, several important buildings in Philadelphia, such as the 2nd Bank of the United States and Girard College, also reflect the broad early-nineteenth-century American interest in the ancient Greek world. In fact, many of the plantation houses in the American South were not in the Greek Revival style, and many enslaved African subjects labored on small farms that had no attendant "Big House," as conventional conceptions of plantation architectures commonly include. Walcott notes the common Greek Revival style of government architecture in Washington, D.C., in "The Star-Apple Kingdom." See notes 32.13 and 312.16.

177.16 Athens, Sparta, Troy—three powerful cities of the ancient Greek and Mediterranean world that have namesake counterparts in the American South related to American slavery and the Trail of Tears. Athens, Georgia, is a university town located in the northeastern part of the state (the site of the University of Georgia) that has a large number of Greek Revival buildings; it is also houses the Morton Theatre, the first African American–owned and operated performance hall. Athens escaped the notoriously destructive Union March through Georgia during the Civil War; after the war, during Reconstruction, it became a headquarters for the Freedmen's Bureau. Sparta, Greece, was known for its martial culture and rivalry with Athens. Sparta, Georgia, is a modest town south of Athens, Georgia, between Augusta and Macon. Troy is an ancient city in Turkey and location for Homer's *The Iliad*. Troy, Alabama, is a town in the southeastern part of the state. Troy University was founded there in 1887. See notes 3.2, 6.1, 8.9, 14.5, 16.14–15, 17.5–6, 24.6, 31.4, 32.13, 177.4, 177.20, 178.6, and 284.4.

177.20 headed for Oklahoma—Oklahoma is the American state west of the Mississippi River that was the end point of the Trail of Tears. Situated just north of Texas, the state combines American southern and western culture. There remains a large American Indian population, but the land rush brought a large number of European settlers. The word "Oklahoma" is Choctaw in origin and joins the words for people, *okla*, and red, *humma*. Before statehood, the area was simply termed "Indian Territory." The climate can be harsh and many residents departed from its Dust Bowl in the early twentieth century. See notes 177.4, 177.8–9, 177.16, and 178.6.

178.6 terror—the term "terror" derives from the period of mass murders, the Reign of Terror, habitually by guillotine, in the French Revolution. Many people lingered in prison for years, some without trial, and died within its walls. The terror here refers to lynching, the murder of African Americans, usually by hanging after a period of torture, by white throngs. This was a systemic practice in the United States and was particularly common in the Reconstruction South in the nineteenth century, though it occurred at an accelerated rate well into the twentieth century. The perpetrators of such crimes were often protected within or representatives of the white power structures in their local communities. While a firm etymology for the term "lynching" remains unclear, it is associated with the practices of Charles Lynch (1736–1796), a Virginia colonist and son of an Irish indentured servant, who punished loyalists, colonists who were loyal to the British, during the American Revolution without due process. See notes 87.20 and 178.7–8.

178.6 oaks along red country roads—the Georgia state tree is the live oak. Live oaks (*Quercus virginiana*) are in the "red oak" group. They are known for their enormous canopies, which are resistant to high winds and pressured weight, even those of extreme force. Indigenous to the American Gulf and Atlantic south as well as Cuba, their tops can be exponentially larger in diameter than their height. Georgia's red clay soil predominates in the northern part of the state. Red Clay is also the name of the Cherokee nation's final seat of self-governance on the border of

Tennessee and Georgia. The state of Georgia in 1832 had forbidden the Cherokee from practicing self-governance, but the Cherokee moved across the state line in 1837 when they were forced onto the Trail of Tears. See notes 177.4, 177.16, and 177.20.

178.7–8 silk-cotton tree . . . Afolabes hung—the silk cotton tree (*ceiba*) is common in tropical zones and is named for the cotton-like filaments that it generates. These trees can grow to eighty feet, and they yield flowers for several months a year. They provide a lithe timber that is relatively easy to whittle and carve and is often used to produce canoes because of its buoyancy. In plural form, Afolabe, Achille's father to whom he journeys in *Omeros*, represents the descendants of the African diaspora, particularly those in the United States who were lynched. See notes 83.20 and 178.6.

178.8–9 hooded clouds / guarded the town squares with their calendar churches—the Ku Klux Klan, the American white supremacist hate organization founded after the American Civil War, wear white hoods and robes during their raids. Known for the burning of crosses, the Klan is highly associated with white Protestant church members who attempted to suppress African Americans after Emancipation and who were growing uncomfortable with the newly multiethnic America, following waves of immigration in the late nineteenth and twentieth centuries. See notes 178.6 and 178.7–8.

178.19 aspens—a North American poplar tree from the family *Salicaceae* known for its tremulous leaves and greenish grey bark; it grows to between sixty and ninety feet, depending on the type. Some of the variations can reproduce asexually when necessary, so a nearby male or female tree is not required for reproduction.

178.21 lindens—several varieties of deciduous trees, such as a common lime tree (*Tilia europaea*). The American linden (*Tilia americana*) is known for its height of up to 130 feet and its pleasing floral aroma. Thus it is popular with bees. The Carolina linden (*Tilia caroliniana*), common in the southeastern United States, produces an excellent honey.

179.19 Colonel Cody's circus—William Frederick Cody or Buffalo Bill Cody (1846–1917). Cody traveled around the country putting on cowboy-themed shows and became famous for his Wild West Show. Despite his popular image, Cody was a conservationist and even advocated for the rights of American Indians. Due to the death of his father, Cody worked from a young age. His fame is based, in part, on his adventures as a U.S. Army scout and buffalo hunter along the frontier. In demand as a hunter and scout, he had an intense familiarity with the geography of the West. He served in the American Civil War. When he visited New York in 1872 he was convinced to appear on stage by Ned Buntline, the pseudonym of E.Z.C. Judson (1823–1886), who originated "dime store" fiction and wrote several novels that immortalized Cody. In 1883, he produced what became known as "Buffalo Bill's Wild West and Congress of Rough Riders of the World." The show toured both the United States and Europe for several years with an enormous cast and featured dramatic reenactments of western adventure including a stagecoach holdup, target shooting, and war dances. Both Annie Oakley, the stage name of Phoebe Ann Mosey (1860–1926), the famed pistol handler and shooter, and Sitting Bull, Tatanka Iyotake (1831–1890), the Dakota chief, appeared in the show at various points. See notes 161.6–7. 161.11.164.16, 164.21, 174.15, and 181.21.

180.3 Catherine Weldon—see note 176.6.

180.5 loon—see note 169.6.

180.15 Versailles—see notes 31.26–27.

180.18 the papers the Sioux . . . folded—the Fort Laramie Treaties of 1851 and 1868 attempted to settle territory disputes between the Sioux nation and the American government. Yet, the American government repeatedly flouted the treaties. A gold rush in the Black Hills in the 1870s only increased settler and prospector incursion. Hostilities culminated in the Battle of Little Big Horn in 1876 when the Sioux and Cheyenne defeated General Custer and his troops. Although this was a decisive military victory for indigenous peoples, the loss of their land, livelihood, and way of life proved to be an ultimate, if momentarily deferred, defeat in the war against American expansion and territorial seizure. See notes 164.16, 164.21, 175.12, 176.3, 176.6, 181.16–17, 182.10, and 182.15.

181.2 Battle of the Saints—see notes 28.21, 31.26–27, 32.5, 32.6, 34.21, 43.1, 43.10, 81.19–20, 84.1, 92.12–13, 99.21–100.5, and 100.9.

181.3 new Eden—the Caribbean. In his essay "Muse of History," Walcott examines the history of the Caribbean amid a series of alternatives. He famously rejects the fathers who participated in both sides of the historical transaction (the buying and selling of enslaved peoples) that brought his ancestors to the Caribbean; yet, he avers that the Caribbean is a dynamic bequest for its peoples today. See notes 12.25, 63.8, 97.2, 248.23–24, and 308.15.

181.8 ghost dance—see notes 164.16, 164.21, 175.12, 176.3, 176.6, 180.18, 181.16–17. 182.10, and 182.15.

181.12 Catherine Weldon—see note 176.6.

181.16–17 Dakotas, / the Sioux, and the Crows—American Indian nations that were brutally treated by European settlers and the U.S. government. The Dakotas were part of the Sioux nation. See notes 164.16, 164.21, 174.15, 175.12, 176.3, 176.6, 180.18, 182.10, and 182.15.

181.21 Blackfoot—an American Indian nation that includes three distinct yet intimately affiliated peoples: the Piegan/Peigan, the Piikuni/Kainah, and the Siksika. The Siksika literally translates as Blackfoot and are the group for which the larger nation is named. They were hunters and highly successful warriors in the northern Plains but currently reside in Alberta, Canada, and the U.S. state of Montana. When the buffalo were largely exterminated in the late nineteenth century, the Blackfoot fought off starvation by turning to other means of subsistence such as agriculture. See notes 161.6–7. 161.11.164.16, 164.21, 174.15, and 179.19.

181.22 When the Crow sets his visage on Death—Crow vision quests were sometimes integrated into a Sun Dance; the Crow believe that they will secure a vision of death for an enemy to avenge the death of a Crow. The Sun Dance became widespread, from Canada to Texas, during the late nineteenth century, and though its origins are unclear, it was a coalescing ritual ceremony for the Plains nations that occurred in late spring and early summer. Dancers would seek visions as they refused food and water for several days, often enduring ritual piercings. The U.S. Bureau of Indian Affairs banned the Sun Dance from 1883 to 1934. It had come to take place on the 4th of July, American Independence Day, and had served as a counter marker of indigenous peoples' resistance to the celebration of the European setters/immigrant Americans. See notes 174.15 and 182.10.

182.10 Great Wind—the Sioux creation narrative explains that an Old Man had a daughter who joined with Wind and produced the four directional airstreams that are aligned with the compass points of North, South, East, and West; in conjunction with the Great Sun, they govern creation. The Sioux also believe that a supreme force sometimes appeared enveloped in a "Great Wind" as a means of protection and that to connect with this force, they needed to conduct ceremonies such as the Sun Dance. See notes 164.16, 164.21, 175.12, 176.3, 176.6, 180.18, 181.16–17, 181.22, and 182.15.

182.12 Hebron—a city in the West Bank, currently governed by the Palestinian authority. The city is important in both Islamic and Jewish tradition because of its affiliation with Abraham. There are many small rivers that course through Palestine and Israel, one of which is the Hebron River, which extends from the West Bank to Gaza and into the sea, though at a certain point it becomes the Besor River.

182.14 Catherine Weldon—see note 176.6.

182.15 Indian agent—a functionary of the Bureau of Indian Affairs, the U.S. government agency responsible for administering reservations and American Indian peoples. In the nineteenth century, the Bureau and its European settler agents were notorious for manipulation and thievery. Today such agents, called superintendents, are American Indians. In Walcott's *The Ghost Dance*, the Indian agent is named Major James McLaughlin. In the play, his allegiances are torn between the Sioux and the U.S. government and further fictionalized with a personal intimacy with Catherine Weldon. This character is based on the actual Indian agent James McLaughlin (1842–1923), who spoke Sioux, married a half– American Indian, and wrote a book called *My Friend the Indian*, published in 1910. McLaughlin ordered the arrest of Sitting Bull (1831–1890), who was killed during the attempt to arrest him. See notes 164.16, 164.21, 175.12, 176.3, 176.6, 180.18, 181.16–17, and 182.10.

CHAPTER XXXVI

182.16 sic transit Gloria—Latin for "passing glory"; from the phrase "sic transit Gloria mundi," which means "the glory of the world passes."

Emily Dickinson (1830–1886) uses the phrase in her 1852 poem, "Sic transit gloria mundi," which critiques received educational practices and Christopher Columbus (1451–1506).

183.8 Bayeux of ivy—the Bayeux tapestry is an embroidered work that celebrates the Norman invasion and conquest of England in 1066. It bedecked the thirteenth-century Gothic cathedral in Bayeux, France, for centuries during special celebrations. The details of the tapestry form a convincing, elegant narrative, and it is adorned with elaborate borders.

183.17 that sky's Canaletto's—the Venetian painter Canaletto, Giovanni Antonio Canal (1697–1768), gained fame for his striking and adroit depictions of cities, particularly London and Venice, though he also worked in the opera houses of Venice and Rome, painting backdrops and scenery. He was also adept at painting rural estates amid elaborate panoramas. See notes 68.26, 72.9, and 204.16.

183.17 that empty bench Van Gogh's—Vincent Van Gogh, the Dutch painter (1853–1890), known as a postimpressionist, whose prominent brush strokes amid thick layers of paint are highly distinctive and arresting. His technique has greatly influenced modern painters, particularly the Abstract Expressionists. Walcott refers to Van Gogh in *Another Life*; he is also a prominent character in his play, *O Starry Starry Night*. See note 87.12.

183.26 *The Gulf Stream*—an 1899 painting by Winslow Homer (1836–1910), an American painter known for his landscapes and marine paintings. This painting depicts a single figure of an African man on board a boat with a broken mast and torn sail. Sharks circle the bloody water surrounding the boat. In the distance, on the horizon, a large ship rests offering no rescue while a water spout threatens. Homer was born in Boston where he became a lithographer and an illustrator. During the Civil War, he worked for *Harper's Weekly*. He painted in both watercolors and oils, and he became increasingly fascinated by the sea, painting the Atlantic from the Canadian maritime to the Caribbean. This painting hangs in the Metropolitan Museum of Art in New York.

184.1 Guinea—a West African country, formerly termed French Guinea, that borders the Atlantic Ocean and several other states (Guinea-Bissau, Senegal, Mali, Côte d'Ivoire, Liberia, and Sierra Leone); one of the largest markets for the slave trade, dating to the Portuguese presence in the fifteenth century. See notes 122.16–17, 127.7, 129.14–15, 130.8, 150.1–2, 149.6, 150.1–2,189.3, and 224.15.

184.2 another Homer's hand—Winslow Homer (1836–1910), who painted *The Gulf Stream*. See note 183.26.

184.7 a sea whose rhythm swells like Herman Melville—Herman Melville (1819–1891), the nineteenth-century American writer best known for the novels *Moby Dick* and *Billy Budd*. His fiction often animates his life on the sea, which he undertook because of the falling fortunes of his family. Ultimately, the financial instability of his writing career was ameliorated with an appointment as a U.S. customs inspector for New York Harbor. See notes 184.9, 184.11, 184.22, and 185.8; 12.

184.9 Having for the imperial colour ... dusky tribe—a quotation from Herman Melville's (1819–1891) *Moby Dick* (1851) that describes the whiteness of the whale and the "superiority" of white men. See note 142.1, 184.7, 184.11, 184.20, 184.22, and 185.8; 12.

184.11 Lawd, Lawd, Massa—lines from *Black Folk Tales*, particularly "High John, the Conqueror," a story of an enslaved African subject outsmarting his master. Zora Neale Hurston (1891–1960) also records such language in her *Mules and Men*, a study of African American folklore. Walcott uses these lines to address Herman Melville. See notes 184.7, 184.9, 184.22, and 185.8; 12.

184.14 the museum—the Boston Museum of Fine Arts, established in 1876, originally in Copley Square; however, in 1909, the museum moved to Huntington Avenue, where it remains today, though now expanded significantly. Dramatic columns are a striking feature of the institution's façade.

184.15 the State House dome—the cornerstone of the Massachusetts State House in Boston, the seat of state government, was laid in 1795, though the dome was not gilded until 1906. See note 184.15 below.

184.15 Saint Gaudens's—Augustus Saint-Gaudens (1848–1907), the noted Dublin-born American sculptor, from a French father and an Irish mother, who designed the 1897 monument on Boston Common to Colonel Robert Gould Shaw (1837–1863) and the "54th Massachusetts Colored Regiment." This monument celebrates the Free African American soldiers and their colonel, who are famed for their bravery in battle as they attempted to take Fort Wagner in Charleston, South Carolina, during the American Civil War. Half of the regiment was killed during this battle. The Confederate victors buried Shaw with his fallen men, thinking him a disgrace, but Shaw's family, who were abolitionists, declined all attempts to move him; they considered his burial with the free African American 54th Regiment soldiers both appropriate and an honor. Saint-Gaudens' bronze monument sits across from the Massachusetts State House. See note 184.15 above.

184.20 Ahab—the ship's captain in *Moby Dick* who is obsessed with finding and killing the white whale that took his leg. He so closely identifies with the ship and the quest that when he loses his leg he compares himself to a ship without a mast. See notes 142.1, 184.7, 184.9, 184.11, 184.22, and 185.8; 12.

184.22 Queequeg—South Pacific character from Herman Melville's (1819–1891) *Moby Dick* (1851). He is a harpooner aboard the ship, *Pequod*, and represents the figure of the so-called noble savage, an idealized stereotype; he is described as a former cannibal. See notes 184.7, 184.9, 184.11, 184.20, and 185.8; 12.

184.23 sic transit—see note 182.16.

185.8; 12 Melville's book . . . Bible—Biblical allusions, criticism, and interpretation feature heavily in Herman Melville's (1819–1891) *Moby Dick* and are prominent in scholarly treatments of his work. See notes 184.7, 184.9, 184.11, 184.20, and 184.22.

185.13 sanderlings—a small shorebird; a wading bird; a sandpiper (*Calidris alba; Crocethia alba*). They shelter in the winter on beaches. See note 88.16–21.

186.8 lobster-yawls—a small fishing boat, rigged with gear to catch lobsters.

186.9 Homer (first name Winslow)—see note 183.26.

186.10 the mackerel-shoaled / sky—a mackerel sky is dotted with rows of small, white clouds, as in the pattern of spots on the back of a mackerel (*Scomber scombrus*); such clouds usually indicate moisture in the atmosphere. A shoal is a shallow body of water. See notes 157.7 and 157.14–15.

186.11; 23 Marblehead—a five-mile-square town on the northeastern coast of Massachusetts; it sits on a coastal outcrop. This promontory partly shelters Boston Harbor from the rough seas of the North Atlantic. See note 280.8.

186.20 My father—see note 68.21.

187.5 The World's Classics—see note 71.11.

187.11 your mother—Alix Walcott (1894–1990), Derek Walcott's mother, a teacher and ultimately the headmistress of a Methodist grammar school in Castries. See notes 61.10, 68.21, 69.13, and 167.12.

187.17 Dominate, Dominus—the etymology of "dominate," meaning "to rule over," derives from the Latin *dominus*, "Lord" or "God." See note 112.22.

❖ Book Five

SUMMARY

The journey opens outward again in the fifth book, which that charts the narrator's journey to Europe. He lands in Portugal and moves quickly to Britain. From Lisbon to London, the narrator traces the routes of European slave ships. He finds in London the representation of British maritime power and global domination, repeatedly invoking the "meridian" of Greenwich, the instrument through which the British organized time with Greenwich Mean Time (GMT) as the origin, the center of the globe, the zero hour. While the narrative begins across the Atlantic in Lisbon, Portugal, almost immediately, Walcott moves the location to the southernmost point of the Caribbean, Port of Spain, Trinidad, just across the Gulf of Paria from Venezuela and the continent of South America. This radical switch in movement suggests a shifting and shadowing of character and location. The antipodal movement then reverses, and Portugal is again the entry point for Europe. Yet, Portugal is not the final destination. We are brought to the center of London and Charing Cross with a gesture of recognition of the well-known markers of the fading empire. Images of central London give way to an enticing vision of GlendaLough, County Wicklow, south of Dublin and the home of Maud Plunkett, and the subsequent quick crossing of the Irish Sea to rural Ireland. Walcott enters Ireland, Britain's first colony, to encounter the historical precedent for further island domination by the British. He acknowledges the centuries of troubled colonial history and its contemporary refraction of sectarian violence while celebrating the "Muse of our age's Omeros . . . true tenor of the place," James Joyce (200.17–18). In fact, Walcott places his own character, Maud Plunkett, among Joyce's characters from "The Dead," as Joyce, cast in the dye of the New World, indigo, leads them all in song. The images of Ireland move from the rural west of the island and transition gradually to Dublin. The portrait of Ireland is at once literary and sacred; Walcott blesses himself with the voice of Joyce just as he acknowledges the troubled religious divisions in the country. The wake of the departure from Ireland ripples to the Mediterranean and back to the Caribbean. Finally, the narrative moves again across the Atlantic to the United States. It is in this final movement in the book that the narrator claims to "reenter my reversible world" (207.4). This new world is one that has sold the ancestors on an auction block and used their skills to enrich a nation that dominates and dislocates indigenous peoples at home and abroad. The Sioux nation and Catherine Weldon's futile attempts to ensure their independence are connected through the Ghost Dance, the spiritual movement that promised a messiah who would rid the Plains of settlers and restore the warrior dead. The search for home and restoration continues, but now the quest is positioned in terms of Weldon herself. The narrator looks for her at her old eastern address, but he is met only with isolation and anonymity.

ANNOTATIONS

CHAPTER XXXVII

189.1 I crossed my meridian—The term "meridian" derives from the Latin *meridianus* or "midday." The meridian hour is 12 noon. It is a made-up line that circles the globe north/south in orientation or longitude separating time zones. The Greenwich Meridian runs through London and was established in 1884 as the longitude of zero because it is the site of the well-known British Observatory. In 1493 Pope Alexander VI (Rodrigo Borgia) (1431–1503), a notoriously corrupt pontiff, granted a meridian of absolute control to Portugal and Spain over Africa and the New World. The latitude and longitude of St. Lucia are 13° 53' north of the equator and 60° 68' west of Greenwich.

189.3 mud-caked settlement founded by Ulysses—Lisbon, capital city of Portugal. According to the ancient myth, the city was founded by Ulysses (Odysseus) after the Trojan War. Its original name, *Olisipo* or

Ulyssipo, suggests such a connection, but scholars find the likelihood of the Phoenicians as the original settlers probable but not incontrovertible. The folk belief of an ancient Greek connection for the city's founding remains strong. Yet even today, the prominence of the city centers on its enormous port, which is at the mouth of the Tagus River as it empties into the Atlantic Ocean. Its strategic position at the mouth of the Mediterranean Sea and just north of Africa allowed Portugal to prosper greatly from the enslavement of African subjects and their subsequent trade to the New World. See notes 122.16–17, 129.14–15, 130.8, 189.4, and 201.16.

189.4–5 the nesting sills of Ulissibona . . . 'Lisbon'—the landscape in the city of Lisbon is quite steep, and seven hills have terraced sides with sills of rock providing stability to the perilous mounts. Residents of Lisbon profess a folk belief that their seven terraced hills evoke the seven hills of Rome. See notes 189.3 and 201.16.

190.2 Port of Spain—the capital of Trinidad and Tobago, the southernmost nation in the Caribbean archipelago, though the state includes these two large islands and several smaller ones. The city, on the island of Trinidad, is located on the Gulf of Paria, across from Venezuela. On a clear day, the mountains of Venezuela are visible and provide a dramatic view from the city's Grand Savannah, a central park. Port of Spain is the country's cultural center, with vibrant communities predominantly of African and Indian descent, as well as its commercial hub, with its broad economic base. During a brief period (1958–1962), Port of Spain served as the capital of the Federation of the West Indies.

190.11 Madeira—one of two Portuguese islands in the North Atlantic off the coast of Morocco. Agriculture predominates today, but historically, the island was a critical point for the provisioning of European slave ships before their stops in Africa and subsequent transatlantic journeys. Madeira also refers to the wine, grown on the island in its rich volcanic soil. A unique fortification method raises the alcohol content of this wine considerably, giving it a tremendous ability to tolerate heat. It was thus ideal for the Atlantic trade routes. Madeira is noted as a sacramental wine in *Another Life*. See note 127.7.

190.16 Vincentian—The inhabitants of St. Vincent and the Grenadines in the Windward Islands of the Caribbean. The island of St. Vincent is just twenty miles south of St. Lucia. The term "Vincentian" also refers to an order of Roman Catholic priests known for their missionary work with impoverished communities and their focus on education. See notes 6.13, 32.5, 59.14, and 301.27.

190.21 arpeggio—musical notes in a quick sequence during a performance, from the Italian, *arpa*, for harp.

191.1 meridian—See note 189.1.

191.5 Pope Alexander's decree—See note 189.1.

191.11 antipodal—geographical opposite, on the reverse side of the world and/or diametrically opposed. See note 99.4.

191.21 coins of the olives showed us their sovereign's face—the Portuguese frequently included olive branches on their currency, particularly the *centavos*, or "cent," through the twentieth century, but olive branches have appeared more generally on coins since Roman times. Sovereign refers to both an absolute ruler and a coin, equivalent to one pound Sterling, that was minted in Britain beginning in the late fifteenth century but discontinued in the early twentieth century. See notes 45.13, 122.16–17, and 189.3.

192.9 port of Genoa—Genoa, or *Genova*, a port on the North West coast of Italy south of Milan. This port is, and has been since the Middle Ages, Italy's most significant location for importing and exporting goods. It offered a gateway first to the Mediterranean and ultimately to the Caribbean and wider Americas. Christopher Columbus (1451–1506) was born in Genoa. Corsica and Sardinia were once Genovese colonies.

192.14 flotilla—a designation for an assemblage of similar seafaring vessels, larger than a squadron but smaller than a fleet.

192.18 stone Don in the opera—Wolfgang Amadeus Mozart's (1756–1791) opera *Don Giovanni* stages the legend of Don Juan, the notorious womanizing nobleman. He seduces a young woman and murders her father. The myth of Don Juan has reappeared consistently and includes treatments by George Gordon, Lord Byron (1788–1824), in *Don Juan*, and Jean Baptiste Poquelin Molière (1622–1673), in *Dom Juan, ou le festin de pierre* (Don Juan or the Stone Feast). The Spanish Baroque dramatist (and monk) Tirso de Molina (1579–1648) originated the play version of the Don Juan tale with his *El burlador de Sevilla*; Walcott wrote a version of this play, *The Joker of Seville*.

192.20 pennons—see note 161.16.

192.22 cuirasses—body shell or covering worn to protect the human torso, constructed variously of bronze, leather, iron, and steel.

193.5 Levantine—an area in the Eastern Mediterranean that historically includes countries from Greece to Egypt but also refers to the maritime basin of the sea that those countries border. The term originates with the period of the Crusades and derives from the French *lever*, "to rise." It became associated in Europe with those eastern countries over which the sun rises.

193.6 Alexander's meridian—See 189.1.

193.10 fado—a style of Portuguese folk song noted for its delightful expression of profound melancholy; commonly performed in bars and cafés.

CHAPTER XXXVIII

193.13 Charing Cross—an area in central London, at the intersection of Strand and Whitehall, to the north of Trafalgar Square. There are also railway and subway stations of the same name and location. The Anglo-Saxon *cerring* or "bend" (perhaps evoking the curve of the nearby Thames) is joined with the final cross that Edward 1 (1239–1307) erected for his beloved, Queen Eleanor [of Castille] (1246–1290), upon her death to designate this spot. This nexus is considered the geographical center of London, from which all distances in Britain are measured. See notes 30.25, 193.21, 194.4, 194.9, and 195.4.

193.14 Underground—the subway; London's extensive labyrinthine underground transport system, most often referred to as the "Tube." The system originated in the 1860s but was not nationalized until after World War II. The name "Tube" refers to one of the original methods of construction and design. Rather than dig from street level and then cover the reinforced passageway as in the earliest methods of subway construction, a subsequent "Tube" system used an underground burrowing technology that did not disrupt the street level above.

193.15 scrofulous—scrofula is a particular bone and glandular form of tuberculosis, more common in pediatric cases of the disease.

193.21 National—the National Gallery borders Trafalgar Square, overlooking the Nelson's Column. It contains Britain's national collection of European paintings from the thirteenth through the nineteenth centuries. The building was opened in 1838 after funding was provided by Westminster Parliament to house bequests to the nation from private collectors. See notes 30.25, 193.13, 194.5, 194.9, and 195.4.

194.3 red double-deckers—London's distinctive two-tiered, bright red public buses. The paradigmatic type, called the Routemaster, began service in 1956. Such buses remain a mainstay of transportation in London.

194.4 from pigeon-stirred Trafalgar—Trafalgar Square is named after the naval victory of Horatio Lord Nelson (1758–1805) at the Battle of Trafalgar in 1805. A crucial victory for the British in the Napoleonic wars that propelled Britain into global maritime domination, the battle was fought off the coast of Spain at Cape Trafalgar between Gibraltar and Cádiz. Nelson perished in the battle from enemy fire while on board his ship, the HMS *Victory*. Nelson's Column, a monument to him, dominates the paved square. Grand in scale, this monumental public plaza is surrounded by dramatic architecture (and is where pigeons commonly congregate). On the north side of the square is the National Gallery and St. Martin-in-the-Fields. The Mall, off the square, extends to Buckingham Palace, the London residence of the British monarch. South of the square are Whitehall and the Houses of Parliament. Pigeons predominate and automobiles circle the space. Nelson is included in the Middle Passage section of "The Schooner Flight." See notes 30.25, 193.13, 193.21, 194.9, and 195.4.

194.5 Gryphons on their ridge—also spelled griffin; ancient mythic creature with the head and wings of an eagle and the body of a lion, sometimes used as decoration in architecture. Often the roadways into the city of London (the core of the larger metropolis) are decorated with griffons, which are thought to confer protection.

194.7 Isle of Dogs running over Westminster bridge—the Isle of Dogs is an area in the East End of London that was home to thriving docklands until the 1970s, when the area went into decline. It was refurbished in the 1990s and now is home to Canary Wharf, Britain's tallest office tower, a noted center of commerce and finance. Westminster Bridge spans the River Thames just south of Trafalgar Square, several miles from the Isle of Dogs proper.

194.9 St. Martin-in-the-Fields—an eighteenth-century Anglican church located in Trafalgar Square; designed by James Gibbs (1682–1754), the Scottish architect, who strikingly juxtaposed Baroque and Palladian forms. Famous for opening its doors to homeless people and charity endeavors, the church is now known for its classical and jazz concerts. It is home to the Academy of St. Martin-in-the-Fields, cofounded by the renowned conductor, Sir Neville Marriner (1924–). See notes 30.25, 193.13, 193.21, 194.4, 195.4, 196.24, 197.17, and 211.7.

194.15 *Odyssey*—one of two epic poems (the other is *The Iliad*) attributed to the Greek poet Homer. *The Odyssey* depicts Odysseus' (Ulysses in Roman myth, see note 201.16) journey back to Ithaca, after the ten-year Trojan war, to his son, Telemachus and his wife, Penelope, who has been resisting pressure to marry. Her suitors have long since presumed Odysseus dead. The epic is profoundly influential in world literature as a tale of wandering and return. The story is filled with fantastic elements and unique challenges that greet the hero, all of which give him the opportunity to test himself. These include his meeting with the Cyclops, Polyphemus, Circe and her swine, Calypso's enticements, and the narrow passage between Scylla and Charybdis. His return is first noted by his aged but loyal dog, Argos. Subsequently, Odysseus reveals himself to Eumaeus, the swineherd. He then plans the elimination of the suitors. Before Odysseus' return, Telemachus undertakes a journey to find news of his father; this journey serves to protect the young man from the plots of the suitors who see him as a likely successor to the throne. There are two poets noted in the epic: Phemius, the court singer at Odysseus' home palace on Ithaca, and Demodacus, the singer of the Phaeacian King Alcinous, both of whom are applauded by Homer for their craft. Subsequent to the publication of *Omeros*, Walcott wrote *The Odyssey: a Stage Version*. See notes 130.5, 153.1, 201.16, 203.11, and 232.21.

195.4 Embankment—the Victoria Embankment of the River Thames, on the north side of the river, near Charing Cross and Trafalgar Square; designed by the engineer Joseph William Bazalgette (1819–1891). The embankment runs along the thoroughfare between Westminster and Blackfriars Bridges. On the south side of the Thames in this area is the Albert Embankment, also designed by Bazalgette. See notes 30.25, 193.13, 193.21, 194.9, and 195.4.

195.14 All-Hallows by the Tower—a church; the oldest Christian house of worship in London, All-Hallows is presently Anglican but was first built as the Saxon Abbey of Barking in 675 and subsequently added to and restructured several times between the eleventh and fifteenth centuries. It overlooks the Tower of London. Roman pavement was uncovered beneath the church in the early twentieth century. Bombed during World War II, the remaining towers, walls, and original arch were preserved in the rebuilding effort. Given its proximity to the tower, the church was often where the bodies of executed prisoners were taken. See note 197.8.

195.16 ginkgo—a unique species of tree indigenous to China, also known as the Maidenhair (*Ginkgophyta*). The leaves are the shape of an extended fan and produce large seeds that are often used as herbal supplements.

195.22 Houses of Parliament—the building that houses the legislature of the British government, also known as the Palace of Westminster. The current Gothic Revival building—the preferred style of the head architect, Charles Barry (1795–1860)–was under construction from 1837 to 1860. Big Ben, the celebrated clock, decorates St. Stephen's Tower. The building contains both the House of Commons and the House of Lords. See note 196.16.

195.23–24 Outer Provinces—area outside of but surrounding the central London metropolis. Given the intense damage to the city during World War II, the British government reconstructed the city after the war in a manner that protected the central city from overdevelopment and moved some of the London population to peripheral communities.

196.13 The meridian of Greenwich—see note 189.1.

196.15 Shoreditch—an inner-city area east of central London, once very working class and down-at-heel, with a history of skilled trades such as carpentry and printing. The area is now gentrified and more fashionable, with trendy bars and nightlife.

196.16 Big Ben's iron flower—the clock atop the Houses of Parliament on St. Stephen's Tower on the north end of the building; the iron flower refers to the clock face that has hour and minute hands of nine feet and fourteen feet in length, respectively. The clock remains accurate and is set based on the time of the Greenwich Observatory. See note 195.22.

196.19 Abbey—Westminster Abbey, adjacent to the Houses of Parliament. So many famous writers, musicians, and monarchs are buried there that the church is almost overwhelmed with tombs, including an area called Poet's Corner where both Geoffrey Chaucer (ca. 1342/43–1400) and Robert Browning (1812–1889) are laid to rest (among many others). Gothic in style and completed over many centuries, the abbey is the location for the crowning of British monarchs and important state functions. The location previously housed a Benedictine monastery.

196.20 St. Martin-in-the-Fields—See note 194.9.

196.24 St. Paul's—a cathedral (Anglican) located in the City of London. Built by Sir Christopher Wren (1632–1723) in the late seventeenth century on a site that has had a church on it since the seventh century. Wren's design altered considerably during construction and incorporated neoclassical and Baroque elements. Its striking, high dome was inspired by St. Peter's Basilica in Rome and marks the London vista. Its cross reaches 366 feet high. See notes 32.10, 194.4, and 211.7.

197.1 Glen-de-Lough—a glacial valley in County Wicklow, Ireland. See notes 25.4–5, 198.15, 199.1, 200.5, and 200.9.

197.4 Corn Exchange—a London building where a grain market took place up until the nineteenth century, though corn exchanges functioned in other cities as well. The London Corn Exchange is on Mark Lane, next to the Stock Exchange, and near St. Paul's Cathedral.

197.8 red double-decker—see note 194.3.

197.8 Bloody Tower—the Tower of London, a Norman construction (1078); an historic landmark in the east of central London alongside the river Thames and Tower Bridge. The dominating white square fortress of the tower is often referred to as bloody because of the many beheadings that have taken place there, including the supposed murder of two young princes in 1483. The fortress has housed inmates accused of treason or other crimes. It has also been used as a mint, an animal keep, a royal palace, and a repository for arms and now the crown jewels. It is protected today by the Yeoman Warders or Beefeaters of the Tower, who are widely recognizable for their Tudor-style uniforms. See note 195.14.

197.10 Serpentine—the Serpentine River (also known as the Serpentine Lake) is in Hyde Park in London. It is an enormous lake that curves noticeably. Part of this water body stretches into the adjacent Kensington Gardens; this section is known as Long Water. The Serpentine is a popular recreational area and continues for a significant length of Hyde Park.

197.13 Margate Sands—Margate is a coastal resort town in county Kent, popular with day-trippers from the east of London. The beach is known as Margate Sands. It became a popular resort in the eighteenth century due to the unusually fine quality of the sand.

197.16 National Gallery—See note 193.21.

197.17 Palladian Wren—Palladian is a style of architecture named after sixteenth-century Italian architect Andrea Palladio (Andrea di Pietro della Gondola) (1508–1580), who is known for his design of highly symmetrical buildings, particularly villas. Christopher Wren was the architect of St. Paul's and used Palladian forms in his design for that cathedral. See notes 194.9 and 196.24.

197.20 St. Paul's—See note 196.24.

197.23 the Downs—a chalk hill landscape of unusual beauty west of London, noted for its rolling hills, pastures, woodlands, and heaths. The top of the Downs is such a surprising and remarkable landscape zone that orchids can be found. There are archeological indications of early human life in the area, but currently it is used largely for grazing small farm animals.

197.24 the pillars on Salisbury Plain—Stonehenge, the famed primeval monument with standing stones; pillars arranged in circles. The origin or original purpose of Stonehenge remains a mystery. The remarkable formation of the monument and the stones themselves are thought to date from 3000–2000 BCE. Large sarsen and smaller blue stones were used in the formation; the blue stones originated in Wales, roughly one hundred miles away.

197.26 Brixton—area in South London where a large immigrant population from the Caribbean settled during the 1950s and 1960s. Currently it is a multiethnic area with approximately 24 percent of its residents of African and/or Caribbean descent. It has a young and fashionable image, with a vibrant nightlife and a fairly young population. It is home to the famous "Electric Avenue" and Brixton Market, where Caribbean products are sold.

CHAPTER XXXIX

198.1 curraghs—also curaghs or coracles; small, somewhat broad boats constructed of a light weight lathe or wicker frame that are covered with tarred canvas or sealed animal skins to form their hulls. They are often used off the coast of Ireland, particularly in the Irish western shores and the Aran Islands, though they also have a history of use in Wales. Identified with an impoverished peasant culture close to the sea, they are referred to in John Millington Synge's description of life in *The Aran Islands*. The term derives from both the Irish *curach* and Welsh *curwgl*.

198.3 broken abbey—ruins common in Ireland of medieval monastic communities. The ruins of the abbeys range from the spectacular Clonmacnoise in the center of the country, County Offaly, to less well-known sites that collectively reflect the era when Irish monks helped to preserve written Christian culture, often in Latin, the language of the Roman Catholic Church. The histories of these settlements and religious communities vary. Clonmacnoise, on the bank of the River Shannon, was founded in roughly 545 CE by St. Ciaran; this location had become renowned by the tenth century for the transmission of knowledge. Many of the abbeys, now in ruins, were also important destinations for pilgrimages.

198.4 tonsured hill—shaved, deforested hill. Tonsure is commonly associated with religious orders; the shaving of hair is viewed as a sign of devotion and a marker of difference from the larger society.

198.5–6 Pilgrims following monks footpath—there are three large pilgrimage sites in Ireland: Clencolmcille, Mt. Croagh Patrick, and Lough Derg. All are associated with saints, either Patrick or Colmcille, and the spread of Christianity in Ireland. Pilgrims commonly ascend to the top of the hill/mountain or venture to the island (in the case of Lough Derg).

198.9 square Celtic cross—a religious symbol of Christianity with two intersecting lines at right angles that signifies the crucifixion; a conventional Latin cross, with a traditional Celtic symbol of a circle that interconnects the two horizontal and two vertical lines.

198.15 slit of a tower—the round Tower at Glendalough originally housed a bell and provided refuge when inhabitants were under duress. See notes 25.4–5, 197.1, 199.1, 200.5, and 200.9.

198.18 old language of Ireland—Irish or what some readers might recognize as Gaelic. The indigenous language of Ireland is related to Welsh, Breton, and Scots Gaelic, though it is distinct from all the other Celtic tongues. Although English as a language was well established in Ireland within the Pale—the geographic term for the area in the east surrounding Dublin under British control since the Statutes of Kilkenny in 1366 demarcated British "civilization" against Irish "savagery"—the dominance of Irish speakers in Ireland remained until the Great Famine of the late 1840s. The victims of the famine, both the dead and those forced to emigrate, were overwhelmingly located in the west of the country and thus Irish speaking. Only after the famine did Ireland become a majority English-speaking country.

199.1 wood with a lake . . . hooded hills—Glen-da-lough—a very free translation informed by a physical description of the setting of Maud Plunkett's place of origin, Glen-da-Lough. See notes 25.4–5, 197.1, 198.15, 200.5, and 200.9.

199.2–3 shame of disenfranchisement—the Penal Laws of the eighteenth century imposed on the majority of native Irish, Roman Catholics, by a parliament comprising minority Protestants who identified with the English crown. These laws discriminated against Catholics overtly through the denial of property rights, economic opportunities, laws of inheritance, and civic representation. The Penal Laws were slowly dismantled but were overturned entirely with the Catholic Emancipation Act of 1829.

199.9 Glen-da-Lough's obelisk—see notes 24.5, 197.1, 198.15, 199.1, 200.5, and 200.9.

199.10 alder—a tree commonly known as birch, from the family *Betulaceae*, common in cold climates of Europe and North America.

199.10 aspen—see note 178.19.

199.14–15 nation / split by a glottal scream—the historic division of Ireland between the native indigenous population, overwhelmingly Roman Catholic, and the foreign colonial British presence, Protestant in faith after the establishment of the Church of England by King Henry VIII (1491–1547). Though the first incursion into Ireland from the larger island to its east came with the Anglo-Norman invasion of 1159.

199.16 Celtic rune—the Celts in fact did not create runes; these alphabets made of characters were used by Germanic peoples from the third to the thirteenth century in Northern Europe. Yet, the term also signifies a poem in its secondary meaning, with the word *runo* meaning "poem" in Finnish. In this sense, the remaining lines of the stanza suggest an allusion to W. B. Yeats' "Man and the Echo," when the poet questions if his production of *Cathleen Ni Houlihan* at the Abbey, Ireland's National Theater, had consequences beyond his imagining and resulted in death for some Irish volunteers during the 1916 Easter Rising, a rebellion Yeats memorializes in his poem, "Easter, 1916."

199.26 Shem from a Shaun—the two central male characters, shifting representations of principal figures, from James Joyce's *Finnegans Wake*, Books I and III, respectively. Shem the Penman and Shaun the Postman are twin brothers who signify opposing drives yet linked consciousnesses. Shem is a bohemian artist who critiques his practically minded brother, the civil servant, a bore. See notes 98.20, 200.11, 200.12, 200.16, 201.7, 201.11, 201.12–14, 201.16, 209.18, and 297.17.

200.2 tinker—an Irish Traveler; a member of an itinerant community that performs manual labor or low-skilled work. Although historians see no evident connections between the Romany of mainland Europe and the Irish Travelers, the communities share similar practices. The origins of the Irish Travelers remain mysterious, though because they only appear in historical accounts after the mid-nineteenth century, scholars have suggested they are the descendants of peasants displaced and set to wandering during the famine of the late 1840s.

200.5 Sugar Loaf Mountain—a mountain in County Wicklow, Ireland, just north of Glen-da-Lough, Maud's home county. It is also the name of a mountain overlooking Rio de Janeiro and Guanabara Bay in southern Brazil. See notes 24.9, 25.4–5, 197.1, 198.15, 199.1, and 200.9.

200.7 orange hour—the Orange Order, a Protestant loyalist organization founded to commemorate the Protestant William III of Orange's (1650–1702) defeat of the Catholic James II (1633–1701) in the Battle of the Boyne in 1690. The annual commemoration of the victory and its attendant parades in mid-July, viewed as incendiary in the Catholic communities in the North of Ireland, is termed "marching season."

200.9 Glen-da-Lough's tower—the tower amid the early Christian ruins is round with a height of over one hundred feet and a fifty-two-foot circumference; it stands notably higher than its surroundings. See notes 25.4–5, 197.1, 198.15, 199.1, and 200.5.

200.11 bloomed—refers to Leopold Bloom, the everyman hero of James Joyce's (1882–1941) *Ulysses*, a modern epic set in Dublin to commemorate Joyce's first walking out with his life partner and eventual wife, Nora Barnacle (1884–1951). Bloom is a cuckolded advertising salesman, a "Jewish hero in a Catholic country within a Protestant Empire"; his exile and wandering throughout the day characterize the modern condition of an alienated metropolitan existence. Joyce undertook his own version of wandering and exile as he convinced Nora, an uneducated young woman from Galway working as a maid in Finn's Hotel, to leave Dublin with him and move to the Continent just a few months after what has become immortalized as Bloomsday, June 16, 1904. Bloom is referenced in *Another Life*. See notes 98.20, 199.26, 200.12, 200.16, 201.7, 201.11, 201.12–14, 201.16, 209.18, and 297.17.

200.12 Liffey—the river that dissects Dublin separating the north side, historically more impoverished, from the more affluent south side, the location of Trinity College and University College Dublin, Joyce's alma mater. The river is relatively slow-moving but dominates the cityscape and is a common reference point. A bridge that crosses the Liffey at Usher's Island, a quay on the south side where Joyce' famous short story, "The Dead," is set, has recently been named for the author. The river originates in County Wicklow and empties into Dublin bay fifty miles later. See notes 98.20, 199.26, 200.11, 201.7, 201.12–14, 201.16, 209.18, and 297.17.

200.16 Anna Livia—Anna Livia Plurabelle, the central female character in James Joyce's (1882–1941) *Finnegans Wake*. She is the mother of Shem and Shaun and a representation of the Liffey River. A washerwoman, she populates the pages of the text at several key moments, but her striking monologue in Book I, chapter 8, with its appropriately musical and fluid language, reminds readers of rebirth, renewal, and the maternal. At once beautiful and unsightly, Anna Livia is a woman who has lived long and suffered but who endures eternally. See notes 98.20, 199.26, 200.11, 200.12 201.7, 201.11, 201.12–14, 201.16, 209.18, and 297.17.

200.17 our age's Omeros, undimmed Master—Walcott greets Joyce much like Dante greets Virgil, his guide through the *Inferno*, as his "master."

200.19 I blest myself in his voice—a recognition of and/or desire for paternal (and poetic) inheritance. Walcott echoes the Stephen Dedalus in the "Proteus" chapter of *Ulysses* as he recalls being recognized in Paris as his father's son because of his voice. In *The Aeneid*, Virgil's hero, Aeneas, is described, by Evander in the Book VIII, as having a voice similar to that of his father, Anchises. Seamus Heaney (1939–2013) depicts a similar intersection with James Joyce (1882–1941) in *Station Island*. See notes 98.20, 199.26, 200.11, 200.12, 201.7, 201.12–14, 201.16, 209.18, and 297.17.

201.1 "There's a bower of roses by Bendemeer's stream"—See notes 56.11, 56.16, and 201.2.

201.2 Moore—Dublin-born Thomas Moore (1779–1852), an Irish poet well known for both his "oriental romance," *Lalla Rookh*, and his collection of poetry set to traditional music, *Irish Melodies*. A lawyer by training, he served the British crown in Bermuda, though very briefly, as the Registrar of the Admiralty Prize Court on the island. He wrote a small number of poems related to his Bermuda experience. He is perhaps most widely known outside of Irish literary circles for his friendship with George Gordon, Lord Byron (1788–1824). Byron gave his memoirs to Moore, who torched them and then produced his own version of Byron's days. See notes 56.11 and 56.16.

201.7 The Dead—the title of the final short story in James Joyce's (1882–1941) *Dubliners*. Set during an annual epiphany party, the story ends with a common image of human mortality; snow is falling across the land and the protagonist, Gabriel Conroy, is contemplating a journey westward into the symbolic afterlife. "The Dead" thus include not only Gabriel but all of the characters in the story, the two elderly aunts and the fellow party-goers, from Mr. Browne and Freddy Malins to Gretta Conroy and Bartel D'Arcy. In the story Gabriel has three confrontations with women: Lily the servant; Miss Ivors the nationalist; and Gretta, his wife. Through these confrontations Gabriel is able to experience his epiphany of human connectedness and the universal experience of death. See notes 98.20, 199.26, 200.11, 200.12, 201.12–14, 201.16, 209.18, and 297.17.

201.7 wick-low shade—see note 25.4–5.

201.11 bright doors and cobbles—the brightly colored doors of Dublin's Georgian Town Houses that line the stone streets surrounding many public squares throughout the city. Built in the eighteenth century with rather uniform coloring originally, the most well-known houses with a collection of striking doors now surround Merion Square; the doors sport geometric patterns topped by a semicircular window fashionable during the Georgian period.

201.11 Mr. Joyce—James A. Joyce (1882–1941), Irish writer and author of *Dubliners, A Portrait of the Artist as a Young Man, Ulysses*, and *Finnegans Wake*. Joyce's works move from a more conventional realism in *Dubliners* to the innovative proto-postmodernism in *Finnegans Wake*. He is known for his experimental style and for characters that often display nuanced interior psychological development. Although he lived in exile in continental Europe as an adult, all of his works remain centered in Ireland. His most famous novel, *Ulysses*, is known for its dramatic reimagining of the ancient myth of Odysseus' wandering and return as the modern alienated journey of Leopold Bloom across the metropolis of Dublin in a single day. Walcott clearly admires Joyce and his works. This affection is evident not only in *Omeros* but also in *Another Life* and even the short poem, "Volcano," where he notes Joyce's famed fear of thunder. See notes 98.20, 199.26, 200.11, 200.12, 201.7, 201.12–14, 201.16, 209.18, and 297.17.

201.12–14 Howth—the coastal promontory northeast of Dublin; it is the setting for a critical scene of youthful union in James Joyce's *Ulysses*, remembered later in life by Leopold Bloom in the "Lestrygonians" chapter and by his wife, Molly, in the final moments of the "Penelope" chapter. The name "Howth" originates with the Danish, *hoved*, or "head." This hill of Howth also appears in the opening lines of *Finnegans Wake*. See notes 98.20, 199.26, 200.11, 200.12, 201.7, 201.11, 201.16, 209.18, and 297.17.

201.16 Martello—the Martello Tower in Sandycove, a coastal town south of Dublin. Joyce lived in this particular tower briefly in 1904 with Oliver St. John Gogarty (1878–1957), the model for his character Buck Mulligan, and set his opening chapter of *Ulysses*, "Telemachus," in the same location. The young hero, Stephen Dedalus, is cast out of the tower and loses his keys to a visiting amateur English ethnographer, Haines, who has come to study the "primitive" Irish. The towers were constructed between 1804 and 1806 by the British to defend their strategic positions across the globe, including Ireland, against a possible French invasion. The towers take their name from the location of the first tower built in Cape Mortella, Corsica.

201.16 Ulysses—the Roman name for the wandering Greek hero, Odysseus. James Joyce (1882–1941) takes the Roman name for his modern epic *Ulysses* (1922) set in Dublin in 1904. The three main characters—Stephen Dedalus, a young dissolute student; Leopold Bloom, an advertising salesman; and his wife, Molly (Marion Tweedy) Bloom, a singer and mother—are linked in the intricate web Joyce creates of his "dear, dirty Dublin." The work is dramatically challenging and innovative as it shatters nineteenth-century realist conventions of the novel. *Ulysses* is structured in three parts: the *Telemachiad*, surrounding Stephen Dedalus; the *Wandering*, charting Bloom's day: and the *Nostos* or Return, coming home to find Molly in bed. Ulysses is noted in Walcott's "Origins" and his "Epitath for the Young." Ulysses also appears repeatedly in the works of the Guyanese writer, Wilson Harris (1921-). Odysseus is referenced in Walcott's "A Sea-Chantey" and *Another Life*. In *Another Life*, he transforms the noun Ulysses into a verb. See notes 98.20, 199.26, 200.11, 200.12, 201.7, 201.11, 201.12–14, 201.16, 209.18, and 297.17.

201.16 one-eyed Ulysses—James Joyce (1882–1941) is often pictured with an eye patch. He endured multiple surgeries to correct his vision, all of which ultimately failed. By the time he was writing *Finnegans*

Wake, he was nearly blind. See notes 98.20, 199.26, 200.11, 200.12, 201.7, 201.11, 201.12–14, 209.18, and 297.17.

201.17–18 mail packet / . . . wake glittering like keys—refers to James Joyce's (1882–1941) *Finnegans Wake.* The *Wake* opens with an early allusion to the Castle atop Howth Head. One of the central male characters is a mailman, Shem the Postman. The work concludes with a mention of "they keys to," which suggests the circularity of the work; it ends with its beginning anew, potentially unlocking the linguistic inscrutability of fiction. See notes 98.20, 199.26, 200.11, 200.12, 201.7, 201.11, 201.12–14, 201.18, 209.18, and 297.17.

201.18 the Head—the Head of Howth. See notes 201.12–14.

CHAPTER XL

201.20 Aegean—See notes 31.4, 32.13, 204.5, 230.13, and 281.19.

202.5 oleander—see note 164.6.

202.10 sea lace—see note 82.9–10.

202.11 bridal lilac—lilacs are flowering shrubs(*S. vulgaris*) that produce elongated flower clusters, commonly of pale to deep purple, yellow, and white. Indigenous to Southeastern Europe and Asia, the size and flowers of the plant can vary based on the climate. Its flowers are commonly used in Western weddings. The larger varieties can reach nearly twenty feet in height.

202.12 Odysseus—see notes 130.5, 153.1, 194.5, 201.16, and 232.21.

202.22 Calypso—see notes 64.19, 194.15, and 229.5.

203.3 trireme—a fifth-century BCE naval vessel common to the eastern Mediterranean, particularly of the Greeks and Phoenicians; a light ship, used on shallow coastal and open waters, propelled by oars and square sails. The Greeks commonly navigated in sight of land.

203.6 Helen—see notes 8.9, 11.4, 17.5–6, 24.6, 34.20, 35.18, 36.21, 62.27, 153.1, and 298.9.

203.7 Circe—see note 64.19.

203.11 dream of Ithaca—the vision of Odysseus while on his wandering to return to his home kingdom of Ithaca. See notes 130.5, 153.1, 194.15, and 232.21.

203.15 mattock—an agronomic instrument for digging, a hoe.

203.18 sea swift—see notes 8.3, 88.21, 239.16, and 242.15.

203.21 chrysalis—the hard, fixed shell stage, *pupa*, in the maturity of a butterfly or moth. From the Greek, *khrysos*, for "gold," a strategic locus of metamorphosis. See note 62.19.

203.23 Odysseus—see notes 130.5, 153.1, 194.5, 201.16, and 232.21.

203.26 head for the horns of an island—the Pitons of St. Lucia, see notes 30.19, 40.21, 59.13, 103.3, 227.10, and 289.8.

204.5 Andros to Castries—Ándros is a Greek island in the Aegean Sea. Ándros is also the largest island in the Bahamas. Castries is the capital of St. Lucia. See notes 31.4, 32.13, 230.13, and 281.19.

204.6 Margarita or Curaçao—both islands in the far southern Caribbean Sea. Margarita Island is a mere twelve miles north of Venezuela. Curaçao is an island just thirty-seven miles north of Venezuela. See notes 77.14–15 and 155.25–26.

204.9 Ulysses—see notes 189.3, 200.11, and 201.16.

204.13 Istanbul's spires—Turkish city formerly known as Constantinople and Byzantium that sits on the edge of the Mediterranean Sea. Its architecture reflects its complex history and vibrant cultural heritage. There are many Byzantine churches with spires, the largest of which is the Hagia Sophia, a well-known and dramatic sacred structure that like many former churches was transformed into a mosque with the ascendancy of Islam. The spires of the city today are mostly minarets or towers connected to the city's many mosques.

204.14 Saracen . . . scimitar—Saracen is a follower of Islam; the term came into general usage in Western Europe during the Crusades and is used in the French epic poem, *Le Chanson de Roland*. A scimitar is a sword with a curved blade.

204.16 lowering Venice . . . gondolier—Venice, a city of canals and former maritime power that dominated trade for a millennium, sits amid a inlet on the Adriatic coast of Northern Italy. The city is sinking as waters advance and its land diminishes. Gondoliers are the captains of the keel-free boats that navigate the city's waterways, controlling an oar at the stern. See notes 68.26, 72.9, and 183.17.

205.3 Velázquez—Diego Rodríguez de Silva Velázquez (1599–1660); a Spanish painter known for his insightful and humanistic depictions. His *Las Meninas* is a masterful rendition of an informal view of a royal court; the king and queen are visible in a mirror, while their young daughter and her caretakers occupy the center of the painting.

205.6 Schubert—Franz Peter Schubert (1797–1828), Austrian composer, whose music is famed for coalescing the emotive qualities of Romanticism while maintaining traditional forms.

205.6–7 Duchamp's *The Bride . . . Bachelors*—Marcel Duchamp (1887–1968), French Modern artist, who shattered conventional expectations for visual art. In his *The Large Glass, or The Bride Stripped Bare by Her Bachelors, Even*, he rejected traditional visual markers and instead interpreted male/female intimacy through industrial geometry using metal and glass.

205.7 Dada—artistic movement in the modernist literary and artistic period, begun in 1916 and in vogue until the early 1920s in Europe and North America. Dada has variously been interpreted to mean "nonsense" and "hobby horse" (from the German). Dadaists reject formalism and conventionality. They embrace spontaneity, found objects, and assembled words. The movement incorporates visual and literary art, particularly poetry.

205.8 Celan and Max Jacob—Paul Celan (Paul Antschel) (1920–1970), a Romanian Jewish poet who survived a concentration camp. Both of his parents died during World War II. After the war while living in Paris, he wrote in German and captured the manifest sorrow of surviving the war in mid-century Europe. He committed suicide in 1970. Max Jacob (1876–1944), French Breton Jewish poet who converted to Roman Catholicism in 1915 but was imprisoned and died in a concentration camp during World War II. He was a surrealist poet who was part of the bohemian scene in Paris in the 1920s, known for his friendships with many Cubist painters.

205.12 The World's Great Classics—see note 71.11.

205.17 Caesar—a Roman Emperor, tyrant, dictator, or ruler. The term stems from the rule of Julius Caesar (100–44 BCE) and his adopted heir Augustus (Octavian) (63 BCE–14 CE), who took Caesar's name. There are several well-known busts of Augustus with a damaged or missing nose. The terms "Kaiser" and "Tsar," German and Russian, respectively, are transliterations of Caesar.

205.21 naiads—from Greek myth; water nymphs affiliated with freshwater, suggesting lightness and kind approval.

CHAPTER XLI

206.9 demos . . . cracy—a play on the etymology of democracy from the Greek *demokratia*; *demos* means "common people" but is linked with the origin of the word "district" and/or "demotic," signifying the everyday. *Ocracy* is linked with *kratos* which means "rule."

206.17 *fasces*—the Latin plural form of *fascis*, or "bundle." A Roman symbol denoting power and control, made from a bundle of sticks with an axe or blade distended from the top. The symbol signifies authority, particularly the Roman Republican form. The term inspired Benito Mussolini (1883–1945) to name his party the Fascist Party; the party used a *fasces* as a symbol beginning in 1919.

206.18 Republic—a republic is a country or state that places sovereignty with the people who then usually elect representative leaders. Republics are not led by a hereditary monarch; they are led in whole or part by the citizens of the state. Plato's (428/427–348/347 BCE) *Republic* is a dialogue with his teacher, Socrates (470–399 BCE); the work examines the possibility of being just.

207.1 Solons—legislators, from the Greek, after the Athenian lawmaker and poet, Solon (630–560 BCE), who is known for his expansion of government from mere nobility to a broader population of the wealthy.

207.15 Gloucester—city in the west of England, on the River Severn, with a population of approximately 125,000. The Romans called the city "Glevum." Gloucester, Massachusetts, is roughly thirty miles north of Boston. This city has been a vibrant maritime center for centuries and houses large seafaring fleets.

207.16 Iroquois—a linguistic designation that includes a set of American Indians such as the Cherokee, Huron, Mohawk, and Oneida, among others. Their territories reached from Ontario, Canada, through New York and into Pennsylvania. There is also an Iroquois Confederacy of an even wider American Indian group of nations that persisted from

1600 to 1784 and adeptly maneuvered the British and French against each other during the European contest for the colonization of North America.

208.8 Catherine—see note 176.6.

208.9 Shawmut—the Shawmut Peninsula, on which the city of Boston now stands, in Massachusetts.

208.10 Concord, contagious vermilion—town twenty miles from Boston, the location of the first inland Puritan settlement. The town is also famed for the Battle of Lexington and Concord, the first in the American Revolution, in April 1775. The "Concord Hymn" of Ralph Waldo Emerson (1803–1880) commemorates the battle. In the nineteenth century, the town served as a hotbed of cultural and creative activity. The vermilion suggests the Redcoats, the nickname for British troops, who were easily spotted by the rebelling colonists. See notes 90.13 and 209.24.

208.14 George—see note 93.6–7, 103.26–27, and 257.17.

208.18 seine—see note 52.27.

209.4 pennons—see note 161.16.

209.7 Hussars—a light cavalry corps, European, who often served as lookouts and guides, known for their elaborately decorated livery.

209.13–14 The Book . . . Leviathan's hide—in the Bible, Leviathan is a mythic sea creature, a serpent. The figure and term were also used by Thomas Hobbes (1588–1679) as the title for his 1651 examination of the relation between religious devotion and government. Leviathan is noted in Walcott's "A Sea-Chantey."

209.16 Catherine—see note 176.6.

209.18 The nightmare cannot wake—in James Joyce's (1882–1941) *Ulysses*, Stephen Dedalus, the young artist, laments his inability to escape the nightmare of history. Joyce's phrase appears as an epigraph for Walcott's "Muse of History" essay. See notes 98.20, 199.26, 200.11, 200.12, 201.7, 201.11, 201.12–14, 201.16, 201.16, and 297.17.

209.22 Transcendental New England—Transcendentalism is the belief that the ideal spiritual state goes beyond the actual, physical state, and that the individual achieves insight through personal reflection rather than through religious ritual or dogma. Transcendentalism was at the center of the American Renaissance and is strongly associated with the New England states, the home of its founders and many followers. See notes 90.13, 208.10, 209.23 and 209.24.

209.23 Thoreau—Henry David Thoreau (1817–1862), Transcendentalist American writer and philosopher of nature and its relation to the human condition; an abolitionist. He is perhaps most known for his philosophy of civil disobedience, or resistance to government through nonviolent means. See notes 90.13, 208.10, 209.22, and 209.24.

209.24 Emerson—Ralph Waldo Emerson (1803–1882), American writer, philosopher, and orator, and friend of Thoreau. He is known for his "Self Reliance" and his 1836 *Nature*, which helped to inspire Transcendentalism. A central figure in the American Renaissance of the early nineteenth century, Emerson became known as the "Sage of Concord." See notes 90.13, 208.10, 209.22, and 209.23.

CHAPTER XLII

211.4 finical—fussy, picky in an extreme fashion; derives from finicky, meaning "overly fine."

211.7 Baroque—a heavily ornamented, dramatic, and complex style, commonly used to describe the European music, art, sculpture, and architecture of the early seventeenth century. See notes 194.4 and 196.24.

212.2 Warsaw—capital city of Poland. Located on the Vistula River, 230 miles south of the Baltic Sea and in the eastern core of the nation.

212.2 Cracow—also Krakow; a large city in southern Poland on the Vistula River that has been a cultural and artistic center dating back to the seventh century. In World War II, fifty-five thousand of the city's Jewish residents were forced into a ghetto from where they were sent to Nazi death camps. See note 212.15.

212.15 Zagajewski—Adam Zagajewski, (1945–) Polish poet living in Cracow, a member of the Solidarity movement, whose work famously resisted political hegemony and martial law. His poems frequently lament Polish history. See notes 212.2.

212.15 Herbert—Zbigniew Herbert (1924–1998), Polish poet and dramatist, who asserted family ties to the metaphysical poet George Herbert (1593–1633). Zbigniew Herbert was part of the Polish resistance in World War II and one of the best known and most translated Polish poets. See note 212.15 below.

212.15 Milosz—Czeslaw Milosz (1911–2004), Polish poet and Nobel Laureate in Literature in 1980. He translated some of Zbigniew Herbert's poems. He was famously critical of writers and intellectuals accommodating political oppression in any form but particularly the Communist regime in Poland. See note 212.15 above.

212.17 the Charles—the Charles River separates Boston from Cambridge, Massachusetts. The river runs for eighty miles from Middlesex County to Boston Harbor. In the city, it is popular with local rowing clubs.

212.24 Catherine Weldon—see notes 176.6.

213.1 ghost dance—See notes 164.16, 164.21, 175.12, 176.3, 176.6, 180.18, 181.16–17, 182.10, and 182.15.

213.6 Great Plains—a vast expanse of prairie in the American Midwest and West that goes from the Mississippi River basin west to the Rocky Mountains, covering many states and reaching from Canada to Mexico. See notes 161.11, 174.15, 176.6, 181.21, 181.22, and 182.10.

CHAPTER XLIII

213.17 Parkin farm—see note 176.3.

214.6 Ghost Dance—see notes 164.16, 164.21, 175.12, 176.3, 176.6, 180.18, 181.16–17. 182.10, and 182.15.

214.15–16 dribbling sacks condemned by the army—the U.S. army's distribution to American Indians of blankets and cloth that were infected with small pox. The distribution of infected materials was a tactic used to suppress indigenous peoples and remove them from their lands. See notes 164.16, 164.21, 174.15, 175.12, 176.3, 176.6, 180.18, 181.16–17. 182.10, and 182.15.

214.18 Crows, Sioux, Dakotas—see notes 164.16, 164.21, 174.15, 175.12, 176.3, 176.6, 180.18, 181.16–17, 182.10, and 182.15.

215.8–9 ecstasy of their own massacre ... Ghost Dance—see notes 164.16, 164.21, 175.12, 176.3, 176.6, 180.18, 181.16–17, 182.10, and 182.15.

215.12 Sioux, Dakotas, Crows—see notes 164.16, 164.21, 174.15, 175.12, 176.3, 176.6, 180.18, 181.16–17, 182.10, and 182.15.

215.16–24 I pray . . . fanged growl—these lines repeat several key phrases from Achille's journey to Africa on page 145.

216.9 Cody's circus—see notes 161.6–7, 161.11, 164.16, 164.21, 174.15, 179.19, 181.21.

217.13; 18 Catherine—see note 176.6.

218.4 Ghost Dance—see notes 164.16, 164.21, 175.12, 176.3, 176.6, 180.18, 181.16–17, 182.10, and 182.15.

218.9 Wild geese—multiple varieties of waterfowl including geese and swans. The term also refers to Irish exiles forced abroad, in 1690 in particular, though the term has come to stand for any Irish exile for political action and to Irish in service of Catholic regimes outside of Ireland from the late seventeenth to the twentieth centuries. See note 88.16–21.

218.10 the Charles's—see note 212.17.

219.21 glaucous—a botanical term for a blue-green color.

❖ Book Six

SUMMARY

The penultimate, sixth, book returns to the Caribbean and St. Lucia in full narrative force. St. Lucia is the object and final destination of the quest. Here, Walcott returns home. Hector's death in his taxi, the Comet, becomes a moment for questioning the place of poetry and the making of art from misery while rejecting facile nostalgia. Yet, the sea and its presence as both liquid history and maternal point of origin serve as a rhythm of reassurance and continuity amid change and loss. Achille invokes an ancestral African river. Ma Kilman remembers the seed for the cure for Philoctete carried by the swift from Africa. The swift has brought a powerful entity that will root in St. Lucia and provide a salve for the wounds of history. Her death after releasing the seed from her claws and finding respite on the shore is one of transformation. She becomes a bleached bone, reminiscent of Os, of the Conch shell's invocation, and of indigenous cultures' use of bone for flutes. Ma Kilman submerges Philoctete's wound in the bath of rootedness and lava that gurgles from the earth. He is cured. Major Plunkett takes Maud to her last Mass. Memories of Plunkett's empire and his service to it surround the couple. Maud's death from cancer is followed with a service at the cathedral. Her casket is covered with the shroud she has embroidered with birds, images of worldly transcendence and Atlantic wanderings. As the Mass ends Achille, who is seated with Philoctete (a figure who is healed though scarred), is approached by Helen. She tells Achille that she will return home to him, a reconciliation that suggests reunion as much as the coming forth of progeny.

ANNOTATIONS

CHAPTER XLIV

221.1 San Fernando to Mayagüez—two cities that occupy opposite zones of the extended arms of the Caribbean archipelago. San Fernando is a city in Trinidad on the Gulf of Paria, approximately thirty-five miles south of the capital of Trinidad and Tobago, Port of Spain. Named for Ferdinand VII (1784–1833) of Spain, the city is known for its oil fields and attendant energy industries. Mayagüez is a city in Puerto Rico, on the western side of the island, known for its deep port and fishing as well as a local university campus.

221.7 bitter history of sugar—the transition from a tobacco to a sugar economy prompted the European settlers in the Caribbean to exponentially increase their dependence on enslaved African subjects. See note 58.22.

221.9 the Indian diaspora—the indentured workers from the Indian subcontinent that arrived in the Caribbean after the emancipation of enslaved African subjects. This diaspora continued for many years, roughly from 1845 to 1917. Trinidad and Guyana are the predominant destinations for this diaspora in the Caribbean. See notes 156.8, 156.9, and 156.10–11.

222.13 Achille . . . Hector—see notes 6.1, 8.4, 8.9, 10.25, 16.14–16, 17.5–6, 24.6, 34.20, 53.4, 83.20, 146.15–16, 150.12, 175.13–14, 228.25, 296.2, 298.9, and 320.7–16.

222.14–15 Helen / as my island—see notes 8.9, 11.4, 17.5–6, 24.6, 34.20, 35.18, 36.21, 62.27, 153.1, and 298.9.

223.3 military barracks—the colonial British army barracks at the top of Morne Fortune that overlook Castries. These barracks currently house Sir Arthur Lewis Community College. The Colonial Governors' Graveyard rests within the precinct of these buildings, though it is obscured by more recent buildings of wooden construction. See notes 42.20, 58.10, and 314.27–315.1.

223.5 *Vent Noël*—from the French; "Christmas wind" suggests the French version of "Jingle Bells," *Vent d'hiver.*

223.7 laurier cannelle—see note 3.4.

223.9 Morne—see notes 42.20, 58.10, and 314.27–315.1.

223.11–12 jackfish … accra—Accra is a fried dough or fritter that is commonly made with pieces of saltfish mixed in the dough. For jackfish, see note 50.11.

223.14 Morris chair—William Morris (1834–1896), British designer and poet who was known for integrating myth into his designs. He is best known today for his textile and wallpaper patterns. The Morris chair, a reclining chair with arms made of wood, was designed not by William Morris but by his firm, Morris and Company, in 1866.

223.16 lace curtains—the phrase "Lace-Curtain Irish" suggests those Irish emigrants who have striven toward upper-middle-class respectability, even if they did not have the economic or social means through which to achieve it. Lace curtains provide a veneer of social ascent.

223.17 Ithaca—see notes 130.5, 194.15, 203.11, and 232.21.

223.19 twin-headed January—Janus, the Roman god of doorways; frequently found on entryways and exits and associated both with inceptions and with looking backward and forward at once. He is often pictured as two-faced. The month of January is named for him. Walcott is himself a twin who was born in January.

224.1 breadfruit—the fruit of the breadfruit tree (*Artocarpus communis*). Europeans introduced the tree to the Caribbean to provide an easy food source for enslaved peoples. The tree originates in the South Pacific. The fruit itself is small and round with a green or yellow outer layer.

224.3 Battle of the Saints—see notes 28.21, 31.26–27, 32.5, 32.6, 34.21, 43.1, 43.10, 81.19–20, 84.1, 92.12–13, 99.21–100.5, and 100.9.

CHAPTER XLV

224.7 one side of the coast plunges—the eastern side of St. Lucia has a dramatic landscape and seascape junction, between the crashing waves of the Atlantic and the liminal zone of the beach.

224.11 Dennery—town on the Atlantic side of St. Lucia. See notes 4.8 and 11.4.

224.13 African breakers—the waves that have moved across the

Atlantic, large and rolling. They originate off the West African coast and make their way across the Atlantic; they often reach the Caribbean with enormous force. See note 224.7.

224.14 rocks with their lace—sea lace. See note 82.9–10.

224.15 Dakar—capital city of Senegal, known for its protected port that has been a prominent commercial and trading nexus for centuries. The name means "tamarind tree" in the local Wolof tongue, *dakhar*. See notes 129.14–15, 150.1–2, and 184.1.

224.16 wings of frigates—see notes 19.6, 43.18, and 65.5.

224.20 Comet—see note 53.4.

225.2 zouk—a highly produced form of music characterized by French Creole/Kwéyòl languages(s) and sound innovation in the Caribbean; internationally known, but particularly prominent in Martinique, Guadeloupe, St. Lucia, and Dominica. The origins are traced to the band, *Kassav'*, which was formed in Guadeloupe in the late 1970s; both this band and this music are mentioned in Maryse Condé's (1937–) *Crossing the Mangrove*, which is set in Guadeloupe. See notes 24.14, 81.19–20, 92.12–13, and 121.6.

225.14–15 Madonna / of the Rocks . . . blue hood—painting by Leonardo da Vinci (1452–1519), known also as the *Virgin of the Rocks*; painted between 1483 and 1486 and now in the collection of the Louvre Museum in Paris. The painting is known for its pyramidal composition featuring the Madonna (in a blue wrap/hood), the infant Christ, John the Baptist, and an angel. Walcott notes in *Another Life* that the composition of this painting was an inspiration for Gregorias/St. Omer in his altarpiece depiction(s). See note 225.20.

226.9 small flag of the island—see note 17.23.

225.20 cerulean mantle—a intense blue or cobalt color, from the Latin *caelum*, for "sky." In the Roman Catholic Church, traditionally the Virgin Mary is represented wearing blue whereas in the Eastern Orthodox Church she is represented habitually in red. A mantle is a cloak or covering, commonly without sleeves, from the Latin *mantellum* for "cloak." See note 225.14–15.

225.21–22 lace / of foam—sea lace. See note 82.9–10.

226.2 his arc was over—the arc or tail of a comet, usually made of dust but sometimes including plasma and created by radiation, though not all comets generate such tails or arcs. See note 53.4.

226.8 African combers—See note 224.7.

226.18 Comet—see note 53.4.

227.10 hotel development—Walcott has a long history of questioning the development of hotels in the Caribbean for both environmental and socioeconomic reasons. In *Another Life*, he laments them overtly with a repetition of the word "hotel." More recently, he has openly campaigned against hotel development in the Pitons area; he is critical not only because of the environmental impact but also because the large-scale resorts mimic colonial plantation power structures and social dynamics. Walcott also condemns the exploitation of tourism in the Caribbean in his *The Antilles: Fragments of Epic Memory*. See notes 30.19, 40.21, 59.13, 103.3, and 289.8.

227.13–16 My craft . . . a canoe—Walcott compares writing poetry to carpentry and building a canoe such as those built on the opening pages of *Omeros*. The link between writing and harvesting elements from the natural world is evident in Walcott's "Forty Acres: a Poem for Barack Obama" and evokes Seamus Heaney's (1939–2013) comparison of writing poetry to working on the bog in "Digging." See notes 3.1 and 5.6.

227.21 amber, the afterglow of an empire—a resin that preserves whatever is in its grasp, often yellow or brown and less commonly green or red.

227.27 Praslin? That heron—a district, town, bay, and nature preserve on the eastern side of St. Lucia. It is also the name of an island in the Seychelles in the Indian Ocean. See notes 28.25, 49.6, 90.7–8, and 227.27.

228.14 Micoud—a town on the eastern side of St. Lucia, several miles south of Praslin and north of Vigie.

228.16 Hector's—see notes 8.9, 16.14–15, and 53.4.

228.25 dried calabashes of fake African masks for a fake Achilles—a market for fake African masks, newly and locally produced and without an actual African provenance, is supported by the tourist trade. See notes 6.1, 8.4, 8.9, 10.25, 16.14–16, 24.6, 83.20, 98.22, 146.15–16, 150.12, 175.13–14, 228.25, 296.2, 298.9, and 320.7–16.

229.1 who needed art in this place—as a young man Walcott was strongly influenced by the St. Lucian artist and writer Harry Simmons (1914–1966), who believed in the absolute necessity of creating an indigenous art in St. Lucia. Simmons proposed a network of "Little Galleries" to make art creation and viewing a part of everyday life on the island. These local, little galleries would be akin to the "Little Magazines" of the early twentieth century that featured avant-garde work from outside of the traditional literary establishment. Simmons was an important figure in the intellectual circles of St. Lucia in the early twentieth century.

229.5 calypso—a musical form originating in the Eastern Caribbean islands, Trinidad particularly, that features a ballad form and witty lyrics, now associated with steel bands that perform during Carnival. The singers will often use multiple languages and registers of language(s) to comment upon political and social intrigues. This form of music originated with the *cariso* tradition when enslaved subjects would gather and sing during the Lenten season. Walcott wrote a series of articles on calypso for the *Trinidad Guardian* when he was a young, struggling writer. Although he has considered these articles mere journalism, in fact they display a nuanced and analytical perspective on this vibrant cultural tradition. Calypso is also the name of the sea nymph who keeps Odysseus on her island for many years and who releases him only when the gods intervene. See notes 64.19 and 194.15.

229.8 like any Eden—see notes 12.25, 63.8, 97.2, 181.3, 248.23–24, and 308.15.

229.9 Hewannorra (Iounalao)—see notes 5.2, 92.5, and 92.15.

229.12 Greece or Hawaii—two extremes of geography, the first in the Eastern Mediterranean, the second in the Pacific, that are well known as tourist destinations. Greek culture has been influential globally through its ancient myths, literature, and political structures. Hawaiian culture has been much more isolated. The indigenous peoples of Hawaii are thought to have emigrated from Polynesia. Their culture, though altered, has survived the onslaught of American Christian missionaries in the late eighteenth and nineteenth centuries. However, ownership of Hawaiian lands is now largely in the hands of the descendants of missionaries and settlers.

230.2 man-o-war—see notes 19.6, 43.18, and 65.15.

230.6 had a nice woman—Helen. See notes 8.9, 11.4, 17.5–6, 24.6, 34.20, 35.18, 36.21, 62.27, 153.1, and 298.9.

230.11 Serengeti—a large plain of grasslands and woodland savannah in northern Tanzania, bordering Kenya and the Masai Mara National Reserve. It is a protected nature and wildlife refuge and a UNESCO world heritage site. Zebra, wildebeest, gazelle, and lion freely wander this roughly 5,700-square-mile area.

230.13 Scamander—see notes 31.4, 32.13, 35.16, 204.5, and 281.19.

230.18–19 "Omeros," / as in a conch shell—the invocation. See notes 12.25 and 14.10–12.

230.21 myrmidons—see note 10.25.

231.18 furies—Greek goddesses of vengeance, also called the Eumenides, often three in number, they pursued justice particularly for blood crimes committed within a family. They figure prominently in Aeschylus' (525/524–456/455 BCE) trilogy, *The Oresteia*, which charts the demise of the House of Atreus.

231.20 *Mer* was both sea and mother—See note 14.10–12.

CHAPTER XLVI

232.3 sea almond—see note 4.1.

232.7–8 gunwal . . . fathoms—see note 44.25.

232.14 ancestral river—see notes 52.24, 133.9–10, and 139.17.

232.17 compère—French and St. Lucian Kwéyòl for comrade or godfather, commonly used in Anancy (Caribbean folk) tales to suggest a close relationship.

232.21 carried an oar / to the church and propped it—in *The Odyssey*, after the journey to the underworld, Odysseus returns to Circe's isle to bury Elpenor, a member of his crew, who fell from Circe's roof while drunk; Odysseus places Elpenor's oar on his pyre. The oar also suggests one of the prophecies of Tiresias in *The Odyssey*, who foretells of a second journey Odysseus will make subsequent to his return to Ithaca. Odysseus will carry an oar into the inland hills and valleys of Greece where he will encounter people who do not recognize the implement and are thus unaware of the sea. Odysseus will place the implement in the earth and then sacrifice to the gods, particularly Poseidon, the god of the sea. Ezra Pound (1885–1972) uses the prophecy of Odysseus' second journey with the oar in his *Canto XXIII*. See notes 130.5, 153.1, 194.15, and 203.11.

233.3 hull of the gommier—his boat. See note 5.6; 20.

233.12 seine—see note 52.27.

234.22 the heron—see note 49.6.

235.7 moonlit meridian—see note 189.1.

235.14 Bon Dieu, aie, waie—a lamentation, from the French and St. Lucian Kwéyòl; sorrowful and surprised, "Good God, ai, waie."

CHAPTER XLVII

236.11 la Messe—French and St. Lucian Kwéyòl, meaning "the Mass"; the liturgy of the Roman Catholic Church.

236.13 the wafer—see notes 58.7–9 and 62.17.

236.19 her beads—rosary beads, from the Latin *rosarium* for "rose garden," a Roman Catholic ritual practice of prayer in which each bead signifies a prayer, usually 15 groups of 10 prayers yielding 150 Hail Marys, signified by small beads, and other prayers, namely the Our Father, signified by larger beads. Practitioners finger the individual beads during the recitation of each prayer to mark their devotional progress.

236.20 Hail Mary—see note 236.19.

236.20 marigolds—an annual and common flowering plant from the *Asteraceae* family, native to the Americas, though there is an African variety. The plant has yellow, red, and orange flowers.

236.21 anemone—see note 9.21.

236.22 watercress—a plant (*Nasturtium officinale*) that grows in or near water and has small white flowers and delicate flavorful leaves.

236.22 sacred heart of Jesus—in the Roman Catholic Church, the representation of the heart of Jesus serves as a devotional object or image; often pictured glowing and surrounded by thorns. There is a Roman Catholic sodality, a devotional society, that takes the Sacred Heart as its iconographic image of the divine.

236.23 anthurium . . . logwood—all of the genus of *Anthurium* of tropical plants, common in the Caribbean, with flat, heart-shaped red leaves that open to reveal a petite staff of bright yellow or red. See note 6.17.

236.24 aloe—a succulent plant in the *Asphodelaceae* family, common in desert areas, known for its healing properties related to skin ailments.

237.5 sybil—see notes 58.5 and 106.19.

237.6 Mimosa—a large group of plants, shrubs, and some trees, of the genus *Mimosa*, that are common in tropical areas, with feather-like leaves. Some varieties are known to respond to external stimuli such as bright sun or physical stroking.

237.14 palanquins of umbrella yams—a couch or chaise-like platform that could be carried aloft on poles to transport a dignitary. See note 140.10.

238.21 a language she could not recognize—see note 18.3.

238.23 antipodal—see notes 99.4 and 191.11.

238.24 sea troughs—deep fissures in the earth's surface under the sea. A notable one in the Caribbean is the Cayman Trench (aka Bartlett Trough); it runs from Cuba toward Central America and reaches a depth of over twenty-five thousand feet. Such troughs often feature apertures to release pressure but are also associated with earthquakes.

238.24 ospreys—see note 88.16–21.

239.2–3 Bight / of Benin—see notes 129.14–15, 145.5, and 149.6.

239.12 horned island—St. Lucia's Pitons. See notes 30.19, 40.21, 59.13, 103.3, 227.10, and 289.8.

239.16 bleached bone—the bones of the sea swift, after death and decomposition, are bleached by the sun. See notes 8.3, 88.21, and 242.15.

CHAPTER XLVIII

240.6 carapace—the hard, bone-like shell that covers the body of lobsters, tortoises, and crabs to protect them from predators.

240.18 dung beetle—any number of insects from the *Scarabaeidae* family that burrows into feces, feeds on the waste matter, and if female, generates and places larvae into the feces. A symbol of regeneration for the ancient Egyptians, the scarab, a dung beetle, associated with the sun, is a common motif in ancient Egyptian art.

241.12 *per mea culpa*—from the Latin, meaning "for my fault."

241.14 camphor—a white or even translucent substance from the camphor tree that is used to soothe skin inflammation, treat infections, and ward off pests. It is also used to produce celluloid.

241.26 sea grapes—see notes 17.7 and 63.17.

242.3 bilge . . . manchineel—see notes 9.15 and 10.23.

242.10 host . . . Mary—see notes 58.7, 62.17, 225.14–15, 225.20, and 310.13

242.15 African swallows—varieties of hirondelles, such as the cliff swallow (*Hirundo pyrrhonota*), cave swallow (*Hirundo Fulva*), and barn swallow (*Hirundo rustica*), regularly migrate through the Caribbean and have been spotted recurrently on St. Lucia. The African river martin or swallow (*Pseudochelidon eurystomina*) habituates the Congo River. See notes 8.3, 88.21, and 239.16.

242.16 cotton tree—the silk cotton tree or the kapok tree. See note 178.7–8.

242.21–22 Erzulie / Shango, and Ogun—see notes 52.21, 52.22, and 52.23.

243.10 nettle—a stinging plant with spines that injure any who handle it without care, from the genus *Urtica*; the word is also a verb meaning "to irritate."

243.14 caverned prophetess—see notes 58.5 and 106.19.

244.1; 24 language of her great-grandmother—see note 18.3.

244.17 coal-baskets—see notes 37.13, 104.6, and 120.6; 9.

245.2 original cave—of the Sybil, see notes 58.5, 106.19, and 245.16.

245.13 obeah—see note 58.5.

245.16 Cumae—a Greek colony in Italy founded in 750 BCE, approximately twelve miles from Naples, known for its Sybil or prophet. The colony was taken over by Rome in 338 CE but was ultimately destroyed in the thirteenth century. Greek ruins can be found in the area; the cave of the Sybil also remains. See notes 58.5 and 106.19.

CHAPTER XLIX

246.17 O: the scream—see notes 12.25 and 14.10–12.

247.14 corolla—see note 4.4.

248.2 *In God We Troust*—see note 8.4.

248.5 sea anemone—see note 9.21.

248.7 swamp lily—a type of water lily, also called a lizard's tail; a member of the *Nymphaeaceae* family.

248.8 sea almond—see note 4.1.

248.9 barracoon—see note 151.12.

248.21 Choiseul—refers to Choiseul, a village on the southern part of the island, named after the French minister Étienne-François de Choiseul (1719–1785) under Louis XV (1710–1774). Choiseul has both a cemetery and the oldest church on the island, the French Rivière Dorée Catholic Church. The name of the church literally means "golden river"; yet there is also a reference to an Arawak/Aruac word for a type of soft wooded tree from which a canoe can be made, duru, or now in Caribbean English, a dorey. Walcott references this church in chapter 1 of "Tales of the Islands." See note 269.1–2.

248.23–24 Adam . . . Eden. And the light was the first day's— from the book of Genesis, in the Bible, the first several chapters of which provide an account of the primeval creation of the earth and the residents of the Garden of Eden. See notes 12.25, 63.8, 97.2, 181.3, and 308.15.

249.3 banyan—tree (*Ficus benghalensis*). The East Indian tree has roots that grow from the branches down to the earth, creating a wide and dramatic protective canopy.

249.10 barrack arches on the Morne—see notes 42.20, 58.20, and 314.27–315.1.

249.13 Malebolge—see notes 59.18 and 137.7.

249.21 interior light like Lucia's—see notes 64.21.

250.2 Circe—see note 64.19.

250.14 breadfruit—see note 224.1.

CHAPTER L

251.3 allamanda—see note 65.8.

251.9 The Rodney—see notes 28.21, 32.5, 32.6, 34.21, 39.21, 43.1, 43.10, 43.13, 79.18, 81.19–20, 81.21, 92.12–13, 99.21–100.5, and 100.9.

251.15 Putney—a district of London in the Wandsworth borough in the southwest area of the city. Putney became fashionable in the seventeenth and eighteenth centuries and remains an affluent area known for rowing.

251.16 chrysanthemums—flowering plants of the *Asteraceae* family, primarily cultivated in subtropical zones. They have small colorful flowers of red, orange, yellow, and pink and are commonly called mums.

251.18 his tom—a common cat, male; the term "tomcat" has come to suggest a male on the prowl for sexual adventure. See note 27.3.

251.20 bombsites—the Battle of Britain was fought between the German Luftwaffe and the British Royal Air Force during World War II. After a more general air campaign across the island, the Germans bombed London nightly for nearly two months in the fall of 1940. This period became known as the "Blitz," an abbreviation derived from the German term *blitzkrieg*, for "lightening war," the rapid and overwhelming style of warfare the Germans used to overtake much of Europe before the Allies halted their advances.

251.21 Trafalgar—see notes 30.25, 193.13, 193.21, 194.4, 194.9, and 195.4.

252.7–8 Strand ... Kensington—see notes 193.13 and 197.10.

252.19 Tumbly and Scott—see note 101.34.

253.14 Marble Arch—an area of London adjacent to the northeastern section of Hyde Park and its famed Speakers' Corner. The park was originally a hunting green for British monarchs, but in 1851 it became the site for the Great Exhibition and the famed Crystal Palace. The actual arch for which the area of Marble Arch is named previously stood near Buckingham Palace. The architect John Nash (1752–1835) designed the Marble Arch in 1828 as a grand entrance for Buckingham Palace.

253.15 his island's market—see notes 37.13, 104.6, and 120.6.

253.20–21 News / of the World—a sensational tabloid newspaper that was founded in 1843. In the 1940s it was the newspaper with the largest circulation in the world. Rupert Murdoch's (1931–) News Corporation purchased it in 1969. Due to a phone hacking scandal in 2011 that reached the highest levels of its editorial and managerial staff, the newspaper ceased publication in July 2011.

253.21 Thames—see notes 193.13, 195.4, and 197.8.

254.16 water-lily—see notes 248.7 and 266.4.

254.17–18 ginger- / lilies—synonym of garland flowers, of the *Zingiberaceae* family. The association with ginger comes from the plant's rhizomatic root system that resembles the gnarly and intensely flavored root.

254.22 Queen Anne's lace—see note 62.18.

CHAPTER LI

255.14 Rover—see note 26.11.

256.17; 22 honky—white person, disparaging.

257.10 the cathedral—Cathedral of the Immaculate Conception in Castries, St. Lucia. See note 120.15–16.

257.12 the Memorial—in Derek Walcott Square in central Castries facing the Central Library; made of imposing white painted concrete that memorializes fallen St. Lucians, most of whom served as members of the British West Indies Regiment, who fought in World Wars I and II. The names of these men are inscribed on the central column in two brass plaques. Those who served and died during World War II were pilots. During World War II, a Nazi submarine sank two ships in Castries Harbor. St. Lucia was a significant location for the Lend-Lease program that allowed the Americans to offer material support to the British before the Americans' official entry into the war with the bombing of Pearl Harbor. The memorial in Castries is the location for the island's Remembrance Day service every November. See notes 30.24 and 262.1.

257.16 library—the Central Library of Castries, St. Lucia. See note 120.18.

257.17 Georgian trim—a style of architecture and ornamental decoration prevalent during the reign (which began in 1714) of Britain's King George I (1660–1727) but widely popular until the 1830s through the reign of King George IV (1762–1830). The style varies but is often characterized by symmetry and refined ornamentation and is noted for its Palladian influence and neoclassical aesthetic. This movement began as a rejection of previous Baroque styles. See notes 93.6–7, 103.26–27, and 197.17.

257.22 Lisbon—see notes 155.23–25, 189.3, and 189.4–5.

258.9 binnacle—the base on which a compass stands or is mounted, often on a ship, that can serve as a means of protection and at times illumination from below.

259.7 Bread of Heaven—manna; a gift from the heavens, in the book of Exodus, that sustained the Israelites through their many years in the desert. "Bread of Heaven" is also the name of a popular gospel song.

260.1–2 oleanders . . . orchids—orchids (*Orchidaceae*); flowering plants with striking yet delicate blooms. They are notoriously difficult to cultivate but are suited to the tropical Caribbean climate. See note 164.6.

260.6 bridal magnolias—the flowers of the magnolia tree or shrub, from the family *Magnoliaceae*, are commonly used for wedding bouquets; the flowers, with six to twelve petals of white, pink, and sometimes purple, are pleasingly aromatic.

260.8 Bendemeer's stream—see notes 56.11, 201.1, and 201.2.

CHAPTER LII

260.17 Seychelles—see notes 28.25, 90.7–8, and 227.27.

260.20 Macaulay . . . Gibbon—Thomas Babington Macaulay (1800–1859); British politician and author of the five-volume *History of England* (1849–61) as well as *Lays of Ancient Rome* (1842) who served the British Empire in India from 1834 to 1838 during the transition from commercial to governmental control. He is noted and reviled for his instructions on colonial education. Edward Gibbon (1737–1794), British historian and author of *The Decline and Fall of the Roman Empire* (1776–88), a work in many volumes that charts the intricacies of political history in that empire. In 1770, he published *Critical Observations on the Sixth Book of the Aeneid.*

261.4 aisling—an Irish Gaelic word and now Hiberno English term for a dream or vision. The word also signifies a seventeenth- and eighteenth-century Irish genre, a dream vision poem. Irish poets wrote aislings in support of the Catholic James II (1644–85). Seamus Heaney (1939–2013) entitled a poem in his 1975 collection, *North*, by this name.

261.19–24 Provinces, Protectorates . . . Secretaries—a litany of geographic and service designations within the British Empire.

262.1 poppies . . . wreaths—red poppy flowers are used to memorialize fallen soldiers, particularly on Armistice, now Remembrance Day, every November. The practice dates to World War I and the Canadian John McRae's (1872–1918) 1915 poem "In Flanders Fields," which describes the Belgian countryside covered with poppies between the crosses on the graves of the dead. Wreaths are also commonly bestowed on graves and memorials during Remembrance Day ceremonies. Walcott describes wearing a poppy in *Midsummer*. See notes 30.24 and 257.12.

262.3 dromedaries under Lawrence—the Arabian camel (*Camelus dromedaries*) with one hump, common in Africa, India, and the Middle East and domesticated for use in the desert as a means of transport and sustenance; strongly associated with Bedouin culture and the Arabian Peninsula. For Lawrence, see notes 23.10 and 31.13.

262.8 Dragoons—European soldiers, commonly cavalry. The term originates in the sixteenth century for the short musket that these troops carried. In the nineteenth-century British army, a light cavalry was termed a "light dragoon regiment." In the twentieth century, these dragoons replaced their horses with armored vehicles such as tanks.

262.12 Rock of Ages—a popular Christian hymn by the Anglican cleric Augustus Montague Toplady (1740–1778); also the name of a 1972 album by The Band, the Canadian-American rock group that served as a backup group for Bob Dylan (Robert Zimmerman) (1941–).

262.13 Zouave—see note 87.12.

262.16 Airs from Erin—see note 56.16.

262.19 laburnums—popularly called golden chain, poisonous trees or shrubs with clusters of drooping flowers from the *Fabaceae* family; indigenous to southern Europe.

262.20 Mafeking relief—also Mafikeng, a garrison town in South African, close to the Botswana border, established by the British military that the Boers besieged during the Boer War, Oct 1899–May 1900; its release from the siege was cause for much public celebration in Britain.

262.22 Gordon—British governor general of the Sudan, Charles George Gordon (1833–1885), who died during the Mahdists' siege of the British at Khartoum. Considered a martyr to the empire who had served in the Crimea, China, and North Africa, Gordon was celebrated in Britain. However, Gordon was included in Lytton Strachey's (1880–

1932) *Eminent Victorians*, a volume that questioned and complicated such conventional opinions.

262.22 Khartoum—the capital of Sudan from the Arabic, *Al-Khurṭūm,* meaning "elephant's trunk," sits at the intersection of the White and Blue Niles. It was founded as a military outpost during the nineteenth century and was contested between the Egyptians and the British, though the British held this location until Sudanese independence in 1956. See note 262.22 above.

262.23 *The World's Classics*—see note 71.11.

262.24 Benares—a city, also called Varanasi, in the Uttar Pradesh state of India. This city sits on the Ganges River; Hindus designates it as a sacred city. The city has been a center of arts, learning, and spiritualism for centuries.

262.25 His will be done, O Maud, His kingdom come—from the Christian prayer, the Our Father, central to the Roman Catholic Mass. See notes 236.11 and 236.19.

263.2 Rangoon to Malta—Rangoon is the former Anglicized name for Yangon, the former capital of Myanmar (previously known as Burma). In 2006, the Myanmar government moved the capital to Naypwidaw. Malta is the island nation in the Mediterranean Sea that is actually comprised of five islands, of which the island of Malta is the largest. Its culture reflects the diversity of influences accumulated over millennia. In 2004, Malta joined the European Union.

263.4 laudanum—a drug commonly prescribed through the nineteenth century for various ailments; opium dissolved in alcohol.

263.5 Jordan—river that begins at Mount Hermon on the border of Syria and Lebanon. Its course also separates in part Israel, the West Bank (Palestine), and Jordan. According to Christian teaching, the waters of the Jordan served as an important location for baptism.

263.11 Victoria Regina—Queen Victoria. See notes 25.17, 26.9, 103.26–27, and 195.4.

263.15 Embankment—see note 195.4.

263.21 Ulysses—see notes 189.3, 200.11, and 201.16.

263.22 Telemachus—The son of Odysseus and Penelope. He remains home as a child on Ithaca while his father ventures off to the Trojan War. He is manipulated by the suitors but seeks news of his father and remains loyal to him. See note 201.16.

CHAPTER LIII

264.11 vertiginous irises—a variety of garden flowers (*Iridaceae*) that are known for their beauty and often deep bluish purple flowers. Common in the Mediterranean.

264.19 Glen-da-lough—see notes 25.4–5, 197.1, 198.15, 199.1, 200.5, and 200.9.

264.21 the disenfranchisement no hyphenating rook—see note 199.2–3.

266.4 Les Nympheas—*Water Lilies*, a large series of murals originally meant to span eighty feet in the Orangerie of the Tuileries Palace in Paris. These paintings by the impressionist painter Claude Monet (1840–1926), inspired by his garden and pond at Giverny in northern France, are considered masterpieces. These works are profoundly intense depictions of nature. See note 248.7.

266.15 baize—a type of fabric, akin to felt, commonly used to cover billiards and game tables. The word is derived from the French, *bai*, a red/brown color, though the fabric is now most commonly green. See note 87.9.

266.24 a martin—the Caribbean martin (*Progne dominicensis*) travels to St. Lucia during the spring and fall and resides in St. Lucia during the summer breeding season.

266.25 black frigate bird—see notes 19.6, 43.18, and 65.5.

267.5 Saltibus—a village in southwestern St. Lucia that is known for the surrounding area's stunning waterfalls.

267.9 bitterns and herons—a bittern, from the family *Ardeidae*, is comparable to but smaller than a heron and noticeably more plump. See note 49.6.

267.24 Coal Market—see notes 37.13, 104.6, and 120.6; 9.

CHAPTER LIV

268.2 cockatoo hair—a parrot from the *Cacatuidae* family with a highly visible crest, native to Australia and the South Pacific region, that often perches on the tree line. In Australian slang, a "cockatoo" is a look-out for nefarious activities.

268.13 Troumasse—a river that flows from the heights of the rain-forest preserve to the eastern side of St. Lucia, passing a town of the same name close to the shore and emptying into Troumasse Bay and subsequently the Atlantic.

268.13 heron—see note 49.6.

269.1 heights of Saltibus—see note 267.5.

269.1–2 D'Elles Soeurs . . . LaFargue—La Fargue is a town in Cho-iseul, St. Lucia. It is close to the River Doree and is southwest of Saltibus. Walcott invokes D'Elles Souers in *The Prodigal* (80). See note 248.21.

269.12 R.S.M.—Regimental Sergeant Major, a rank in the British Army.

269.16 Kipling's requiem—Rudyard Kipling (1865–1936), Brit-ish writer, who is known for his support of British imperialism. While he did not publish a work entitled "Requiem," he did publish a "Reces-sional." However, Kipling's requiem suggests the collapse of the British Empire and a definitive end for the author of the infamous "The White Man's Burden."

270.19 Battle of the Saints—see notes 28.21, 31.26–27, 32.5, 32.6, 34.21, 43.1, 43.10, 81.19–20, 84.1, 92.12–13, 99.21–100.5, and 100.9.

271.3 Olympian games—the ancient Greek athletic competition that was held every four years as a part of a religious festival; according to Greek myth, these games were founded by Heracles. The modern (with the late nineteenth-century resurgence) Olympic Games now include both summer and winter sports.

271.5 *Ville de Paris*—see notes 28.21, 32.5, 32.6, 34.21, 39.21, 43.1, 43.10, 81.19–20, 81.21, 92.12–13, 99.21–100.5, and 100.9.

271.19 Trojan War—see notes 3.2, 6.1, 8.9, 14.5, 16.14–15, 17.5–6, 24.6, and 31.4.

272.6 breadfruit—see note 224.1.

CHAPTER LV

272.12 pillars of Scotch—a Scotch attorney; a tree or shrub, the *Clusia rose*. Indigenous to the Caribbean, these grow to thirty feet in height and produce white flowers and a vibrant orange fruit.

272.12 red sorrel—a sourwood or sorrel tree (*Oxydendrum arboretum*). Indigenous to the southeastern United States, these trees grow to seventy-five feet in height and generate white flowers.

272.12 sea-moss—an aquatic animal species(*bryozoan*) that lives suspended in water (there are both freshwater and saltwater varieties) and collects nutrients through its tentacles that appear plant-like. Their shape, color, and size vary.

272.21 ginger beer—an alcoholic drink, popular in the Caribbean (and long associated with British culture). The drink is made of ginger, sugar, yeast, and other additives that vary depending on the producer. The dark and stormy, a cocktail popular in Bermuda and the Caribbean, joins ginger beer with rum.

273.1 black pudding, souse—a blood sausage paired with pickled meat, a common savory delight in the Anglophone Caribbean.

273.18 fifes—see note 143.11.

273.21 Bight of Benin—see notes 129.14–15, 145.5, and 149.6.

273.25 *paille-banane*—a pay-bannann; a costume made of banana leaves for ritual folk-dance enactments and celebratory of African heritage. It is commonly worn by men but evocative of a feminine or androgynous performance of gender(s).

273.26 calabash—see note 98.22.

274.2 anemone—see note 9.21.

274.4 mansards—a type of roof that has a dramatic steep slope underneath a flat top level; named for the French architect who popularized the style, François Mansart (1598–1666).

274.9 Boxing Day—the day after Christmas, December 26; a public holiday in Britain and many Commonwealth countries that commemorates the ritual of giving to the poor and those in service.

275.15 *pomme-Cythère*—see note 162.14.

275.16 the apple of Venus—see notes 11.4, 100.11, 114.10, and 314.12; 21.

275.16 *Ville de Paris*—see notes 28.21, 32.5, 32.6, 34.21, 39.21, 43.1, 43.10, 81.19–20, 81.21, 92.12–13, 99.21–100.5, and 100.9.

276.14 fife-chac—see notes 53.10 and 143.11.

276.15 *Un! Deux! Trois!*—French, "one! two! three!"

276.19 calabash—see note 98.22.

277.14 fifes—see note 143.11.

277.15 hummingbird's wings—see note 88.16–21.

277.20 runnels—see note 48.6.

❖ Book Seven

SUMMARY

The final, seventh, book of *Omeros* opens with the head of Homer transformed into a coconut floating in the Caribbean Sea. The poet converses with the head about the nature of the epic, the import of poetry, and the journey across the sea. Walcott identifies the voice of Homer with the ocean. St. Lucian history provides a reminder of the location and its past. Achille and Philoctete take to the sea. They encounter a whale that lifts their boat and rights their course for shore. Major Plunkett consults Ma Kilman for a séance with his dead wife, Maud. He seeks reassurance and forgiveness. Ma Kilman offers him both, with a gesture from heaven as a place as green as Maud's beloved Ireland. Seven Seas is in the No Pain Café when Ma Kilman's niece, Christine, arrives to help in the shop. Helen's coming child, which may be either Hector's or Achille's, is the source of a disagreement in naming. Achille will raise the child and wants an African name; Helen prefers no such name and delays the decision until the christening. The final chapter in the work includes an invocation, an epic convention that calls upon the muses for inspiration. Walcott's placement of such an invocation at the opening of the final book rather than in the first book suggests that the narrative continues as a circular, eternal song. Walcott writes, "I sang of quiet Achille, Afolabe's son. . . . I sang our wide country, the Caribbean Sea" (320.7; 320.16). He does not invoke the gods but acknowledges the singer as the master of the tale and of his subject. The final book of *Omeros* is an assemblage of the work as a whole. It reaches back to the points of origin, the strategic positions on the journey, and wraps them in a circular pattern of the historical past and contemporary present. The circularity of the narrative is one of the key elements of the final book. The rhythms of the past, the continuity of the present, and the promise of the future endure at once. The sea, the narrative, and the world persist in this simultaneous "epilogue" (321) and invocation that refuses narrative closure and celebrates Walcott's beloved St. Lucia. The final movements in *Omeros* become an incantation of the ongoing sea and waves. Achille returns from the sea with a fresh catch; he hauls *In God We Troust* onto the beach and unloads. He washes himself, though the sea smell rightly remains. The No Pain Café in the distance is illuminated. Although Achille's final step in the journey is inland, the waves continue their unrelenting movement, and thus the narrative begins again.

ANNOTATIONS

CHAPTER LVI

280.8 marble head—head of Homer, drawn from Ovid's (43 BCE– 17 CE) treatment of the head of Orpheus in his *Metamorphoses*. Both Rainer Maria Rilke (1875–1926) and H.D. (1886–1961) have reimagined Orpheus more recently. Orpheus was the reputed son of Calliope, the muse of epic poetry. After his death and dismemberment, Orpheus' head and lyre are cast into the water; the head continues to sing even after death. The head and the lyre land on the island of Lesbos, where an oracle is established. The ability of the head to speak after death also evokes the figures in Dante's (1265–1321) ninth circle of the *Inferno* as well as distorted cries in T. S. Eliot's (1888–1965) "Little Gidding." Walcott converses with Ovid in "The Hotel Normandie Pool" and in *The Fortunate Traveller*. He also invokes the marble head in "From This Far." See notes 12.25, 14.5, 186.11; 23, 283.17, 283.21, and 288.21.

    281.7 chiton—see note 15.11.

    281.19 drumming cave—the cave of Philoctetes is located, according to custom, near Kaviria on Lemnos (now Límnos), a Greek island in the Aegean. It is underwater but is accessible by ferrying to the area and swimming/diving. See notes 3.2, 31.4, 32.13, 204.5, and 230.13.

    282.10 light of St. Lucia—see note 64.21.

    282.15 sybil—see note 58.5.

282.17 St. Martin-in-the-Fields—see notes 194.4 and 194.9.

282.20 Thames—see note 193.13, 195.4, and 197.8.

282.24 Aegean's chimera—see notes 31.4, 32.13, 204.5, 230.13, and 281.19.

283.4–5 Medusa's shield—Medusa, the Gorgon of ancient Greek myth, with a head covered in snakes rather than hair, was decapitated by Perseus. However, in one version of her story, her head was placed on the shield of Athena, the goddess of war, because Medusa's severed head had the power to transform anyone who gazed upon it into stone.

283.11 frigate bird—see notes 19.6, 43.18, and 65.5.

283.15 desert shaman—see notes 146.18, 164.16, 164.21, 175.12, 176.3, 176.6, 180.18, 181.16–17, 182.10, and 182.15.

283.17 Homer meant joy—the earliest accounts of the name "Homer" link the biographically elusive epic poet with a particular location as well as with the idea of following and blindness. The joy associated with the name in this line relates to the contemporary experience of a reader's pleasure. See notes 12.25, 14.5, 280.8, 283.17, 283.21, and 288.21.

283.20 laurier cannelles—see note 3.4.

283.20 pages of rustling trees—from Virgil's (70 BCE–19 CE) *Aeneid*, Book VI, where the poet describes verses as written on leaves. In the section entitled "The Estranging Sea" of *Another Life*, Walcott compares epics on paper to leaves.

283.21 Master, I was the freshest of all your readers—the modern poet, Walcott, speaks to the ancient oral epic poet, Homer. See notes 12.25, 14.5, 280.8, 283.17, 283.21, and 288.21.

284.4 Thebes? Athens?—Thebes is the ancient Greek city (now Thíva) associated with Oedipus, particularly in Aeschylus' (525/524–456/455 BCE) *Seven Against Thebes* and Sophocles' (496–406 BCE) treatments of the Oedipus myth in *Oedipus the King*; the ancient city was famed for having seven gates. Athens (now Athínai) was the center of the Ancient Greek world, known for its arts, culture, political thought, architecture, and enduring global influence. It remains the capital city of modern Greece. See notes 14.18, 32.13, and 177.16.

284.9 Helen—see notes 8.9, 11.4, 17.5–6, 24.6, 34.20, 35.18, 36.21, 62.27, 153.1, and 298.9.

284.11 Ten years war—the Trojan War. Walcott uses this phrase to describe the Trojan War in "Map of the New World." See notes 3.2, 6.1, 8.9, 14.5, 16.14–15, 17.5–6, 24.6, and 31.4.

CHAPTER LVII

285.5 the ferryman—Charon, the gloomy ferryman of Greek myth who is the son of the Night; he ferries the dead across the Rivers Acheron and Styx to the underworld. He appears in Book 6 of *The Aeneid*. Walcott refers to Charon in "A Village Life." See note 287.7.

285.7 marble—see note 280.8.

285.8 startled dog—Cerberus, the vicious three-headed dog of Greek myth, who guards the underworld and prevents the dead from escaping their ultimate destination.

285.10 no wake—see notes 199.26, 200.16, 201.11, 201.16, and 209.18.

286.2 my father—see note 68.21.

286.14 calypso—see notes 64.19, 194.15, and 229.5.

286.16–17 "In the mist of the sea . . . Greek ship anchor"—a mocking account of conventional epic writing, presenting a conventional view of St. Lucia.

286.21–287.4 "It was a place of light . . . a healing place"—the mockery of the conventional writing in the above passage is undercut with the appreciation of the wondrousness of St. Lucia, told from the perspective of the blind poet.

287.7 charred ferryman—a play on Charon, the ferryman. See note 285.5.

288.1 Marigot—the capital city of the French side of the island of Saint Martin. The island is among the Leeward Islands in the Caribbean archipelago. The French side of the island occupies a unique position within the French Overseas Departments. The other part of the isle, officially a separate state, takes its name from the Dutch, Sint Maarten.

288.7 Troy—see notes 3.2, 6.1, 8.9, 14.5, 16.14–15, 17.5–6, 24.6, and 31.4.

288.10 Comte de Grasse—see notes 28.21, 32.6, and 43.10.

288.11 Menelaus—see notes 17.5–6, 24.6, 34.20, and 298.9.

288.21 irisless eyes—the head of Homer, or Orpheus, as a marble statue that floats to the island. Ancient Greek sculptures sometimes have smooth eyes rather than a circle to indicate an iris. See notes 12.25, 14.5, 280.8, 283.17, 283.21, and 288.21.

CHAPTER LVIII

289.1 Soufrière—see notes 59.13, 59.14, and 289.8.

289.3 Messrs. Bennett & Ward—see note 60.7–8.

289.4 blind guide—Homer. See notes 12.25, 14.5, 280.8, 283.17, 283.21, and 288.21.

289.7 Lucia's eyes—see note 64.21.

289.8 Pool of Speculation—the real estate speculation close to the Pitons is based upon the resort/spa structures that commonly feature pools. Yet, historically, the sulfur pits or baths of Soufrière, have also been a spot for speculative investment meant to extract local resources, such as those of Bennett & Ward/Wood. The baths in sulfur pits are thought to be medicinal; visitors can take the waters there if they can withstand the heat. Walcott's pool of speculation thus evokes the precisely fitting punishments joined with damnation both in Dante's (1265–1321) *Inferno* and Ezra Pound's (1885–1972) *Canto XIV*. See notes 59.14 and 60.7–8.

289.11 Hephaestus or Ogun—the Greek god of fire, son of Hera and Zeus, who famously crafts the shield of Achilles. For Ogun, see note 52.23.

289.14 malebolge—signifies the final descent into the underworld. Unlike the intersection with the shade of Walcott's father or the journey to Africa that serves as a journey to a non-Christian past, this quest witnesses the damnation of several figures, including Hector, who is punished for his forsaking of the sea for facile profit on land, a curious inverse of the punishment of Ulysses in Dante's (1265–1321) *Inferno*, who is in the eighth circle because he left his island only to be shipwrecked (a final end for the hero that Dante creates himself). See notes 59.18 and 137.7.

289.15 traitors—those who sell St. Lucia for tourists and foreign investment, otherwise known as the extraction of resources for foreign profit. See notes 59.14, 60.7–8, and 289.8.

290.18 stone head—see note 280.8.

290.19 nightingale—see notes 88.16–21, 152.10, and 313.24.

290.23 goat bleating down from the theatre steps—the origins of the theater in ancient Greece derive from the practice of religious festivals, especially those of Dionysus; such festivals would have commonly had an animal sacrifice as a part of their ritual celebrations. The word "tragedy" derives from the ancient Greek, *tragōidía*, or "goat song."

291.6 unthreading foam—sea lace. See note 82.9–10.

291.10 he does not go; he sends his narrator—begins the passage where Seven Seas compares Walcott to Homer, the poets, and their journeys. Seven Seas then operates as Virgil to Walcott's Dante, a journey's guide.

291.11–12 two journeys / in every odyssey—see note 232.21.

291.27 circle yourself and this island with this art—see note 229.1.

292.2 Malebolge—see note 59.18.

292.4–7 Hector in hell . . . comet—see note 53.4.

292.17–18 god river, / the god snake—see notes 52.24 and 139.17.

292.22 Bennett & Ward—see note 60.7–8.

292.27 tree of Eden—see notes 12.25, 63.8, 97.2, 181.3, 248.23–24, and 308.15.

293.16 the shit they stewed in—from Dante's (1265–1321 CE) *Inferno*, in the third circle of upper Hell, the Gluttons, those who ingest more than is essential commit the sin of incontinence and thus exist in waste and filth for eternity; they are akin to swine.

294.8 to use other eyes, like those of that sightless stone—see note 280.8.

294.9 Soufrière—see notes 59.13, 59.14, and 289.8.

CHAPTER LIX

295.3 bittern—see note 267.9.

295.6 sea-almond's branches—see note 4.1.

295.9 sybils—see notes 58.5.

295.24 Cap's bracing headland—see note 20.7.

295.27 Golden Fleece—see note 36.6.

296.1 Gilgamesh—warrior hero of the ancient Mesopotamian epic who is both human and divine. Gilgamesh, king of Uruk, creates havoc in his city until the gods send his double Enkidu to tame him. The two go on a journey to murder Huwawa, who has taken over the cedar forest. After they kill him, Ishtar desires Gilgamesh, but he rejects her. Enraged, she goes to the higher gods for revenge and convinces the Bull of Heaven to ravage Uruk. Gilgamesh and Enkidu kill the bull. The gods are furious and decide Enkidu must perish. Gilgamesh laments his friend with poetry as he confronts his own mortality. He searches for the secret of eternal life, and he discovers the man who survived the flood. Gilgamesh is sent to a plant whose leaves grant eternal life; Gilgamesh takes it but falls asleep near water. A serpent emerges from the water and takes the plant. Gilgamesh returns to Uruk. Gilgamesh is brash and arrogant; Enkidu is sorrowful and resigned.

296.2 the Iliad—one of two epic poems (the other is *The Odyssey*) attributed to the Greek poet Homer, *The Iliad* depicts the rage of Achilles and its consequences; it deals with the aftermath of the abduction of Helen, the slaughter of Hector, and a relatively brief period during the fight for Troy. The central hero of *The Iliad* is Achilles, who must choose between a short glorious life or a long anonymous one. This martial epic is noted for its battles and movements juxtaposed with profoundly moving scenes of despair. The pride and anger of Achilles drive the narrative. Famously beautiful scenes depicting the making of Achilles' shield and the comparison of the stars in the sky with the number of fires on the shore to warm the troops relieve the narrative from a bleak, battle focus. The Trojan hero, Hector, kills Patroclus, who is wearing Achilles' armor and is thus mistaken for the great hero. Hector subsequently battles Achilles and loses. Achilles drags Hector's body around the walls of Troy. Yet, ultimately, Achilles returns the body to Priam, Hector's father and king of Troy. The Greeks are able to enter the city walls with the false gift of the Trojan horse that conceals the Greeks inside. Helen, who has resided in Troy with Paris throughout the epic, though she suspects the ruse, does not inform the Trojans of the Greek trick. See notes 3.2,

6.1, 7.1, 8.9, 10.25, 14.5, 16.14–15, 24.6, 31.4, 34.20, 35.18, 99.4, 130.3, 146.15–16, 152.14–15, 153.1, 177.16, and 194.15.

296.7 Guinea—see notes 129.14–15, 149.6, 150.1–2, and 184.1.

296.15 branching from the white ribs of each ancestor—see notes 149.14–15 and 239.16.

296.22 palanquins of Portuguese man-o'-wars—see notes 19.6, 43.18, and 65.15.

297.1 anabasis—*Anabasis Kyrou* (*Upcountry March* or the *Expedition of Cyrus*), written by Xenophon (430–350 BCE); the ancient Greek historian's account of the expedition of Greek soldiers against the Persians. Both sides were led by brothers: the Greeks by Cyrus the Younger (423–401 BCE) and the Persians by Artaxerxes II (d. 358/9 BCE). Anabasis is the inverse of epic katabasis. See note 137.7.

297.14 Troy—see notes 3.2, 6.1, 8.9, 14.5, 16.14–15, 17.5–6, 24.6, and 31.4.

297.17 mirror of History—evokes the famous phrase in James Joyce's (1882–1941) *Ulysses* that describes Irish art as a servant's broken mirror. See notes 98.20, 199.26, 200.11, 200.12, 201.7, 201.11, 201.12–14, 201.16, and 209.18.

297.22–23 Troumasse River—see note 268.13.

297.25 man-o'-war's—see notes 19.6, 43.18, and 65.15.

298.4 wings of the frigate—see notes 19.6, 43.18, and 65.5.

298.9 the rage of Achilles—from the opening lines of *The Iliad*. The poet asks the gods for inspiration to sing the rage of Achilles, Peleus' son. As the epic opens, we learn that his anger has derived from a dispute with Agamemnon over the young woman Briseis. See notes 6.1, 8.4, 8.9, 10.25, 16.14–16, 17.5–6, 24.6, 83.20, 146.15–16, 150.12, 175.13–14, 228.25, 296.2, 298.9, and 320.7–16.

298.19 rust in one sufferer—the wound of Philoctetes. See notes 3.2, 9.20, 17.7, and 18.15

299.5 Cyclops—see note 13.7.

299.11 Lawrence crossing the sand—see notes 23.10, 31.13, and 262.3.

CHAPTER LX

299.20 frigates—see notes 19.6, 43.18, and 65.5.

300.4 Aruac—see notes 3.1, 5.2, 92.5, 92.15, 162.14, and 164.16.

300.5 egret, or parrots—see notes 49.12.

300.9 sybil—see note 58.5.

300.17 robbed by thirty mile seines—see note 52.27.

300.26–27 marlin . . . albacore—see notes 157.14–15.

301.3 Caribs in the deep silver mines—after the arrival of the Europeans, the indigenous peoples of the Caribbean and Latin America were forced to extract minerals, particularly silver, from mines. The methods of this extraction were both brutally cruel to the Caribs and damaging to the environment. This forced labor was often related to forced displacements. For example, in 1797, the British removed with force four thousand Caribs from St. Vincent. They were resettled in Central America. Walcott notes the Carib's forced labor and mining of silver in "The Schooner Flight." See notes 3.1 and 6.13.

301.7 Soufrière—see notes 59.13, 59.14, and 289.8.

301.11–12 Aeneas / founding not Rome—see notes 14.5, 95.12, 137.7, and 206.17.

301.15 Anse La Raye, Canaries—see notes 58.25 and 59.13.

301.27 Grenadines—islands of the Lesser Antilles (roughly six hundred in number, some of which have no human residents) spread between St. Vincent and Grenada; the northern islands are a part of, as the name suggests, St. Vincent and the Grenadines, while the southern islands fall under the jurisdiction of Grenada. See note 190.16.

302.1 Soufrière—see notes 59.13, 59.14, and 289.8.

303.3 Baleine—French and St. Lucian Kwéyòl; a "whale." The encounter with the whale suggests Ishmael and Ahab in *Moby Dick* and Shabine in "The Schooner Flight." See notes 72.4–5, 142.1, and 184.7.

303.8 *In God We Troust*—see note 8.4.

CHAPTER LXI

304.1 RSM—see note 269.12.

304.11 *fin de siècle*—French for "end of the century"; usually describes a period of the final years of the nineteenth century and its aesthetic decadence.

304.16 Helen—see notes 8.9, 11.4, 17.5–6, 24.6, 34.20, 35.18, 36.21, 62.27, 153.1, and 298.9.

304.19–20 Etty / or Alma-Tadema—William Etty (1787–1849), English painter of historical subjects, who was particularly drawn to the ancient Greek myths. His skilled treatments of women and goddesses are idealized yet imaginative. Lawrence Alma-Tadema (1836–1912) is the Dutch-born and naturalized British painter who was renowned for his depictions of the ancient Greek and Roman worlds. His subjects are filled with striking details such as fabric, flowers, and architecture that were at times anachronistic. For example, the roses that he so perfectly depicted in the work *A Reading from Homer*, which portrays an enraptured audience listening to a recitation in ancient Greece, were a recently generated hybrid and thus an anachronism. See notes 12.25, 14.5, 280.8, 283.17, 283.21, and 288.21.

305.14;20 Tom—see notes 27.3 and 251.18.

306.13 croton—a plant, tree, or shrub also called variegated laurel (*Codiaeum variegatum*) that is indigenous to the South Pacific. The leaves are brightly colored with pink, white, orange, purple, green, and yellow predominating in the types that have colored leaves. Croton trees can grow up to twenty feet high.

306.19 Glen-da-Lough—see notes 25.4–5, 197.1, 198.15, 199.1, 200.5, and 200.9.

307.2 curlew—see note 89.6; 19.

307.3 knolls and broken castles—see note 198.3.

307.9 gardeuse—see note 58.5.

307.10 the keys—see note 201.17–18.

307.17 sybil—see note 58.5.

308.1 Glen-da-Lough—see notes 25.4–5, 197.1, 198.15, 199.1, 200.5, and 200.9.

308.10 Rover—see note 26.11.

308.11 No Pain Café—see notes 17.7 and 17.13–14.

308.15 serpent's heads—in Western myth, a symbol of temptation from the book of Genesis; the serpent entices Eve to bite from the tree of knowledge. She partakes, and the fall of humanity from the grace of

God and the state of perfection in the Garden of Eden ensues. In a more positive myth, the snake is also a symbol of Damballa, the African Caribbean god, and is associated with rivers, particularly the one Achille encounters in Africa. See notes 12.25, 52.24, 63.8, 97.2, 139.17, 181.3, and 248.23–24.

308.25 He had turned his head away once—Orpheus turns back while he and his beloved Eurydice ascend from the underworld; she disappears and is returned to Hades as a punishment for his rear glance. Walcott refers to Eurydice in "Goats and Monkeys."

309.6 Saltibus—see note 267.5.

309.7 mimosa—see note 237.6.

309.15 flowers of the immortelle—see note 93.15–16.

309.19 Helen—see notes 8.9, 11.4, 17.5–6, 24.6, 34.20, 35.18, 36.21, 62.27, 153.1, and 298.9.

CHAPTER LXII

310.1 Christmas bush—also called poison ash (*Comocladia dodonaea*); bush with sharp green leaves that become crimson as the plant ages. The plant is indigenous to the Caribbean and Latin America.

310.1 red sorrel—see note 272.12.

310.8 vespers—ritual evening prayers in the Christian tradition.

310.13 *Salve Regina*—Latin for Hail Queen; a prayer, anthem, or sacred song written for the Blessed Virgin Mary in the Roman Catholic tradition. This hymn is sometimes performed during vespers services. See notes 100.6, 225.20, and 310.8.

310.18 egrets—see note 49.12.

311.10–11 *In God We Troust* . . . GABBAGE DUMPED HERE—see note 8.4.

311.18 No Pain Café—see notes 17.7 and 17.13–14.

311.20 museum—see notes 43.1 and 81.19–20.

311.21 Battle—see notes 28.21, 31.26–27, 32.5, 32.6, 34.21, 43.1, 43.10, 81.19–20, 84.1, 92.12–13, 99.21–100.5, and 100.9.

311.23–24 Helen / of the West Indies—see notes 8.9, 11.4, 17.5–6, 24.6, 34.20, 35.18, 36.21, 62.27, 153.1, and 298.9.

311.25 immortelle's vermilion—see note 93.15–16.

312.13–14 Pitons . . . breadfruit—see notes 30.19, 40.21, 59.13, 103.3, 224.1, 227.10, and 289.8.

312.16 Greek frieze—a narrow band of sculpture in relief, commonly above columns and architraves but below the cornices on the buildings in classical and Greek Revival styles of architecture. See notes 177.9–11 and 177.16.

312.16 Helen—see notes 8.9, 11.4, 17.5–6, 24.6, 34.20, 35.18, 36.21, 62.27, 153.1, and 298.9.

312.22–23 Paris . . . Venus—see notes 11.4, 100.11, 114.10, and 314.12; 21.

312.23 *pomme-Cythère*—see note 162.14.

313.3; 6 Troy . . . two Helens—see notes 3.2, 6.1, 8.9, 11.4, 14.5, 16.14–15, 17.5–6, 24.6, 31.4, 34.20, 35.18, 36.21, 62.27, 153.1, and 298.9.

313.10 white cowries—marine snails from the family *Cypraeidae.* They often have a bulge on the back of their shells, which are sleek but have tiny teeth-like elements in their openings. The shells are desirable as jewelry because of their lustrous white, tan, and speckled coloring.

313.15 sanderlings—see notes 88.16–21 and 185.13.

313.18 brown dove—doves, from the family *Columbidae,* are a smaller form of the common pigeon; their coloring ranges from white and grey blue to reddish brown. See notes 4.9 and 153.8.

313.18 black grackle—also called crow or blackbird, the Carib grackle (*Quisicalus lugubrus*) is common in the Caribbean and parts of northern Venezuela, Guyana, and Brazil.

313.18 herons like ewers—wide-mouthed or broad-necked herons. See note 49.6.

313.22 African swallow—see notes 8.3, 88.21, 239.16, and 242.15.

313.22 finch from India—either the green tiger finch (*Amandava formosa*), from the family *Estrildidae,* or possibly the red-whiskered bulbul (*P. jocosus* or *Otocompsa jocosa*), from the family *Pycnonotidae.* Both varieties are native to India. See note 88.16–21.

313.24 Chinese nightingales—the red-billed leiothrix (*L. lutea*) are also called the Chinese robin or Chinese nightingale; from the family *Timaliidae.* The bird is commonly caged and is prized for its melodic singing. See note 88.16–21 and 152.10.

313.25 Persian falcon—shahbaz, the symbol of Iran under Cyrus II

(590/580–529 BCE), was a bird; the term translates as "royal falcon." The prefix, *shah*, from the Persian, means "king." Falcons are predatory birds in the *Falconidae* family. See note 88.16–21.

313.26 saw the sand turn green—see notes 23.10, 31.13, and 262.3.

313.27 man-o'-war—see notes 19.6, 43.18, and 65.15.

314.2 nightjars, finches, swallows—see notes 88.16–21 and 242.15.

314.4 fort—see notes 28.21, 32.5, 32.6, 34.21, 39.21, 43.1, 43.10, 43.13, 81.19–20, 92.12–13, 99.21–100.5, and 100.9.

314.7 both navies—the British and French. See notes 28.21, 31.26–27, 32.5, 32.6, 34.21, 43.1, 43.10, 81.19–20, 84.1, 92.12–13, 99.21–100.5, and 100.9.

314.12; 21 Mars—Roman god of war and protector of Rome. The planet Mars is fourth from the Sun with two attendant moons, Phobos and Deimos, the progeny of Mars and Venus, according to legend. See notes 14.5, 95.12, and 206.17.

314.18 Redcoat—see notes 90.13, 208.10, and 209.24.

314.27–315.1 Frenchmen / and British listening in their separate cemeteries—the military cemetery at Morne Fortune, first opened in 1782, includes both French and British soldiers and even a number of colonial governors. The governors are all British: Major General David Stewart (1772–1829), Major General George Mackie (1777–1831), Major General James Farquaharson (1775–1834), Sir Harry Thompson (1857–1902), and Sir Ira Simmons (1917–1974). The section where the British colonial governors are buried is well maintained and overlooks Castries Harbor; it is located behind several buildings, which are now a part of Sir Arthur Lewis Community College, on the road approaching the Morne. The French cemetery fell into disrepair after the British "won" St. Lucia ultimately; all the French markers, monuments, and aboveground tombs have been removed or have decayed into the earth. See notes 42.20 and 58.20.

315.7 The Battle of the Saints—see notes 28.21, 31.26–27, 32.5, 32.6, 34.21, 43.1, 43.10, 81.19–20, 84.1, 92.12–13, 99.21–100.5, and 100.9.

315.9 Rodney—see notes 28.21, 32.5, 32.6, 34.21, 39.21, 43.1, 43.10, 43.13, 79.18, 81.19–20, 81.21, 92.12–13, 99.21–100.5, and 100.9.

315.11 Croix de Guerre—French for "War Cross," a French military award for bravery in service of the French nation during World Wars I and II, though the recipient need not be a French citizen. It is an equal-sided Maltese cross, hung from a ribbon, with crossed blades and the female head of the French Republic on one side, suggestive of the figure of Marianne.

315.24 Iounalo—see notes 5.2, 92.5, and 92.15.

CHAPTER LXIII

316.9 new Helen—see notes 8.9, 11.4, 17.5–6, 24.6, 34.20, 35.18, 36.21, 62.27, 153.1, and 298.9.

316.13–15 Statics . . . Maljo Didier—see notes 9.12, 104.11, and 105.13–14.

316.14 migrant picker—migrant farm laborers harvest the citrus and sugarcane crops grown in Florida, particularly in central Florida surrounding Lake Okeechobee. The U.S. State Department issues Caribbean migrants nonimmigrant one-year worker H2-A visas (for temporary agricultural workers). These employees are paid wages significantly below the national standard. Generally growers shortchange workers by underestimating the amount of harvested produce or cane, since the workers are paid by the weight rather than by their time in the fields. Walcott refers to Florida citrus in his "In a Green Night."

317.8; 16; 20 Statics—see notes 9.12, 104.11, and 105.13–14.

317.8 Cherokee—see notes 177.4, 178.6, and 207.16.

317.18 Choctaw—see notes 177.4, 177.8–9, and 177.20.

318.1 Helen—see notes 8.9, 11.4, 17.5–6, 24.6, 34.20, 35.18, 36.21, 62.27, 153.1, and 298.9.

318.16 *songez*—French, meaning "to consider or muse over a subject, idea, or object."

318.19 chanterelle—also chantrelle, chant wèl, or chantwell; a female singer of the Belaire or Bèlè, a folk dance of social satire, comment, or praise, common in St. Lucia, Dominica, and Trinidad. The singers and dancers are all women, whereas the drummers are usually men. The dancer sometimes dances in a backward direction and communicates with the drummer through gestures and movement to change or call for a particular beat. See note 107.4–6.

318.20 the river griot, the Sioux shaman—see notes 146.18, 164.16, 164.21, 175.12, 176.3, 176.6, 180.18, 181.16–17, 182.10, and 182.15.

318.21 harp—see note 190.21.

319.6 sybil—see note 58.5.

319.9–10 swift—see notes 8.3, 88.21, 239.16, and 242.15.

319.14 meridian—see note 189.1.

320.6 laurier-cannelles-see note 3.4.

CHAPTER LXIV

320.7–16 I sang of quiet Achille, Afolabe's son. . . . I sang our wide country, the Caribbean Sea—epic invocation; a convention of the epic tradition, usually at the opening of the poem, when the poet summons the muses or gods for inspiration. The poet utters the phrase "I sang" or "Sing in me" and describes the journey in brief. Walcott's invocation most profoundly engages with that of Aimé Césaire's (1913–2008) litany of refusal, a description of rejecting European forms as the norm, in his *Notebook of a Return to the Native Land*. In the last line of "The Schooner Flight," Shabine is described as singing of the sea. See notes 6.1, 8.4, 8.9, 10.25, 16.14–16, 24.6, 83.20, 146.15–16, 150.12, 175.13–14, 228.25, 296.2, and 298.9.

321.6 Choiseul—see notes 248.21 and 269.1–2.

322.1 the Halcyon—the name of a bird in ancient Greek myth, linked with the solstice. As an adjective, "halcyon" evokes serenity.

322.6 madras—a gauzy, light fabric made of cotton; commonly used for turbans or hairstyling. The term is identified with the Indian city of Madras on the Bay of Bengal. This city, now known as Chennai, was famous for exporting such fabric. See note 156.8.

322.18 *Ville de Paris*—see notes 28.21, 32.5, 32.6, 34.21, 39.21, 43.1, 43.10, 81.19–20, 81.21, 92.12–13, 99.21–100.5, and 100.9.

322.24 alabaster Hellas—a type of white luminous mineral or gypsum that is used in creating forms, particularly in the ancient world. It is often associated with or mistaken for marble. Hellas is the antiquated Greek name for Greece.

323.4 Troy—see notes 3.2, 6.1, 8.9, 14.5, 16.14–15, 17.5–6, 24.6, and 31.4.

323.4 Menelaus—see notes 17.5–6, 24.6, and 34.20.

323.5 Agamemnon—see notes 34.20, 35.18, 152.14–15, and 298.9.

323.6 Helen—see notes 8.9, 11.4, 17.5–6, 24.6, 34.20, 35.18, 36.21, 62.27, 153.1, and 298.9.

323.10 Philoctete's wound—see notes 3.2, 6.1, 8.9, 14.5, 16.14–15, 17.5–6, 24.6, and 31.4.

323.12 Achille—see notes 6.1, 8.4, 8.9, 10.25, 16.14–15, 24.6, 83.20, 146.15–16, 150.12, 175.13–14, 228.25, 296.2, 298.9, and 320.7–16.

323.16 a swift—see notes 8.3, 88.21, 239.16, and 242.15.

323.22 wooly . . . Cyclops's flock—see note 13.7.

323.25 Polyphemus—see note 13.7.

324.1; 15 mackerel—see notes 157.7 and 157.14–15.

324.4 sea fans—a type of coral; an asexual invertebrate (*Gorgonia flabellum*) shaped like a handheld fan at full extension. They are often brightly colored and are found in the shallow waters of the Caribbean.

324.5 lace—see note 82.9–10.

324.12; 23 Achilles—note spelling change. The "s" on the end of the name suggests the Greek hero. See notes 6.1, 8.4, 8.9, 10.25, 16.14–15, 24.6, 83.20, 146.15–16, 150.12, 175.13–14, 228.25, 296.2, 298.9, and 320.7–16.

324.19 *In God We Troust*—see note 8.4.

325.2 He sniffed his name in one armpit—recalls Aimé Césaire's (1913–2008) rejection of heroic performance, placing it in and comparing it to an armpit in *Notebook of a Return to the Native Land*.

325.5 No Pain—see notes 17.7 and 7.13–14.

325.6 dolphin—the common dolphinfish (*C. hippuras*), found in tropical waters and also called mahimahi, sports intense blue and green coloring with gold flecks; it is carnivorous and feeds on smaller fish.

325.7 Helen in Hector—see notes 8.9, 11.4, 16.14–15, 17.5–6, 24.6, 34.20, 35.18, 36.21, 53.4, 62.27, 153.1, and 298.9.

Bibliography

Adolf, Antony. "Contemporary Epic Novels: Walcott, Merwin, Carson and the Birth of a 'New' Genre." *EAPSU Online: A Journal Of Critical And Creative Work* 1 (2004): 159–71.

Aeschylus. *The Oresteia*. New York: Penguin, 1984.

———. *Prometheus Unbound and Other Plays*. New York: Penguin, 1961.

Alighieri, Dante. *The Divine Comedy*. New York: Alfred A. Knopf, 1995.

Allsopp, Richard, ed. *Dictionary of Caribbean English Usage*. Oxford: Oxford University Press, 1996.

Alma-Tadema, Lawrence. *A Reading from Homer*. Philadelphia Museum of Art, 1885.

Antoine-Dunne, Jean. *Time and Space in their Indissoluble Connection: Towards an Audio-Visual Caribbean Aesthetic*. Amsterdam: Rodopi, 2004.

———, ed. *Interlocking Basins of a Globe: Essays on Derek Walcott*. Leeds: Peepal Tree, 2013.

Ashcroft, Bill, Gareth Griffiths, and Helen Tiffin. *The Empire Writes Back*. New York: Routledge, 1989.

Auden, W. H. *The Shield of Achilles*. New York: Random, 1955.

Augier, Adrian. "Walcott: Our Prodigal Son." In *Saint Lucian Literature and Theatre: An Anthology of Reviews*, edited by John Robert Lee and Kendel Hyppolte, 148–50. Castries, St. Lucia: Cultural Development Foundation, 2006.

Austenfeld, Thomas. "How To Begin A New World: Dante In Walcott's *Omeros*." *South Atlantic Review* 71.3 (2006): 15–28.

Baer, William. *Literary Conversations with Derek Walcott*. Jackson: University Press of Mississippi, 1996.

Balme, Christopher B. *Decolonizing the Stage: Theatrical Syncretism and Post-Colonial Drama*. Oxford: Clarendon, 1999.

Basford, Douglas. "Sexual Desire and Cultural Memory in Three Ethnic Poets." *MELUS* 29.3–4 (2004): 243–56.

Baugh, Edward. *Derek Walcott*. New York: Cambridge University Press, 2006.

Baugh, Edward, and Colbert Nepaulsingh, eds. *Another Life: Fully Annotated*. Boulder, Colo.: Lynne Reinner, 2004.

Benítez-Rojo, Antonio. *The Repeating Island*. Translated by James Maraniss. Durham, N.C.: Duke University Press, 1996.

Bergam, Marija. "Transplantations: Vegetation Imagery In The Poetry Of Derek Walcott And Lorna Goodison." *European Journal Of English Studies* 16.2 (2012): 113–24.

Bery, Ashok, and Patricia Murray. *Comparing Postcolonial Literatures Fiction: Dislocations.* London: Macmillan, 2000.

Birbalsingh, Frank. *Frontiers of Caribbean Literature in English.* London: Macmillan Caribbean, 1996.

Bloom, Harold. *Derek Walcott.* Philadelphia: Chelsea House, 2003.

Bobb, June D. *Beating a Restless Drum: The Poetics of Kamau Brathwaite and Derek Walcott.* Trenton, N.J.: Africa World Press, 1998.

Boeninger, Stephanie Pocock. "'I Have Become The Sea's Craft': Authorial Subjectivity in Derek Walcott's *Omeros* and David Dabydeen's 'Turner.'" *Contemporary Literature* 52.3 (2011): 462–92.

Bond, James. *The Birds of the West Indies.* 2nd ed. New York: Houghton Mifflin, 1971.

Boyagoda, Anna. "'Why Should He Be Here, Why Should They Have Come At All?' Transnational Community in Derek Walcott's *Omeros.*" *Atenea* 27.1 (2007): 79–92.

Brathwaite, Kamau. *The Arrivants: A New World Trilogy.* Oxford: Oxford University Press, 1996.

———. "Timehri." In *Is Massa Day Dead?: Black Moods in the Caribbean,* edited by Orde Coombs, 30–44. New York: Anchor Books, 1974.

Breen, Henry H. *St. Lucia: Historical, Statistical, and Descriptive.* London: Longman, Brown, Green, and Longmans, 1844.

Breiner, Laurence A. *An Introduction to West Indian Poetry.* New York: Cambridge University Press, 1998.

Breslin, Paul. "Derek Walcott's 'Reversible World': Centers, Peripheries, and the Scale of Nature." *Callaloo* 28 (2005): 8–24.

———. *Nobody's Nation: Reading Derek Walcott.* Chicago: University of Chicago Press, 2001.

Brontë, Charlotte. *Jane Eyre.* New York: Penguin, 2009.

Brown, Stewart. *The Art of Derek Walcott.* Chester Springs, Pa.: Dufour, 1991.

Bruckner, D.J.R. "A Poem in Homage to an Unwanted Man." *New York Times,* October 9, 1990. Accessed June 13, 2014. http://www.nytimes.com.

Bryce, Jane. "Riffing on *Omeros*: The Relevance Of Isaac Julien to Cultural Politics in the Caribbean." *Small Axe: A Caribbean Journal Of Criticism* 32 (2010): 83–96.

Burian, Peter. "All that Greek Manure under the Green Bananas: Derek Walcott's *Odyssey.*" *South Atlantic Quarterly* 96.2 (1997): 359–77.

Burkitt, Katharine. *Literary Form as Postcolonial Critique: Epic Proportions.* Burlington, Vt.: Ashgate, 2012.

Burnett, Paula. "The Island as Self as World Text in the Work of Derek Walcott and Romesh Gunesekera." In *Routes of the Roots*, edited by Isabella Maria Zoppi, 289–301. Rome: Bulzoni, 1998.

———. "Walcott's Intertextual Method: Non-Greek Naming in *Omeros*." *Callaloo* 28.1 (2005): 171–87.

———. *Derek Walcott: Politics and Poetics*. Gainesville: University Press of Florida, 2000.

Byron, George Gordon. *Don Juan*. Boston: Philip, Sampson & Co, 1858.

Cabet, Étienne. *Voyage en Icarie*. Paris: Bureau du Populaire, 1845.

Callahan, Lance. *In the Shadows of Divine Perfection: Derek Walcott's Omeros*. New York: Routledge, 2003.

Campbell, Danny. *The Trinidad Theatre Workshop: Pioneers and Premières: The Danny Campbell Photograph Collection*. Glencoe, Trinidad; Washington, D.C.: Jett Samm, 1999.

Canny, Nicholas. *The Oxford History of the British Empire*. New York: Oxford University Press, 1998.

Carrigan, Anthony. "Preening With Privilege, Bubbling Bilge: Representations Of Cruise Tourism in Paule Marshall's *Praisesong For The Widow* And Derek Walcott's *Omeros*." *Isle: Interdisciplinary Studies In Literature And Environment* 14.1 (2007): 143–59.

Casteel, Sarah Phillips. "Autobiography as Rewriting: Derek Walcott's *Another Life* and *Omeros*." *Journal of Commonwealth Literature* 34.2 (1999): 9–32.

———. "'One Elegy From Aruac To Sioux': The Absent Presence of Indigeneity in Derek Walcott's Poetry and Drama." *Canadian Review Of Comparative Literature/Revue Canadienne De Littérature Comparée* 38.1 (2011): 106–18.

Césaire, Aimé. *Notebook of a Return to the Native Land*. Translated by A. James Arnold and Clayton Eshleman. Middleton, Conn.: Wesleyan University Press, 2013.

Chamberlain, Edward. *Come Back to Me My Language: Poetry in the West Indies*. Toronto: McClelland and Stewart, 1993.

Chrysostom, Dio. *Dio Chrysostom*. 5 vols. Cambridge: Harvard University Press, 1971.

Cimarosti, Roberta. *Mapping Memory: An Itinerary through Derek Walcott's Poetics*. Milano: Cisalpino, 2004.

Ciocia, Stefania. "To Hell and Back: The Katabasis and the Impossibility of Epic in Derek Walcott's *Omeros*." *Journal Of Commonwealth Literature* 35.2 (2000): 87–103.

Coggins, John, and D. S. Lewis, eds. *Political Parties of the Americas & the Caribbean*. London: Longman, 1992.

Collins, Loretta. "'We Shall All Heal': Ma Kilman, the Obeah Woman, as Mother-Healer in Derek Walcott's *Omeros*." *Literature And Medicine* 14.1 (1995): 146–62.

Condé, Maryse. *Crossing the Mangrove*. New York: Anchor, 1995.

Conlon, Raymond. "D. L. Macdonald's 'Derek Walcott's Don Juans': Walcott's Debt to Tirso De Molina." *Connotations: A Journal For Critical Debate* 6.1 (1996): 123–29.

Conrad, Joseph. *Heart of Darkness*. New York: Norton, 2005.

Creighton, Al. "The Metaphor of the Theater in *The Four Banks of the River of Space*." *Callaloo* 18 (1995): 71–82.

D'Aguiar, Fred. "In God We Troust: Derek Walcott and God." *Callaloo* 28.1 (2005): 216–23.

Darwin, Charles. *The Origin of Species*. New York: Signet, 2003.

Dasenbrock, Reed Way. "Why the Post in Post-Colonial Is Not the Post in Post-Modern: Homer-Dante-Pound-Walcott." *Paideuma: A Journal Devoted To Ezra Pound Scholarship* 29.1–2 (2000): 111–22.

Da Vinci, Leonardo. *Virgin of the Rocks*. Louvre, ca. 1483–86.

Davis, Gregson. *The Poetics of Derek Walcott*. Durham, N.C.: Duke University Press, 1997.

Davy, John. *The West Indies Before and Since Slave Emancipation*. London: Frank Cass, 1971.

DeLoughrey, Elizabeth, and George B. Handley, eds. *Postcolonial Ecologies: Literatures of the Environment*. Oxford: Oxford University Press, 2011.

DeLoughrey, Elizabeth, Renée K. Gosson, and George B. Handley, eds. *Caribbean Literature and the Environment: Between Nature and Culture*. Charlottesville: University of Virginia Press, 2005.

Devaux, Robert J. *Saint Lucia Historic Sites*. Castries: Saint Lucia National Trust, 1975.

De Vere, Aubrey. *Selections from the Poems of Aubrey De Vere*. Washington, D.C.: Library of Congress, 1894.

Dick, Rhona. "Remembering Breen's Encomium: 'Classic Style,' History and Tradition in Derek Walcott's *Omeros*." *Journal Of Commonwealth Literature* 35.2 (2000): 105–15.

Dickinson, Emily. *The Collected Poems of Emily Dickinson*. New York: Barnes and Noble, 2003.

Dodman, David. "A Place or a People? Social and Cultural Geographies of the Anglophone Caribbean." *Social and Cultural Geography* 8.1 (2007): 143–50.

Döring, Tobias. *Caribbean-English Passage: Intertexuality in a Postcolonial Tradition*. New York: Routledge, 2002.

Dougherty, Carol. "Homer after *Omeros*: Reading a H/Omeric Text." *South Atlantic Quarterly* 96 (1997): 335–57.

Doyle, Arthur Conan. "J. Habakuk Jephson's Statement." In *Master Sea Stories*, edited by Austin Philips, Gordon Stair, and W. Clark Russell. New York: E. J. Clode, 1929.

Duchamp, Marcel. *The Bride Stripped Bare by Her Bachelors, Even (The Large Glass)*. Philadelphia Museum of Art, 1915–23.

Dwight, Timothy, and Julian Hawthorne, eds. *The World's Great Classics*. 56 vols. New York: Colonial Press, 1899–1902.

Eastley, Aaron C. "Lifting 'The Yoke of the Wrong Name': How Walcott Uses Character Names to Negotiate a Positive Afro-Caribbean Diasporic Identity in *Omeros*." *African Diasporas: Ancestors, Migrations and Boundaries* (2008): 70–79.

Eliot, T. S. *The Annotated Wasteland*. New Haven: Yale University Press, 2005.

———. *Four Quartets*. New York: Harcourt Brace, 1943.

Ellison, Ralph. *Invisible Man*. New York: Signet, 1995.

Emerson, Ralph Waldo. *The Concord Hymn and Other Poems*. New York: Dover, 1996.

Erickson, Peter. "Artists' Self-Portraiture and Self-Exploration in Derek Walcott's *Tiepolo's Hound*." *Callaloo* 28.1 (2005): 224–35.

Euripedes. *Cyclops*. Oxford: Oxford University Press, 2001.

———. *Iphigenia at Aulis*. Adapted by Donald Richardson. Lanham, Md.: University Press of America, 1988.

———. *Ten Plays*. New York: Bantam, 2001.

Farrell, Joseph. "Walcott's *Omeros*: The Classical Epic in a Postmodern World." *South Atlantic Quarterly* 96 (1997): 247–73.

Farrier, David. "Charting The 'Amnesiac Atlantic': Chiastic Cartography And Caribbean Epic In Derek Walcott's *Omeros*." *Journal Of Commonwealth Literature* 38.1 (2003): 23–38.

Figueroa, Víctor. "Encomium of Helen: Derek Walcott's Ethical Twist in *Omeros*." *Twentieth Century Literature: A Scholarly And Critical Journal* 53.1 (2007): 23–39.

———. *Not at Home in One's Home: Caribbean Self-Fashioning in the Poetry of Luis Palés Matos, Aimé Césaire, and Derek Walcott*. Madison, N.J.: Fairleigh Dickinson University Press, 2009.

Fitzgerald, F. Scott. *The Great Gatsby*. New York: Scribner, 2004.

Frank, David, ed. *Kwéyòl Dictionary*. Castries, St. Lucia: Ministry of Education, 2001.

Friedman, Rachel. "Derek Walcott's Odysseys." *International Journal of the Classical Tradition* 14 (2007): 455–80.

Fumagalli, Maria Cristina. "Derek Walcott's *Omeros* and Dante's *Commedia*: Epics of the Self and Journeys into Language." *Cambridge Quarterly* 29.1 (2000): 17–36.

———. *The Flight of the Vernacular: Seamus Heaney, Derek Walcott and the Impress of Dante*. Amsterdam; New York: Rodopi, 2001.

Fumagalli, Maria Cristina, and Peter L. Patrick. "Two Healing Narratives: Suffering, Reintegration, and the Struggle of Language." *Small Axe: A Caribbean Journal of Criticism* 20 (2006): 61–79.

Gachet F.M.I., Charles. *A History of The Roman Catholic Church in St. Lucia.* Castries, St. Lucia: Infinity, n.d.

Garland, Marie Tudor. *The Marriage Feast.* New York: Putnam, 1920.

Garvey, Marcus. "Keep Cool." In *Penguin Book of Caribbean Verse in English,* edited by Paula Burnett, 22. London: Penguin, 2006.

Gibbon, Edward. *Critical Observations on the Sixth Book of the Aeneid.* London: 1770.

———. *The Decline and Fall of the Roman Empire.* Hertfordshire, U.K.: Wordsworth, 1998.

Gidmark, Jill B., and Anthony Hunt. "Catherine Weldon: Derek Walcott's Visionary Telling of History." *CEA Critic: An Official Journal of the College English Association* 59.1 (1996): 8–20.

Gifford, Don, and Robert J. Seidman. *Ulysses Annotated: Notes for James Joyce's Ulysses.* Berkeley: University of California Press, 1988.

Gikandi, Simon. *Writing in Limbo: Modernism and Caribbean Literature.* Ithaca, N.Y.: Cornell University Press, 1992.

Gill, Dennis. *Commemorative Booklet in Honour of Mr. Derek Alton Walcott.* St. Mary's College, St. Lucia, West Indies, 1992.

Gilroy, Paul. *The Black Atlantic: Modernity and Double Consciousness.* Cambridge: Harvard University Press, 1993.

Glissant, Édouard. *The Poetics of Relation.* Translated by Betsy Wing. Ann Arbor: University of Michigan Press, 1997.

Gray, Jeffrey. "Walcott's Traveler and the Problem of Witness." *Callaloo* 28.1 (2005): 117–28.

Graziosi, Barbara, and Emily Greenwood. *Homer in the Twentieth Century: Between World Literature and the Western Canon.* Oxford: Oxford University Press, 2007.

Greenwood, Emily. *Afro-Greeks: Dialogues between Anglophone Caribbean Literature and Classics in the Twentieth Century.* Oxford: Oxford University Press, 2010.

———. "'Still Going On': Temporal Adverbs and the View of the Past in Walcott's Poetry." *Callaloo* 28.1 (2005): 132–45.

Hamilton, Edith. *Mythology.* New York: Signet, 1969.

Hamner, Robert D. *Critical Perspectives on Derek Walcott.* Boulder-London: Lynne Rienner, 1997.

———. *Derek Walcott.* New York: Twayne, 1993.

———. *Epic of the Dispossessed: Derek Walcott's Omeros.* Columbia: University of Missouri Press, 1997.

———. "From Winslow Homer to Marcel Duchamp and the Fortunate Flaw in Derek Walcott's '*Omeros*.'" *ARIEL: A Review of International English Literature* 31.3 (2000): 75–103.

———. "*The Odyssey*: Derek Walcott's Dramatization of Homer's *Odyssey*." *ARIEL: A Review of International English Literature* 24.4 (1993): 101–8.

Handley, George B. *New World Poetics: Nature and the Adamic Imagination of Whitman, Neruda, and Walcott*. Athens: University of Georgia Press, 2007.

Harmsen, Jolien, Guy Ellis, and Robert Devaux. *A History of St. Lucia*. Vieux Fort, St. Lucia: Lighthouse, 2012.

Harnett, William Michael. *Still-Life—Violin and Music*, Metropolitan Museum of Art, 1888.

H.D. *Helen in Egypt*. New York: New Directions, 1974.

Heaney, Seamus. *The Cure at Troy: A Version of Sophocles' Philoctetes*. New York: Noonday, 1991.

———. *The Government of the Tongue*. New York: Farrar, Straus and Giroux, 1989.

———. *New Selected Poems*. New York: Farrar, Straus and Giroux, 1990.

Heller, Ben A. "Landscape, Femininity, and Caribbean Discourse." *MLN* 111.2 (1996): 391–416.

Henriksen, Line. *Ambition and Anxiety: Ezra Pound's Cantos and Derek Walcott's Omeros as Twentieth-Century Epics*. Amsterdam: Rodopi, 2006.

Henriksen, Line. "'Big Poems Burn Women': Fredy Neptune's Democratic Sailor and Walcott's Epic *Omeros*." *Australian Literary Studies* 20.2 (2001): 87–109.

———. "Who Is F***ing Helen? Representation of Bodies and Voices in Derek Walcott's *Omeros* and Tony Harrison's *V*." *World Literature Written in English* 39.1 (2001): 86–96.

Hesiod. *The Epics of Hesiod*. London: Whittaker, 1861.

Hill, Geoffrey. *New and Collected Poems: 1952–1992*. New York: Mariner, 2000.

Hines, Derrek, ed. *Gilgamesh*. London: Anchor, 2002.

Hirsch, Edward. "An Interview with Derek Walcott." In *Conversations with Derek Walcott*, 50–64. Jackson: University Press of Mississippi, 1996. [rpt. from *Contemporary Literature* 20 (1977): 279–92].

Hobbes, Thomas. *Leviathan*. Cambridge: Cambridge University Press, 1996.

Hoegberg, David E. "The Anarchist's Mirror: Walcott's *Omeros* and the Epic Tradition." *Commonwealth Essays And Studies* 17.2 (1995): 67–81.

Hofmeister, Timothy. "From Homer to *Omeros*: Derek Walcott's *Omeros* and *Odyssey*." *Classical World* 93.1 (1999): 7–27.

Hogan, Patrick Colm. *Colonialism and Cultural Identity: Crises of Tradition in the Anglophone Literatures of India, Africa, and the Caribbean*. New York: State University of New York Press, 2000.

Homer. *The Iliad*. Translated by Robert Fitzgerald. New York: Farrar, Straus and Giroux, 2004.

———. *The Odyssey*. Translated by Robert Fitzgerald. New York: Anchor, 1989.

Homer, Winslow. *The Gulf Stream*. The Metropolitan Museum of Art, 1899.

Hoyle, Fred. *The Black Cloud*. New York: Signet, 1959.

Hurston, Zora Neale. *Mules and Men*. Philadelphia: Lippincott, 1935.

Ismond, Patricia. *Abandoning Dead Metaphors: The Caribbean Phase of Derek Walcott's Poetry*. Kingston, Jamaica: University of the West Indies Press, 2001.

Jaji, Tsitsi. "The Name of the Father, the Name of the Son, and the Name of the Homeric Spirit in Derek Walcott's *Omeros*." *Torre: Revista De La Universidad De Puerto Rico* 10.36–37 (2005): 175–88.

James, Winston. *A Fierce Hatred of Injustice: Claude McKay's Jamaican Poetry of Rebellion*. New York: Verso, 2001.

Jay, Paul. "Fated to Unoriginality: The Politics of Mimicry in Derek Walcott's *Omeros*." *Callaloo* 29.2 (2006): 545–59.

Jesse, Rev. C. *Outlines of St. Lucia's History*. Castries: St. Lucia Archaeological & Historical Society, 1964.

Johnson, Lemuel A. "The Inventions of Paradise: The Caribbean and the Utopian Bent." *Poetics Today* 15.4 (1994): 685–724.

Josie, Peter. *Shattered Dreams: A Political Odyssey in Post-Independence St. Lucia*. Gros Islet, St. Lucia: Star Publishing, 2012.

Joyce, James. *The Critical Writings of James Joyce*, edited by Richard Ellmann and Ellsworth Mason. New York: Viking, 1959.

———. *Dubliners*. New York: Random, 2000.

———. *Finnegans Wake*. New York: Penguin, 1999.

———. *A Portrait of the Artist as a Young Man*. New York: Viking, 1964.

———. *Ulysses: The Corrected Text*. Edited by Hans Walter Gabler, with Wolfhard Steppe and Claus Melchior. New York: Random, 1986.

Kahane, Meir. *Never Again: A Program for Survival*. New York: Nash, 1971.

Keats, John. *The Odes of John Keats*, edited by Helen Vendler. New York: Belknap, 1985.

Keith, Allan R. *The Birds of St. Lucia*. Tring, Herts, U.K.: Natural History Museum and British Ornithologists Union, 1997.

Keizer, Arlene R. *Black Subjects: Identity Formation in the Contemporary Narrative of Slavery*. Ithaca: Cornell University Press, 2004.

King, Bruce. *Derek Walcott and West Indian Drama: Not Only a Playwright but a Company, the Trinidad Theatre Workshop, 1959–1993*. Oxford: Oxford University Press, 1995.

———. *Derek Walcott: A Caribbean Life*. Oxford: Oxford University Press, 2000.

Kipling, Rudyard. *Selected Works of Rudyard Kipling*. New York: Black, 1936.

Knox, Bernard. "Achilles in the Caribbean." *New York Review of Books*. March 7, 1991. Accessed June 13, 2014. http://www.nybooks.com.

Kraus, Joe. "Through Loins and Coins: Derek Walcott's Weaving of the West In-dian Federation." *Callaloo* 28.1 (2005): 60–74.

Lagapa, Jason. "Swearing at—not by—History: Obscenity, Picong and Irony in Derek Walcott's Poetry." *College Literature* 35.2 (2008): 104–25.

Larsen, Svend Erik. "Memory Constructions and Their Limits." *Orbis Litterarum: International Review Of Literary Studies* 66.6 (2011): 448–67.

Lawrence, T. E., trans. *The Odyssey*. Oxford: Oxford University Press, 1991.

———. *Seven Pillars of Wisdom*. New York: Doubleday, 1935.

Lee, John Robert. *Bibliography of St. Lucian Creative Writing*. Castries, St. Lucia: Mahanaim Publishing and Cultural Development Foundation, 2013.

Lefkowitz, Mary. "Bringing Him Back Alive." *New York Times*, October 7, 1990. Accessed June 13, 2014. http://www.nytimes.com.

Lernout, Geert. "Derek Walcott's *Omeros*: The Isle Is Full of Voices." *Kunapipi* 14.2 (1992): 90–104.

Lester, Julius, ed. *Black Folk Tales*. New York: Grove Atlantic, 1969.

Loreto, Paola. *The Crowning of a Poet's Quest: Derek Walcott's Tiepolo's Hound*. Am-sterdam: Rodopi, 2009.

Low, Gail. *Publishing the Postcolonial: Anglophone West African and Caribbean Writing in the UK, 1948–1968*. London: Routledge, 2011.

Lucas, John. "The Sea, the Sea." *New Statesman & Society* 3 (October 5, 1990): 36.

Macauley, Thomas Babington. *History of England*. New York: Penguin, 1979.

———. *Lays of Ancient Rome*. London: Cassell, 1892.

MacDonald, D. L. "Derek Walcott's Don Juans: A Postilla." *Connotations: A Jour-nal For Critical Debate* 6.1 (1996): 103–10.

Makris, Paula. "Beyond the Classics: Legacies of Colonial Education in C.L.R. James And Derek Walcott." *Revista/Review Interamericana* 31 (2001): 1–4.

Mandrell, James. "Response To D. L. Macdonald's 'Postilla': The One and the Same Redux." *Connotations: A Journal For Critical Debate* 6.1 (1996): 111–22.

Marshall, Woodville K. "St. Lucia in the Economic History of the Windward Islands: The 19th Century Experience." *Caribbean Quarterly* 35.3 (1989): 25–33.

Martyniuk, Irene. "The Irish in the Caribbean: Derek Walcott's Examination of the Irish in *Omeros*." *South Carolina Review* 32.1 (1999): 142–48.

Matos, Nicole. "'Join, Interchangeable Phantoms': From Metaphor to Metonymy in Walcott's Omeros." *Small Axe: A Caribbean Journal Of Criticism* 20 (2006): 40–60.

Mayakovsky, Vladimir. *Selected Poems*. Chicago: Northwestern University Press, 2013.

McCrae, John. *In Flanders Field and Other Poems*. New York: G. P. Putnam Sons, 1919.

McGarrity, Maria. "The Gulf Stream and the Epic Drives of Joyce and Walcott." *ARIEL: A Review Of International English Literature* 34.4 (2003): 1–20.

———. *Washed by the Gulf Stream: The Historic and Geographic Relation of Irish and Caribbean Literature.* Newark: University of Delaware Press, 2008.

McKinsey, Martin. *Hellenism and the Postcolonial Imagination: Yeats, Cavafy, Walcott.* Madison, N.J.: Fairleigh Dickinson University Press, 2010.

———. "Missing Sounds and Mutable Meanings: Names in Derek Walcott's *Omeros.*" *Callaloo* 31.3 (2008): 891–902.

McLaughlin, James. *My Friend the Indian.* New York: Houghton Mifflin, 1910.

McMorris, Mark. "Discrepant Affinities in Caribbean Poetry: Tradition and Demotic Modernism." *Contemporary Literature* 47 (2006): 505–22.

McWatt, Mark. *Derek Walcott: An Island Poet and His Sea.* Oxfordshire: Carfax, 1988.

Meerzon, Yana. *Performing Exile, Performing Self: Drama, Theatre, Film.* Basingstoke: Palgrave Macmillan, 2012.

Melas, Natalie. *All the Difference in the World: Postcoloniality and the Ends of Comparison.* Stanford: Stanford University Press, 2007.

———. "Forgettable Vacations and Metaphor in Ruins: Walcott's *Omeros.*" *Callaloo* 28.1 (2005): 147–68.

Melville, Herman. *Moby Dick: Or, The Whale.* New York: Penguin, 2001.

Milton, John. *Paradise Lost.* London: Folio, 1991.

Minkler, Julie A. "Helen's Caliban: A Study of Gender Hierarchy in Derek Walcott's *Omeros.*" *World Literature Today* 67.2 (1993): 272–76.

Moffett, Joe. "On Chapter XLV Of Derek Walcott's *Omeros.*" *Notes on Contemporary Literature* 38.2 (2008): 6–8.

———. "'Master, I Was the Freshest of All Your Readers': Derek Walcott's *Omeros* and Homer As Literary Origin." *Lit: Literature Interpretation Theory* 16.1 (2005): 1–23.

Molière [Jean-Baptiste Poquelin]. *Don Juan and Other Plays.* London: Nick Hern, 1997.

Monet, Claude. *Les Nympheas.* Musée de L'Orangerie, 1918–26.

Moore, Thomas. *The Poetical Words of Thomas Moore,* edited by A. D. Godley. Oxford: Oxford University Press, 1929.

Mozart, Wolfgang Amadeus. *Mozart's Don Giovanni.* New York: Dover, 1985.

Murnaghan, Sheila, and Deborah H. Roberts. "Penelope's Song: The Lyric Odysseys of Linda Pastan and Louise Glück." *Classical and Modern Literature: A Quarterly* 22.1 (2002): 1–33.

Naipaul, V. S. *A Bend in the River.* New York: Vintage, 1989.

Nair, Rukmini Bhaya. *Lying on the Postcolonial Couch: The Idea of Difference.* Minneapolis: University of Minnesota Press, 2002.

Nettleford, Rex. "The Caribbean: The Cultural Imperative." *Caribbean Quarterly* 35.3 (1989): 4–15.

New England Primer. Albany, N.Y.: Joel Munsell's Sons, 1885.

Nwosu, Maik. "Derek Walcott's *Omeros* and the Refiguration of the Caribbean Eden." *Journal of Postcolonial Writing* 44.2 (2008): 127–37.

Oakley, Seanna Sumalee. *Common Places: The Poetics of African Atlantic Postromantics*. Amsterdam: Rodopi, 2011.

O'Keeffe, Georgia. *Black Mesa Landscape, New Mexico/Out Back of Marie's II*. Georgia O'Keeffe Museum, 1930.

Okpewho, Isidore. "Walcott, Homer, and the 'Black Atlantic.'" *Research in African Literatures* 33.1 (2002): 27–44.

Olaniyan, Tejumola. *Scars of conquest/masks of Resistance: The Invention of Cultural Identities in African, African-American, and Caribbean Drama*. New York: Oxford University Press, 1995.

Ovid. *The Metamorphoses*. New York: Penguin, 2004.

Owens, Wilfred. *The Complete Poems*, edited by C. Day Lewis. New York: New Directions, 1965.

Paquet, Sandra Pouchet. *Caribbean Autobiography: Cultural Identity and Self-Representation*. Madison: University of Wisconsin Press, 2002.

Paravisini-Gebert, Lizabeth. *Literature of the Caribbean*. Westport, Conn.: Greenwood, 2008.

Parker, Michael, and Starkey, Roger. *Post-Colonial Literatures: Achebe, Ngugi, Walcott and Desai*. New York: Palgrave Macmillan, 1995.

Paul, Jay. "Fated to Unoriginality: The Politics of Mimicry in Derek Walcott's *Omeros*." *Callaloo* 29.2 (2006): 545–59.

Peyma, Nasser Dasht. *Postcolonial Drama: A Comparative Study of Wole Soyinka, Derek Walcott, and Girish Karnad*. Jaipur: Rawat Publications, 2009.

Phillips, Caryl. *A New World Order: Selected Essays*. London: Vintage, 2002.

Pollack, Eileen. *Woman Walking Ahead: In Search of Catherine Weldon and Sitting Bull*. Albuquerque: University of New Mexico Press, 2002.

Pollard, Charles W. *New World Modernisms: T. S. Eliot, Derek Walcott, and Kamau Brathwaite*. Charlottesville: University of Virginia Press, 2004.

Pound, Ezra. *The Cantos*. New York: New Directions, 1956.

Prince, Mary. *A History of Mary Prince*. New York: Penguin, 2001.

Questel, Victor D. *List of One Hundred Essays by Derek Walcott as they Appeared in the Guardian for the Year 1964*. St. Augustine, Trinidad and Tobago: Victor Questel, 1972.

Ramazani, Jahan. *The Hybrid Muse: Postcolonial Poetry in English*. Chicago: University of Chicago Press, 2001.

———. "The Wound Of History: Walcott's *Omeros* and the Postcolonial Poetics of Affliction." *PMLA: Publications Of The Modern Language Association Of America* 112.3 (1997): 405–17.

Rankine, Patrice D. "Black Is, Black Ain't: Classical Reception and Nothingness in Ralph Ellison, Derek Walcott and Wole Soyinka." *Revue De Littérature Comparée* 4.344 (2012): 457.

Reiss, Timothy J. "Caribbean Knights: Quijote, Galahad, and the Telling of History." *Studies in the Novel* 29.3 (1997): 297–322.

Rembrandt [Harmenszoo Van Rijn]. *Night Watch*. Rijksmuseum, 1642.

Reynolds, Anderson. *The Struggle for Survival: An Historical, Political and Socioeconomic Perspective of St. Lucia*. Castries, St. Lucia: Jako, 2003.

Roberts, Adam. "Dropping The 'H': Derek Walcott's *Omeros* (1990)." *English: The Journal Of The English Association* 51.199 (2002): 45–61.

Robertson, Claire. "Claiming Freedom: Abolition and Identity in St. Lucian History." *Journal of Caribbean History* 34.1–2 (2000): 89–129.

Rodman, Selden. *Tongues of Fallen Angels; Conversations with Jorge Luis Borges, Robert Frost, Ernest Hemingway, Pablo Neruda, Stanley Kunitz, Gabriel García Márquez, Octavio Paz, Norman Mailer, Allen Ginsberg, Vinícius De Moraes, João Cabral De Melo Neto [and] Derek Walcott*. New York: New Directions, 1974.

Rohlehr, Frederick Gordon. *Withering into Truth: A Review of Derek Walcott's The Gulf and Other Poems*. St. Augustine, Trinidad and Tobago, 1969.

Rotella, Guy L. *Castings: Monuments and Monumentality in Poems by Elizabeth Bishop, Robert Lowell, James Merrill, Derek Walcott, and Seamus Heaney*. Nashville: Vanderbilt University Press, 2004.

Saint-Gaudens, Augustus. *Monument to Robert Gould Shaw and the 54th Massachusetts Regiment*. Boston, 1884–97.

Samad, Daizal R. *Cultural Imperatives in Derek Walcott's Dream on Monkey Mountain*. London: Macmillan, 1995.

Sauerberg, Lars Ole. "Repositioning Narrative: The Late-Twentieth-Century Verse Novels of Vikram Seth, Derek Walcott, Craig Raine, Anthony Burgess, and Bernadine Evaristo." *Orbis Litterarum: International Review Of Literary Studies* 59.6 (2004): 439–64.

Scanlon, Mara. "'In the Mouths of the Tribe': *Omeros* and the Heteroglossic Nation." *Bucknell Review: A Scholarly Journal Of Letters, Arts And Sciences* 43.2 (2000): 100–17.

Seacole, Mary. *Wonderful Adventures of Mrs. Seacole in Many Lands*. New York: Oxford University Press, 1990.

Seddon, S. A., and G. W. Lennon. *Trees of the Caribbean*. London: Macmillan, 1980.

———. *Flowers of the Caribbean*. London: Macmillan, 1978.

Seneca, Lucius. *L. Annaei Senecae Tragoediae: Incertorum auctorum Hercules*

(Oetaeus), Octavia. Edited by Otto Zwierlein. Oxford: Oxford University Press, 1986.

Shakespeare, William. *The Riverside Shakespeare.* 2nd ed. Edited by G. Blakemore Evans and J.J.M. Tobin. New York: Houghton Mifflin, 1996.

Simmons, Harold. *Selected Writings of Harold Simmons Manuscript.* Edited by Didacus Jules. Castries, St. Lucia, Folk Research Center.

Sinnewe, Dirk. *Divided to the Vein?: Derek Walcott's Drama and the Formation of Cultural Identities.* Würzburg: Königshausen and NeumDann, 2001.

Sophocles. *Collected Works,* edited by Mark Griffin and Glen W. Most. Chicago: University of Chicago Press, 2013.

St. Hilaire, Aonghas. "Globalization, Urbanization, and Language in Caribbean Development: The Assimilation of St. Lucia." *NWIG* 77 (2003): 65.

St. Omer, Dunstan. *Altarpiece.* Roseau Valley Church, 1973.

———. *Altarpiece/Assumption.* Church of St. Joseph the Worker, ca. 1950s.

St. Omer, Garth. *A Room on a Hill.* Leeds: Peepal Tree, 2012.

Steinbeck, John. *The Grapes of Wrath.* New York: Penguin, 2006.

Stesichorus. "Poems." In *Greek Lyric Poetry,* edited by M. L. West, 87–96. Oxford: Oxford University Press, 2008.

Stewart, Susan. "Derek Walcott's *Omeros.*" *PMLA: Publications of the Modern Language Association of America* 113.1 (1998): 130.

Strachan, Ian Gregory. *Paradise and Plantation: Tourism and Culture in the Anglophone Caribbean.* Charlottesville: University of Virginia Press, 2002.

Strachey, Lytton. *Eminent Victorians.* New York: Modern Library, 1918.

Sturge, Joseph, and Thomas Harvey. *The West Indies in 1837.* London: Hamilton Adams, 1838.

Synge, John Millington. *The Aran Islands.* Boston: John W. Luce, 1911.

Terada, Rei. *Derek Walcott's Poetry: American Mimicry.* Boston: Northeastern University Press, 1992.

Thieme, John. *Derek Walcott.* Manchester: Manchester University Press, 1999.

Thurston, Michael. *The Underworld in Twentieth-Century Literature.* New York: Palgrave, 2009.

Toews, Jennifer. *How Beautiful My Brethren and Sistren: Derek Walcott, Life and Work: An Exhibition.* Toronto: University of Toronto Library, 2011.

Tutuola, Amos. *The Palm Wine Drinkard and My Life in the Bush of Ghosts.* New York: Grove, 2005.

Tynan, Maeve. *Postcolonial Odysseys: Derek Walcott's Voyages of Homecoming.* Newcastle upon Tyne, U.K.: Cambridge Scholars, 2011.

Van Sickle, John. "The Design of Derek Walcott's *Omeros.*" *The Classical World* 93 (1999): 7–27.

Vestal, Stanley. *Sitting Bull: Champion of the Sioux.* Norman: University of Oklahoma Press, 1932.

Virgil. *The Aeneid*. New York: Vintage, 1990.

Walcott, Derek. *25 Poems*. Port of Spain, Trinidad: Guardian Commercial Printery, 1948.

———. *The Antilles: Fragments of Epic Memory*. New York: Farrar, Straus and Giroux, 1992.

———. *The Arkansas Testament*. New York: Farrar, Straus and Giroux, 1987.

———. *The Bounty*. New York: Farrar, Straus and Giroux, 1997.

———. "The Caribbean: Culture or Mimicry?" *Journal of Interamerican Studies and World Affairs* 16.1 (February 1974): 3–14.

———. *Collected Poems: 1948–1984*. New York: Farrar, Straus and Giroux, 1986.

———. *Dream on Monkey Mountain and Other Plays*. New York: Farrar, Straus and Giroux, 1970.

———. *Epitaph for the Young: XII Cantos*. Bridgetown, Barbados: Advocate, 1949.

———. *The Fortunate Traveller*. New York: Farrar, Straus and Giroux, 1981.

———. "Forty Acres: a Poem for Barack Obama." *London Times*. Accessed December 31, 2008. http://www.timesonline.co.uk.

———. *The Haitian Trilogy*. New York: Farrar, Straus and Giroux, 2002.

———. *In a Green Night*. London: Jonathan Cape, 1962.

———. "Isla Incognita." In *Caribbean Literature and the Environment: Between Nature and Culture*, edited by Elizabeth DeLoughrey, Renée K. Gosson, and George B. Handley, 51–57. Charlottesville: University of Virginia Press, 2005.

———. *The Joker of Seville and O Babylon!: Two Plays*. New York: Farrar, Straus and Giroux, 1978.

———. *Midsummer*. New York: Farrar, Straus and Giroux, 1984.

———. *Moon-child: A Play*. New York: Farrar, Straus and Giroux, 2012.

———: *O Starry Starry Night*. New York: Farrar, Straus and Giroux, 2014.

———. *Omeros*. New York: Noonday, 1990.

———. *The Odyssey: A Stage Version*. New York: Noonday, 1993.

———. *The Prodigal*. New York: Farrar, Straus and Giroux, 2004.

———. "Reflections on *Omeros*." *South Atlantic Quarterly* 96.2 (1997): 229–46.

———. "The Road Taken." In *Joseph Brodsky, Seamus Heaney, and Derek Walcott: Homage to Robert Frost*, 93–117. New York: Farrar, Straus and Giroux, 1994.

———. *The Sea at Dauphin: A Play in One Act*. Port of Spain, Trinidad: University of the West Indies, 1954.

———. *Sea Grapes*. London: Jonathan Cape, 1976.

———. *The Star-Apple Kingdom*. New York: Farrar, Straus and Giroux, 1979.

———. *Tiepolo's Hound*. New York: Farrar, Straus and Giroux, 2000.

———. *Walker and The Ghost Dance*. New York: Farrar, Straus and Giroux, 2002.

———. *What the Twilight Says: Essays*. New York: Farrar, Straus and Giroux, 1999.

————. *White Egrets*. New York: Farrar, Straus and Giroux, 2010.

Walsh, William. *Readings in Commonwealth Literature*. Oxford: Clarendon, 1973.

Wieland, James. *The Ensphering Mind: History, Myth and Fictions in the Poetry of Allen Curnow, Nissim Ezekiel, A. D. Hope, A. M. Klein, Christopher Okigbo and Derek Walcott*. Washington, D.C.: Three Continents, 1988.

Williams, Ted. "Truth and Representation: The Confrontation of History and Mythology in *Omeros*." *Callaloo* 24.1 (2001): 276–86.

Wilson, Samuel, ed. *The Indigenous People of the Caribbean*. Gainesville, Fla.: University Press of Florida, 1999.

Woolf, Virginia. *Mrs. Dalloway*. New York: Harcourt, 1981.

Woollard, Penny. "Derek Walcott and the Wild Frontier: *The Ghost Dance*." *49Th Parallel: An Interdisciplinary Journal Of North American Studies* 23 (2009). Accessed December 2, 2013. www.49thparallel.bham.ac.uk.

Wu, Kaishu. "Writing Identities: Home and Inheritance in V. S. Naipaul's (Auto-) Biographical Strategy in *A House For Mr. Biswas* and Derek Walcott's Inter-Generational Memory in *Omeros*." *NTU Studies in Language and Literature* 27 (2012): 105–30.

Xenophon. *Anabasis*. London: Heinemann, 1922.

Yeats, W. B., ed. *The Book of Irish Verse*. New York: Routledge, 2002.

————. *The Collected Poems*, edited by Richard J. Finneran. New York: Scribner, 1996.

Zoppi, Isabella Maria. "*Omeros*, Derek Walcott and the Contemporary Epic Poem." *Callaloo* 22.2 (1999): 509–28.

Zurru, Elisabetta. "Time, History and the Native American Genocide Seen through Catherine's Eyes: A Stylistic Analysis." *Philologia: Scientific-Professional Journal For Language, Literature And Cultural Studies* 8 (2010): 123–32.

Index

Metropolitan Museum of Art, 55, 128

Micoud, 161

Middle Passage, 17, 22, 43, 50, 70, 81, 97, 104, 137

Milosz, Czeslaw, 155

Milton, John, 117

Minotaur, 93

Moby Dick, 129–30, 185. *See also* Melville, Herman

Monet, Claude, 173

Moore, Thomas, 55, 146

Morne, 33, 48, 56, 79, 158–59, 167, 189

Morris, William, 159

Morton Theatre, 122

"Muse of History, The," 3, 83, 125, 153. *See also* Walcott, Derek

Museum, 35–36, 38, 48, 55, 70, 73, 77, 81, 95, 108, 115, 128–29, 160, 187

Native, 4, 23, 26, 34, 62, 81, 104, 111, 143–44, 164, 174, 188, 192

Neoclassical, 140, 169

Netherlands, The, 71–72, 87, 100, 107

New England Primer, The, 114, 118

New Testament, 61, 108

New World, 3, 15, 22, 35, 50, 107, 115, 133–34, 180

No Pain Café, 32, 89, 91, 177–78, 186–87

Northern Antilles, 69, 71

Obeah, 18, 32, 56, 166

Odlum, George William, 89

Odysseus, 17, 19, 21–22, 28–29, 34, 36, 46, 61, 97, 105–6, 133, 138, 147–50, 162–64, 172

Odyssey, The, 11, 19, 21, 28–29, 31, 35, 44–45, 61, 97, 103, 105–6, 138, 163, 182–83

Old Testament, 108

Omeros, definition of, 30

Oranjestad, 72

Orpheus, 178, 181, 187

O Starry Starry Night, 5, 76, 95, 128. *See also* Walcott, Derek

Ovid, 36, 178. *See also* Hotel Normandie

Owen, Wilfred, 37

Pantomime, 31. *See also* Walcott, Derek

Pastime, 115

Petit Piton, 40, 88

Philoctete, 12, 17, 19, 26, 32–33, 59, 83, 98–99, 157, 177–78, 184, 192

Pissarro, Camille, 5, 107

Pitons, 40–41, 57, 150, 161, 165, 181, 188

Placide, 25

Plains Wars, 118

Plunkett, 13–14, 18, 35–37, 41, 69–70, 87–88, 92, 132, 143, 157, 177

Plunkett, Major, 18, 35, 69, 87–88, 157

Plunkett, Maud, 13, 18, 35–37, 60, 70, 79, 132, 143–44, 157, 172, 177

Poe, Edgar Allan, 76

Polyphemus, 28–29, 138, 192

Pope, 24, 61, 76, 89–90, 133, 135

Port of Spain, 52, 132, 134, 158

Postcolonial, 7

Reconstruction, 122–23

Redcoats, 80, 153

Regiment, 36, 129–30, 169, 171

Reign of Terror, 123

Rembrandt, 73

Remembrance, 40–41, 63, 75, 93, 169, 171. *See also* Walcott, Derek

Revival, 68, 121–22, 139, 188

Revolution, 3, 20, 39, 70, 72–73, 80, 82, 86, 107–8, 116, 122–23, 153

Rodney, Admiral, 20, 39, 42–43, 45, 47–49, 73, 81, 86, 89, 167, 189

Rodney Bay, 45, 89

Roman Catholic, 1, 27, 35, 43, 56, 65, 83–84, 86, 94, 107, 110, 112–13, 118, 135, 142, 144, 160, 164, 172, 187

Roman Empire, 29, 88, 170

MARIA MCGARRITY is associate professor of English at Long Island University in Brooklyn, New York. She is the author of *Washed by the Gulf Stream: The Historic and Geographic Relation of Irish and Caribbean Literature* and a coeditor of *Irish Modernism and the Global Primitive,* and she has written articles for numerous journals, including *Ariel: A Review of International English Literatures, The James Joyce Quarterly,* and *The Journal of West Indian Literature.*